FOOTBALL
IN THE SOUTH BAY

DON LECHMAN

THE
History
PRESS

Published by The History Press
Charleston, SC 29403
www.historypress.net

Copyright © 2014 by Don Lechman
All rights reserved

First published 2014

Manufactured in the United States

ISBN 978.1.62619.308.6

Library of Congress CIP data applied for.

*This book is dedicated to my son, David Michael Lechman,
a wide receiver and defensive back for the 1994 Torrance Tartars and
my favorite high school football player of all time.*

CONTENTS

PREFACE

Football in the South Bay includes high schools and community colleges in the southwestern quadrant of Los Angeles County, from San Pedro and the Palos Verdes Peninsula on the south to Westchester and St. Bernard High School in Playa del Rey on the north, and from Carson and Banning High School on the east to the beach cities and their schools on the west. The accuracy of the records and statistics in this book are dependent on those of the schools, conferences and coaches and the due diligence of the author. The results are as accurate as human beings and archives can make possible.

ACKNOWLEDGEMENTS

This book came into being because of the perseverance and faith of my editor, Jerry Roberts. He said I could do it, and, as usual, he was right. I would like to thank everyone who made this book possible: Janet Pearson and Cleoan Ferm of the Torrance Historical Society; Theresa B. Martinez, Linda D. Aust and Tike Karavas of the Redondo Union High School Archives; the Hawthorne Historical Society; Sabrina Skacan of Mary Star of the Sea High; the Manhattan Beach Historical Society; Diane Sambrano of the Centinela Valley Historical Society; the Peninsula Library Archives; the Torrance Library Archives; Mira Costa High; Leuzinger High; Banning High; Carson High; Gardena High; Narbonne High; Lawndale High; Morningside High; St. Bernard High; Hawthorne High; Mary Star of the Sea High; Serra High; Torrance High; El Segundo High; Lennox High alumnus Roy Hand; Athletic Director Ted Dunlap and Vince Kates of Serra High; Athletic Director Mike Kline of Carson; Carson High teacher and statistician Tim Finney; Fran Pullara and Dezri Smith of Chadwick School; Constantine Treantos of Gardena High Library; George Tachibana of Torrance High; Traci Liley of Harbor College Library Archives; Lynn McGuire of the Harbor College Athletic Department; Rafael Guerrero of El Camino College; Eno Attah and Monique Robinson of Morningside; Chris Rubacha and David Elecciri of Carson High; Christina McCole of St. Bernard High; Mike McAvin of Mira Costa High; Kamilah Jackson of Banning High; Chuck Bennett and Tony Ciniglio of the *Daily Breeze*; and coaches Rock Hollis, George Swade, Guy Gardner, Don Morrow,

Gary Kimbrell, Joe Austin, Bob Baiz, Steve Schmitz, Chris Ferragamo, Steve Shevlin, Rich Busia, Greg Holt, Chris Ferragamo, Mike Walsh, Josh Waybright, Brett Peabody, Scott Altenberg, Gary Willison, Tony Urburu, Todd Croce, Mike Christensen, Tim Lenderman and Manuel Douglas. I apologize to anyone I forgot. I want to thank my friend Alex Areyan, whose support and encouragement cannot be measured, and my family: my wife, Pat, for still loving me; my son, David, for providing football moments; my daughter, Laura, and son-in-law, Johnny, for listening to my writing woes; and my grandchildren—Kevin, River and Ariel—for their love of football and, believe it or not, me.

INTRODUCTION

Football is the most popular sport in America. Over 2.5 million boys play youth football. Another 1.1 million participate in high schools, and more than 70,000 play college football. There are over 1,600 players in the NFL and 280 in arena football, not to mention the millions who play pickup games every year.

High school football is a Friday night tradition since the 1920s. California has certainly had its share of the limelight, as De La Salle High School of Concord holds the national record of 151 consecutive games won from 1992 to 2004. The best high school football program as of 2013 is Valdosta, Georgia, with an incomparable record of 876-209-34. Only two California programs rank in the top fifty—Long Beach Poly ranks twenty-sixth with a 743-308-52 record and Bakersfield High School twenty-ninth with a 740-245-43 record.

The South Bay, while not being a mecca of football glory, has certainly had its moments. The 1920s were just the beginning, but the San Pedro Pilots were definitely the best of the decade, going 50-36-6. Next was the Gardena Panthers, who had an excellent 33-20-4 mark; the El Segundo Eagles, who went 31-41-4; and finally Narbonne of Harbor City, which had a fine record of 26-8-1.

The 1930s seemed kind of uneventful except for Inglewood winning the state championship in 1933 and 1934. Narbonne had the best record, with a 35-11-5 mark, while Torrance won twenty-seven. Redondo Union led the show in the 1940s with an incredible 57-19-5 record, including three consecutive state championships from 1942 to 1944! San Pedro High had thirty-four wins in the war-ravaged '40s, while Torrance had thirty-one and Narbonne twenty-seven.

Even with one year unaccounted for, the Banning Pilots rose to the top in the 1950s, going 51-18-7 behind Lefty Goodhue and Paul Huebner. San Pedro excelled with a 49-32-4 docket, while El Segundo also had a fine decade, going 43-28-3. The Torrance Tartars won thirty-eight even though they lost forty-one.

The cream of the crop in the 1960s was definitely the Gardena Panthers, who had an outstanding record of 72-19-4 behind coaches Stan Smith and Dick Enright. Next was a fine decade from Bishop Montgomery, going 45-42, mostly due to George Swade. Banning accumulated forty-one wins even with two years going unaccounted for. El Segundo managed thirty-seven victories, while San Pedro had thirty-four and Torrance thirty-three.

But two superpowers rose out of the ranks in the 1970s. The first was the Carson Colts under Coach Gene Vollnogle, garnering an incredible 88-24-1 record, while neighbor Banning, guided by Chris Ferragamo, went 82-26-1. Just behind was Gardena, under Ralph Vidal and Bob Sugino, who had a superior 65-32-2 decade. Bishop won forty-nine games in the 1970s, El Segundo forty-four games and San Pedro thirty-three.

The 1980s were more of the same, as Carson, behind Vollnogle, accounted for an insurmountable 102-15 record, and Banning chalked up a 94-18-3 tally sheet. Far behind was Gardena with fifty-one wins, San Pedro with forty-nine, El Segundo with forty-six, Bishop Montgomery with forty-two and Torrance with thirty-four.

A new superpower came into being in the 1990s as San Pedro grabbed the spotlight under new coach Mike Walsh with a 97-31-1 record. But Larry Wein of Westchester High followed right behind with a 92-20-1 record and an incredible .819 winning percentage. Carson was still in the hunt, going 73-48-4, and Banning was 66-51-1. That pretty much left everyone else in the dust.

Then the arrival of the twenty-first century brought another new power: Narbonne of Harbor City. The Gauchos joined the traditional powers, running off a 128-57-1 record behind new coach Manuel Douglas. Carson, of course, was still fighting hard with a great 126-63 sheet, and so was San Pedro with a 107-48-1 record. El Segundo had a good decade, winning ninety-one games, while Torrance, behind Rock Hollis, had sixty-six wins. Gardena, led mostly by Marshall Jones, had sixty-five wins, and Banning hung around with fifty-three.

Without a doubt, Carson High School, with 433 victories and a winning percentage of .706 over a fifty-year period, is the supreme football program in the South Bay. Banning High School and Redondo Union are tied for the second-most wins (415), with Redondo having played the most games (863). But as far as the best winning percentage goes, Peninsula High School is second with a .642 percentage and a 166-92-3 record. Third is San Pedro, with a .637 percentage and a 355-127-26 record. Next is Rolling Hills High, which has a .613 percentage but played only twenty-two years. Following the top three in wins are Gardena (367), Serra (358), San Pedro (355), North (347), El Segundo and Mira Costa (317) and West (304). (Westchester High, with 209 wins, might have ended up in the high echelon, but there are twenty-four years that are unaccounted for.)

As far as coaches go, the best is the one and only Gene Vollnogle. He has not only the best record (236-66-1) and the most wins but also the best percentage of all South Bay coaches (.781) other than Ben Camrada (57-14-2), who was involved in only seventy-three games from 1926 through 1936 at Narbonne in Harbor City.

The coach with the second-most wins is Don Morrow of South and Mira Costa, who boasts a docket of 214-90-2. He is followed by Mike Walsh of San Pedro, who has a 209-75-2 record. The second-best percentage, though, belongs to Scott Altenberg of Serra, who has a 142-42-3 record for a .767 percentage. The third-best percentage is owned by Larry Wein of Westchester with .755. Fourth in number of wins is Gary Kimbrell of Miraleste, Rolling Hills and Peninsula with a 180-70-3 record. Fifth is Chris Ferragamo of Banning with a record of 178-57-4 and a mighty .753 winning percentage. That completes the marvelous sextet at the top. The next layer features Larry Wein of Westchester (162-51-3), Fred Petersen at West Torrance (131-60-4), Joe Austin at South and North (128-72-1) and Manuel Douglas at Narbonne (128-55-1).

The top coaches who won fewer than ninety games were led by Camrada with a percentage of .795, Guy Gardner of Palos Verdes at .742 (44-15-1), Steve Schmitz at .736 (88-31-2) and Gary Willison of Chadwick at .649 (73-39-2). Not to be forgotten on this list of underachievers is Edwin Ellis, who lasted an incredible twenty-five years at Chadwick (1941–65), logging a record of 81-39 for a percentage of .675.

As for community colleges, El Camino has certainly made its mark, winning the national title twice under legendary coach John Featherstone and logging a record of 446-230-10 from 1947 through 2013. The only other college in the area, Los Angeles Harbor, has tallied 259 wins, 335 losses and 8 ties since 1951.

Not to be forgotten are the hundreds of players who have gone on to make a name for themselves in college, the NFL or elsewhere. Most notable is Vince Ferragamo (Banning, 1972) who started at quarterback for the Los Angeles Rams in Super Bowl XIV and led after three quarters before losing to the Pittsburgh Steelers, 31–19. George Brett, who started in the backfield for the El Segundo Eagles in 1970, gained his fame as a third baseman for the Kansas City Royals and earned a place in the Hall of Fame.

Pete Beathard, also an Eagle, made quite a name for himself with the USC Trojans before playing eleven years in the NFL. Tim Wrightman of Mary Star, who was named South Bay Player of the Year in 1978, played two years for the Chicago Bears. Jeff Rohrer (Mira Costa, 1970) played six years with the Dallas Cowboys. Steve Sogge of Gardena quarterbacked USC to a national championship. Johnnie Morton of South Torrance played a dozen years in the NFL, mostly with Detroit, while his brother, Chad, had seven years in the NFL as a kick and punt returner. The Ellison brothers from Redondo also did all right, with Keith spending six years as a linebacker and Kevin getting drafted as a defensive back. Scott Laidlaw from Hawthorne was a fine running back with Dallas, while Curtis Conway, also a Cougar, had an exceptional career, spending twelve years in the NFL.

Hundreds more South Bay football players have gone on to fine careers in football and in life, and this book salutes them.

CHAPTER 1

AVIATION HIGH SCHOOL FALCONS

The most remarkable thing about Aviation High School's twenty-three years on the gridiron was the 1976 season, when the Falcons went 11-0-1 under Coach Ron Veres. "This year's team was the finest group of individuals I ever had the honor to coach," Veres said in the 1977 Aviation High School yearbook.

The Redondo Beach school beat St. Monica's of Santa Monica 36–0, Quartz Hill 20–14 and Bellflower 20–19 to go undefeated in the CIF. Led by All-CIF players Don Morrow (Mira Costa's future coach), Dan Clary, Mike Cherney and John McGee, the team's wins included a 15–0 shellacking of El Segundo, a 32–0 victory over Arroyo of El Monte and a 27–6 win over Lawndale.

Aviation, which started football in 1959 and ended in 1981, had many profitable seasons, including going 6-3 in both 1962 and 1963 under Coach Ed Hyduke, 7-2-1 in 1971 and 9-2 in 1978 under Veres and 7-1 in 1979 under Coach Herb Hinsche.

Coaches Pat Crozier, Ernie Reid and Jerry Runnalls launched football at Aviation in 1959 with a 5-1 record. They duplicated this in 1960 with an outstanding team led by Dennis Hearn at halfback, Ernie Reid at tailback, Ken Proctor at quarterback and Dave Wanner at end. There was a letdown in 1961 with a 3-7 record, but Hyduke revived the team in 1962 with a 6-3 season. "Our team had two excellent qualities," Hyduke said in the Aviation yearbook, "the willingness to work and desire to win." Ed Noble, Craig Holmes, Carlos Baca and Richard Reid excelled on offense, while Larry

Rich Payne rushed for 822 yards and was named MVP of the 6-4 Aviation High team in 1977. *Courtesy of Redondo Beach Historical Society.*

Wolfe, Joe Reid and Gary Bartz led the defense. Victims included Beverly Hills (51–6) and Culver City (19–7). This good stuff was repeated in 1963, as the Falcons went 6-3 again behind Chris Sausser, Rick Warren, John Yeater, Bart Wells and Frank Bennett.

Quarterback Mike Taggart, end Terry Stephens, halfback Dave Stelter, center Louis LeRoy and tackle Glen Engle led the team in 1964, even though the record was only 2-7. Hyduke brought the team up to 4-5 in 1965, with Taggart, Greg Runnals, George Morvant, Chuck Arrasmith and Dennis Hicks headlining the team. Hyduke closed out his fine Aviation career in 1966 (38-35-3) with a 5-3-1 record behind Rick Shield, Steve Barnet, Robert Frickman, Larry Jones and Marc D'Ambrosi.

There were only three coaches in Aviation's history, and Ron Veres came next. In addition to his tremendous 1976 season, Veres won seven games in 1971, six in 1977 and five in 1969 and 1972. In 1969, the Falcons had big wins over Mira Costa (14–0), Miraleste (29–0) and El Segundo (18–6). Team MVP was Bill Arrosmith, while Steve Calderon was the outstanding lineman in the Pioneer League.

And in 1971, the Falcons went 7-2 in the Sky League behind quarterback Mark Gesquirre, who threw fifteen touchdown passes; receivers John Crabtree and Jim Kadrmas; and halfback Dave Forrest, who gained 1,047 yards. Among the teams they beat were Hawthorne (7–0), Mira Costa (25–6), Palos Verdes (21–7) and Redondo (19–0).

Denis Haire, Benny Bais and Ron Walton helped the team to a 3-6 record in 1973 and finished under Coach Veres with a 6-4 record in 1977. The Falcons beat Torrance (10–0), Redondo Beach (21–7) and Leuzinger (10–0). MVP Rich Payne gained 822 yards rushing, while Jeff Steuer and Fred Smith were All-League.

Herb Hinsche took over the following year, going an incredible 9-2 in '78 and 7-1 in '79. In '78, they beat El Toro 20–19 before losing to San Clemente, 41–0. After two more seasons, Aviation closed its doors due to declining enrollment in the district, with students going to Redondo Union High School and Mira Costa in Manhattan Beach.

But once a Falcon, always a Falcon. The spirit lives.

Aviation Win-Loss Records

1959: 5-1, Pat Crozier, Ernie Reid
and Jerry Runnalls
1960: 5-1, Ed Hyduke
1961: 3-7, Hyduke
1962: 6-3, Hyduke
1963: 6-3, Hyduke
1964: 2-7, Hyduke
1965: 4-5, Hyduke
1966: 5-3-1, Hyduke
1967: 2-5-2, Hyduke
1968: 1-8, Ron Veres
1969: 5-4, Veres

1970: 2-6, Veres
1971: 7-2, Veres
1972: 5-5, Veres
1973: 3-6, Veres
1974: 1-7-1, Veres
1975: 4-5, Veres
1976: 11-0-1, Veres
1977: 6-4, Veres
1978: 9-2, Herb Hinsche
1979: 7-1, Hinsche
1980: no record, Hinsche
1981: no record, Hinsche

Coaches' Records

1. Ron Veres: 45-47-2 (.489)
2. Ed Hyduke: 33-34-3 (.493)
3. Herb Hinsche: 16-3 (.842)*
4. Pat Crozier, Ernie Reid and Jerry Runnalls: 5-1 (.833)

* incomplete record

Total: 99-85-8 (.536)
(two years unaccounted for)

CHAPTER 2

BANNING HIGH SCHOOL PILOTS

Banning High School of Wilmington—along with its rival, Carson High School—boasts one of the premier football programs in the United States.

The Pilots were at their zenith when Chris Ferragamo—the older brother of former Ram and Nebraska quarterback Vince Ferragamo—took over in 1969. After going 4-4 his first year and winning at the most seven games through 1974, Ferragamo went on a tear in 1975, winning 10, 12, 11, 10, 11, 12, 11, 9, 9, 10, 9 and 11 over the next twelve years for an average of 10.4 wins a year. Incredible!

Banning players who have made a mark in the NFL include quarterback Jeff Griffin (1971) with the St. Louis Cardinals, Vince Ferragamo (1972) with the Los Angeles Rams, Steve Rivera (1972) with the San Francisco 49ers, Danny Reece (1973) with the Tampa Bay Bucs, Frank Manumaleuna (1974) with the Kansas City Chiefs, Freeman McNeill (1977) with the New Jets, Stanley Wilson (1979) with the Cincinnati Bengals, Navy Tuyiasosopo (1983) with the Los Angeles Rams, Courtney Hall (1985) with the San Diego Chargers, Mark Tucker (1986) with the Arizona Cardinals, Tyrone Rodgers (1987) with the Seattle Seahawks, Bob Whitfield (1989) with the Atlanta Falcons and Fred Matua (2001) with the Detroit Lions.

The football program was launched in 1921, when the school supposedly went 0-2. There was no football again until 1925, when Coaches Helback and Sanborn took the Pilots to a 1-4 record; they then went 3-2 in 1926. The best record in the 1930s came in 1931 under Coach Gene Patz (5-3).

Gus Gerson took over in 1932 and coached the team to fifteen recorded victories through 1940. Mark Sampson coached the Pilots in 1941 and 1942, after which football was not resumed until 1948, when Louis Zamperini's brother Pete led a "B" team to a 4-2 record. Pete then coached the varsity team to a 0-7 record in 1949 before Willard Lefty Goodhue took over.

Goodhue recorded a 1-4-1 season in 1950 and then a fine 5-2 season in 1951. The Pilots shut out Narbonne 26–0, and guard Louie Rubio, end Dan Clark, halfback Jack Hernandez, tackle George Mutschler and fullback Charles Boydston all made All-Marine League. The team finished 3-3-2 under Goodhue in 1952 but leapt to 8-1 in 1953 with wins over San Pedro (26–7), Narbonne (13–6) and Gardena (14–0). The team was led by captain Al Aguilar, running back Jim Olarte, Bob Morton, Rudy Krueger and Dan Rinehart. Their only loss was the final game, where they fell 14–12 to Los Angeles High.

Then in 1957, Paul Huebner came on the scene as head coach, going 9-2 and beating University 35–7 and Huntington Park 42–35 before losing to Manual Arts, 23–13, in the playoffs. Huebner was easily Banning's most impressive coach after Ferragamo. His reign had barely started when Banning went 11-0 in 1958, winning the Los Angeles city championship. In the playoffs, the Pilots dusted Jefferson 20–12, Reseda 13–7 and Freemont 59–19. Other great wins were 20–0 over San Pedro and 46–20 over Gardena. Tailback Robert Hernandez was named All-City and the Marine Co-Player of the Year. Left end Danny Spears was All-City, and fullback Loren Dome was All-Marine.

In 1960, the Pilots were 10-1 with another city championship, losing only to Compton, 18–13. In the playoffs, they beat Reseda 21–0, Hollywood 35–19 and Los Angeles High 57–26. Left end Jim Arens and fullback Charles Jackson were All-Marine, and tackle Richard Reed was All-City.

In 1962, the Pilots were 9-2, as tailback John Blakemore was named All-City, and guard Eddie Kapu, tackle Jack O'Malley and fullback Candy Gonzalez were named All-Marine.

In 1969, Ferragamo took over, and the rest is history. Ferragamo had two mediocre years: 4-4 in 1969 and 1-7 in 1972. The rest of the time, it seemed like he rarely lost. (See accompanying story.)

In 1970, a breakout year, the team went 7-1, thanks partly to Chris's younger brother, Vince, who helped the Pilots finish second in the Marine League. The great Frank Manumaleuna was fullback in 1973, when Banning was 6-2. The 1974 team featured such great players as Mike Herrera, Tyrone Sperling, Larry Metheny, Alphonso Williams, Darryl DeCuir and

Coach Paul Huebner (left) and his then-assistant, young Gene Vollnogle, ruled Banning High football from 1957 through 1968, winning more than sixty games and losing only twenty-five. *Courtesy of Banning High School.*

Harland Buckner. The 1975 season brought a 10-3 record as the Pilots lost the championship to San Fernando, 20–8. But they were preparing for their historic 1976–81 run.

Even when the Pilots let down, they were good. They lost the championship to Crenshaw, 26–21, in 1982 but still were 9-1-1 overall. Trent McKay, Eric McKee and Ronnie Barber led key wins over Carson (14–3) and Pacific Palisades (42–7). A "poor" year, 9-1-2, followed in 1983 behind Keith Cooper and Joe Scott.

The year 1984 was a pretty special one; even though they lost the championship, 33–20, to Carson, the Pilots finished 10-2. The great

Michael Herrera was an All-Marine League lineman for Chris Ferragamo's 1974 Banning Pilot team, which finished 7-2. *Courtesy of Banning High School.*

Jamelle Holieway at quarterback was named City Player of the Year. Fullback Leroy Holt; linemen Mark Tucker, Eric Nold and Darryl Lesure; safety Sam Sutherland; and tailback Brett Young were All-League. More of the same came in 1985, when Banning went 9-3 and beat Carson 31–6 for the championship. League MVP Earl Saunders, Mark Tucker and Marvin Pollard led the team.

After Ferragamo moved on, veteran John Hazelton coached one year, going 5-5. Then Joe Dominguez, a former player, took over and had superior years in 1988 (9-3) and 1991 (12-1), losing only to Dorsey in the finals, 33–30. Backs Mark Bautiste and Victor Garcia and lineman Ernie Gamboa were instrumental in the team finishing eighth in the state of California.

Ed Paculba had a good year in 1992, as the team went 7-4 with Damian Hurst scoring fourteen touchdowns with 1,528 all-purpose yards. The Pilots also beat archenemy Carson that year, 17–13.

In John Aguilar's second year as head coach, the Pilots went 10-4, losing only to Taft, 41–29, in the finals. In the playoffs, they beat Roosevelt 56–0, Sylmar 32–20 and Granada Hills 32–20. Outstanding players included All-American Dan Waldrop, All-City Mike Garrison, Marine Defensive Player of the Year Frank Perez, Marine Offensive Player of the Year Chris Howard, Marine MVP Mike Cockrell and Ricardo Robledo and Mike Geluz, both All-Marine. Ed Lalau had two good years in 1999 (8-5) and 2000 (7-4).

Then comes the sad news. Things ain't what they used to be on the old gridiron. These days, 4-7 and 5-5 are good years for the Pilots. A bright spot came when Ferragamo returned to coach his old team in 2006. He ended up going 9-3 in 2007. The Pilots made the playoffs, of course, beating San Fernando 33–8 before losing to Carson again, 27–12. But good wins included a 56–6 pasting of Los Angeles High and making all their league rivals—San Pedro (28–21), Carson (21–0 in the regular season), Gardena (28–0) and Narbonne (31–18)—eat humble pie. Contributing players included Anthony Rodriguez, Josh Limosnero, Carlos Fernandez and Hanipale Suega.

Current coach, John Aponte, led the team to a 5-5 record in 2013 and is hoping for more winning ways like Banning days of yore.

Banning Win-Loss Records

1921: 0-2

1922: no football

1923: no football

1924: no football

1925: 1-4, Helback and Sanborn

1926: 3-2, Helback and Sanborn

1927: 1-5-1, Gene Patz

1928: 2-5, Patz

1929: 1-6, Patz

1930: no record

1931: 5-3, Patz

1932: 2-2-2, Gus Gerson

1933: 0-5, Gerson

1934: 3-3, Gerson

1935: 1-5, Gerson

1936: 3-3, Gerson

1937: 1-2-1, Gerson

1938: 1-2-1, Gerson

1939: 2-3, Gerson

1940: 2-2, Gerson

1941: 1-3, Mark Sampson

1942: 4-1, Sampson

1943: no football

1944: no football

1945: no football

1946: no football

1947: no football

1948: B football only, 4-2, Pete Zamperini

1949: 0-7, Zamperini

1950: 1-4-1, Willard (Lefty) Goodhue

1951: 5-2, Goodhue

1952: 3-3-2, Goodhue

1953: 8-1, Goodhue

1954: 4-3-2, Goodhue

1955: 4-3-2, Goodhue

1956: no record, Goodhue

1957: 9-2, Paul Huebner

1958: 11-0, Huebner

1959: 6-0, Huebner

1960: 10-1, Huebner

1961: 5-3, Huebner

1962: 9-2, Huebner

1963: 3-4-1, Huebner

1964: 1-7, Huebner

1965: 5-3, Huebner

1966: no record, Huebner

1967: 4-3-1, Huebner

1968: no record, Huebner

1969: 4-4, Chris Ferragamo

1970: 7-1, Ferragamo

1971: 7-2, Ferragamo

1972: 1-7, Ferragamo

1973: 6-2, Ferragamo
1974: 7-2, Ferragamo
1975: 10-3, Ferragamo
1976: 12-1, Ferragamo
1977: 11-1-1, Ferragamo
1978: 10-2, Ferragamo
1979: 11-1, Ferragamo
1980: 12-0, Ferragamo
1981: 11-1, Ferragamo
1982: 9-1-1, Ferragamo
1983: 9-1-2, Ferragamo
1984: 10-2, Ferragamo
1985: 9-3, Ferragamo
1986: 11-1, Ferragamo
1987: 6-4, John Hazelton
1988: 11-3, Joe Dominguez
1989: 6-3-1, Dominguez
1990: 9-4, Dominguez
1991: 12-1, Dominguez
1992: 7-4, Ed Paculba
1993: 5-6, Paculba

1994: 6-5-1, Paculba
1995: 5-6, Kenny Stumpf
1996: 0-10, Stumpf
1997: 4-6, John Aguilar
1998: 10-4, Aguilar
1999: 8-5, Ed Lalau
2000: 7-4, Lalau
2001: 3-7, Lalau
2002: 4-7, Lalau
2003: 3-8, Lalau
2004: 2-7-1, Randy Block
2005: 1-9, Mo Espinosa
2006: 4-7, Chris Ferragamo
2007: 9-3, Ferragamo
2008: 4-7, Ferragamo
2009: 4-7, Ferragamo
2010: 1-9, Tim McTyer
2011: 3-7, McTyer
2012: 3-7, McTyer
2013: 5-5, John Aponte

Coaches' Records

1. Chris Ferragamo: 178-57-4 (.753)
2. Paul Huebner: 63-25-2 (.711)*
3. Joe Dominguez: 38-11-1 (.770)
4. Ed Lalau: 25-31 (.446)
5. Willard Goodhue: 21-13-5 (.603)
6. Ed Paculba: 17-15-1 (.530)
7. Gus Gerson: 15-27-4 (.370)
8. John Aguilar: 14-10 (.583)
9. Gene Patz: 9-19-1 (.328)*
10. Tim McTyer: 7-23 (.304)
11. John Hazelton: 6-4 (.600)
12. Mark Sampson: 5-4 (.556)
13. John Aponte: 5-5 (.500)
14. Ken Stumpf: 5-16 (.238)
15. Helback and Sanborn: 4-6 (.400)

16. Randy Block: 2-7-1 (.250)
17. Mo Espinosa: 1-9 (.100)

* incomplete record

Total: 415-282-19, .593
(four years unaccounted for)

COACH CHRIS FERRAGAMO

Chris Ferragamo, older brother of Vince Ferragamo, the former quarterback of the Nebraska Cornhuskers and the L.A. Rams, was one of the best high school coaches in the country during the twenty-two years he was at Banning High School in Wilmington. Chris, now seventy-four, had a record of 174-57-4 for a .749 winning percentage. His Pilots won ten or more games nine times during his career. Ferragamo, who is a product of Banning High School, attended Harbor and Long Beach State. He started coaching in 1963 and taught science in Los Angeles Unified.

Ferragamo's record was only 4-4 his first year, 1969, but it showed a promise of things to come. That year, All-League players included tight end Sam Reece, quarterback and younger brother Vince Ferragamo, cornerback Jim Legaspi and tackle Ben Flores.

Then came 1976 and Banning's historic run. Ferragamo won his first championship with a 12-1 record, crushing Cleveland 34–0, Crenshaw 40–0 and San Fernando 29–0 behind Joey Montijo, future UCLA great Freeman McNeil, Reggie Williams, Jimmy Gasso and Joey Figueroa.

The following year saw the Pilots go 11-1-1 as they beat El Camino Real for the city championship, 24–14. Stanley Wilson was the 4-A Player of the Year with quarterback Fred Hessen, and Polo Faavi outstanding.

In 1978, Banning went 10-2 and beat Carson 7–6 for the championship behind Wilson, John Truitt, Pete Quartararo and Charles Collins.

1979 was business as usual, as Banning beat Bell 46–0, El Camino Real 20–7 and Carson 14–13, their only loss coming to St. Paul, 17–7. MVP fullback Michael Alo, quarterback Jeff Yanez, running back Danny Andrews, guard Paul Gates, center Tony Guzman and wide receiver Todd Sharp all had exceptional years.

But 1980 was very special as the team finished 12-0 in Ferragamo's only undefeated season. Alo and Andrews and halfback Raymond Moret led the team. Taulau Tupua, LaFon Thompson and Dwayne Moore were all-everything. Some of their victims included Carson (26–0 and 26–14), San Pedro (34–8) and Chatsworth (35–2). And the Pilots wiped out El Camino Real 34–12 to win the city championship. There was a "letdown" in 1981, as the Pilots lost one game but won eleven for their sixth consecutive championship. Montel Bryant was all-everything, and Greg Battle was the City Player of the Year.

In 1986, Ferragamo finished up his first stint at Banning by going 11-1, losing only the championship game to Carson, 21–11, after having beat the Colts 37–10 in league. Quarterback Marvin Pollard, lineman Terrance Powe and defenseman Tyrone Rodgers were outstanding.

In 1987, Ferragamo tried to move on to new success as the head coach at Harbor College. But he didn't have a lot of success his first year, going 2-7-1. In September 1988, Paul McLeod of the *Los Angeles Times* visited the Harbor locker room. He noted that Ferragamo was trying to rebuild the Seahawk program after a stellar high school coaching career—and he was doing so while playing four of the state's top-ranked teams in the first five weeks. Ferragamo asked, "If we play teams that we can run over, does that tell us anything about ourselves?" The coach drilled the backfield on play-calling. "He's really good," said Earl Ray Saunders, a former star at Banning.

But things never worked out for Ferragamo at Harbor, where he ended up 1-10 in his second and final season.

In July 1990, Rob Fernas of the *Los Angeles Times* reported that in 1988, a dejected Ferragamo, after losing to Compton College, said, "I thought I was a good coach, but I guess I'm not. This is really the low point of my life." It was understandable that Ferragamo was down after his Harbor experience. He was used to being the toast of the town. "There were times when Chris could have run for mayor of Wilmington," said Harbor College athletic director Jim O'Brien. Then Fernas reported that some questioned Ferragamo's ability to coach at the college level. John Featherstone, the longtime successful coach at El Camino, did not agree. "I think it's unfortunate what's happened in his coaching career," he said. "The coaching fraternity is a tough fraternity. You've got to produce, and you've got to win or, unfortunately you are looked upon as a loser. Chris isn't a loser. He just got caught in a tough situation for a couple of years."

After leaving Harbor, Ferragamo was the offensive line coach at Long Beach City College for a few years before eventually returning to Banning—with his typical success. After going 4-7 in 2006, he quickly righted the ship

Chris Ferragamo won 178 games in twenty-one years as coach of Banning High School, finishing as the second-winningest coach in South Bay history. *Courtesy of the* Daily Breeze.

and had a 9-3 season in 2007, the best for Banning in the last fourteen years. The next two years saw Ferragamo going 4-7 and thinking it was time to quit. "I tried to bring the program out of the doldrums, and I think we did that, but it's time to move the program forward," he said in a *Daily Breeze* newspaper interview. "I want to let young guys come in now to take it to the next level. Someone full of enthusiasm like I was 40 years ago."

Ferragamo said that when he couldn't demonstrate a chop block on the field, he knew it was time to call it quits. He said he needed a break, but "when I was on the field, I was in heaven. I loved every moment of it. I want to help the team as much as I can. It's my life. I want to still be around it."

Now going on seventy-four, Ferragamo is still around Banning, teaching and mentoring whenever he can.

And no matter what has happened in recent years, his guidance and influence on hundreds of young men can never be taken away, nor can his rightful place as one of the greatest coaches ever to grace a California high school football field.

CHAPTER 3

BISHOP MONTGOMERY
HIGH SCHOOL KNIGHTS

Bishop Montgomery High School, an educational landmark in the South Bay, was founded in 1957, the dream of the Reverend William Ford, pastor of nearby St. James Church in Redondo Beach. On February 23, 1958, Cardinal McIntyre dedicated the school to Bishop George T. Montgomery, the first American-born bishop of Los Angeles.

The first football season was in 1960, when Coach George Gaunder took the fledgling Knights to a 2-7 season. Since then, the Knights have not been an overwhelming football factory, but they have had their moments. The best season ever was posted under Coach Bill Norton in 1983, when the Knights went 12-1-1 to become league champions and went to the CIF finals. Second best was 1966 under George Swade, when the Knights finished 11-1. Their third-best season came more recently, when Ed Hodgkiss led them to a 9-2 season in 2010. The Knights have won the league championship seven times and have had lot of players in the pros.

Quarterback Kevin Starkey (1976) played at Long Beach State and then in the Canadian Football League. Running back Bryan Bero (1984) played for the Chicago Bears. Free safety Brandon McLemore (1995) played for the Tennessee Titans. Omar Smith (1996), who was three times All-League as a wide receiver and defensive back, played in the arena football league and is now an assistant coach. Cornerback Stanley Wilson Jr. (2000), son of Stanley Sr., a star at Banning High School and on the Cincinnati Bengals, was a star at Stanford and plays in the Arena Football League. Kicker David Davis (1998) played in the Arena Football League. Offensive lineman Terrence

Pennington (2001) has played with the Buffalo Bills, Atlanta Falcons and New York Giants, while defensive back Josh Jones (2005) has also played in the Arena Football League.

In Bishop's first year, top players included backs Dick Moore, Dick Corwin and Zac Nazarian; linemen Fred Riganti, Tom Martin, Tom Blackburn and Mike Stetson; and end Willard Wells. Things got better fast after Swade arrived on the scene in 1963 and helped the Knights go 5-4. Outstanding players included Russ Moore, Carlos Thompson, Jerry Leninger and Dave Hanson. In 1964, led by Ray Moreay, Mike Crosby, Edward Gilles and Armand Lemieux, Bishop again went 5-4.

But as Swade and his team became acclimated, the Knights turned in an 8-1 year in 1965. That was just the beginning for three-sport man Danny Graham, one of the greatest athletes in BM history. In 1965, Danny was named All-Camino Real League, City Player of the Year and All-CIF 2nd Team Offense. Tom Hanson, Dan Gillespie, Mike Leamy, Pete Trocchiano and Mike Wood were All-League. Great wins over St. Genevieve (39–6), Lennox (39–0), Palm Springs (20–0), Daniel Murphy (32–6) and St. Monica (44–13) highlighted the season.

But Bishop fans hadn't seen anything yet! The following year, Swade and his gang went 11-1. In 1966, Graham was named All-Camino Real League, City Player of the Year, South Bay Player of the Year and CIF Player of the Year. He was named an All-American in 1966 and led his team to wins in the CIF over Rancho Alamitos (41–20) and Magnolia (34–6) before losing to Morningside (37–27), its only loss of the year. Other quality wins came over Mira Costa (32–14), St. Bernard's (30–0), Daniel Murphy (45–6) and St. Monica's (42–12).

The Knights went 6-3 in 1967 behind quarterback Greg Collins, Steve Patterson, Mirke Ramirez and Bill Copeland. And 1968 was even better, as the Knights went 8-2 and were league champions. They beat Mira Costa 7–0, South High 34–07 and Crespi 14–7. Outstanding players included Bill Copeland, Mike McNeil, Greg Reams, Ed Hansen and MVP quarterback Collins.

Mike Antista took over in 1969 and quickly had his best year in 1970, going 8-3 and winning another league championship. The Knights beat Pacifica High School of Garden Grove 14–9 but then lost to West Covina, 21–14, in the CIF semifinals. Outstanding players included quarterback Ken Makos, linebacker Rich Bongard and running backs Rudy Echavvaria and Joe Mastro. Victims included Pius X of Downey (20–7), Lawndale (14–6), Mt. Carmel of Los Angeles (35–0) and St. Bernard's (27–8).

Quarterback Danny Graham, a three-sport star at Bishop Montgomery High School in Torrance, was Camino Real League Player of the Year and an All-American in 1966. *Courtesy of Torrance Historical Society.*

In 2010, Coach Ed Hodgkiss celebrated his first season at Bishop Montgomery with the school's first outright league title since 1983. *Photo by Sean Hiller; courtesy of the* Daily Breeze.

Bill Norton took over in 1977 and quickly made the Knights league champions while posting a 6-4 record. Bishop was also 7-3-1 in 1982, but 1983 was a tremendous year, as the Knights won the most games in their history, going 12-1 and earning another league championship. The Knights were tied with Mary Star of the Sea at midseason but then went on to win every game until the final championship, when they were beaten by Canyon of Canyon Country, 40–24. Incredibly, the year boasted four consecutive shutouts over Serra (24–0), Cantwell (42–0), St. Anthony (42–0) and St. Monica (42–0).

After Norton left, there wasn't much to cheer about for the next (shudder) twenty-six years. Andy Szabatura did the best, winning nineteen games from 1984 to 1988. Finally, Ed Hodgkiss, a former coach of the Los Angeles Avengers of the Arena Football League, made an immediate impact, going 9-2 in 2010. Quality wins were 48–18 over Laguna Beach, 49–21 over Bosco Tech and 65–13 over St. Bernard's. Unfortunately, the Knights met their maker in the first playoff game, losing to Templeton (near Paso Robles), 43–33.

Great individual effort was put in by running back Nolan Plummer, who rushed for an incredible 2,241 overall yards and an even more incredible 9.07 yards a carry in 2010. Quarterback Mark Nguyen passed for 1,634 yards, while wide receiver Pierre Wise had forty-seven receptions. Linebacker Cameron Johnese led the team with seventy-three tackles, while defensive end Christian Holloway had thirteen sacks.

The Knights had another fine year in 2012, going 7-3. They lost to Valley Christian, 38–21, in the playoffs, but not before wiping out Mary Star of the Sea (38–0), Cantwell (34–14) and Bosco Tech (35–14).

The Knights had plenty of outstanding players. In addition to Nolan Plummer rushing for 2,241 yards, Bryce Bero led all quarterbacks when he passed for 2,533 yards in 1983 and 4,645 for his career. Back in 1966, Danny Graham, a future USC player, led the way with twenty-seven touchdowns and had forty-seven for his career. Dan Campbell had a rousing fifty-one receptions in 1983, while Brandon McLemore had fifty-nine in 1994. Carson Carillo had seven interceptions in 1983. Khoury Clark rushed for 376 yards in a game against St. Bernard in 1991. Most yards passing in a single game were thrown by Alex Stellato (423) in 2004 against Torrance. The longest kickoff return was by Matt Burrola, who ran for a ninety-five-yard touchdown against Piux X of Downey in 1989.

With Coach Hodgkiss at the helm, offensive fireworks are just beginning.

Bishop Montgomery Win-Loss Records

1960: 2-7, George Gaunder
1961: 1-7-1, Gaunder
1962: 1-8, Gaunder
1963: 5-4, George Swade
1964: 5-4, Swade
1965: 8-1, Swade
1966: 11-1, Swade
1967: 6-3, Swade

1968: 8-2, Swade
1969: 4-5, Mike Antista
1970: 8-3, Antista
1971: 6-3, Antista
1972: 4-5, Antista
1973: 5-4, Antista
1974: 4-4-1, Antista
1975: 4-5, Tom Hanson

1976: 4-5, Hanson
1977: 6-4, Bill Norton
1978: 1-8, Norton
1979: 3-7, Norton
1980: 5-5, Norton
1981: 1-9, Norton
1982: 7-3-1, Norton
1983: 12-1, Norton
1984: 4-6, Andy Szabatura
1985: 3-7, Szabatura
1986: 3-7, Szabatura
1987: 4-6, Szabatura
1988: 5-5, Szabatura
1989: 3-7, Steve Carroll
1990: 3-7, Carroll
1991: 6-4, Carroll
1992: 2-6-2, Bob Thompson
1993: 3-7, Matt Giacalone
1994: 3-7, Giacalone

1995: 1-9, Mike Sanders
1996: 2-8, Sanders
1997: 0-10, Jimmy Sims
1998: 0-10, Sims
1999: 3-7, Sims
2000: 2-8, Sims
2001: 2-8, Sims
2002: 2-8, Arnold Ale
2003: 0-10, Ale
2004: 3-7, Ale
2005: 3-7, Ale
2006: 3-7, Ale
2007: 1-9, Ale
2008: 3-8, Ale
2009: 1-9, Ale
2010: 9-2, Ed Hodgkiss
2011: 6-5, Hodgkiss
2012: 7-3, Hodgkiss
2013: 5-6, Hodgkiss

Coaches' Records

1. George Swade: 44-23 (.657)
2. Bill Norton: 35-37-2 (.486)
3. Mike Antista: 31-24-1 (.563)
4. Ed Hodgkiss: 27-16 (.628)
5. Andy Szabatura: 19-31 (.380)
6. Arnold Ale: 16-56 (.222)
7. Steve Carroll: 12-18 (.400)
8. Tom Hanson: 8-10 (.444)
9. Jimmy Sims: 7-43 (.140)
10. Matt Giacalone: 6-14 (.300)
11. George Gaunder: 3-14-1 (.194)

Total: 211-324-4 (.395)

COACH GEORGE SWADE

What do Joe Montana, Joe Namath, Dan Marino, Babe Parilli, Rich Gannon, George Blanda and George Swade have in common? They all grew up in the same area of Pennsylvania and went on to become successful quarterbacks in college—and some in the pros.

It might seem like a stretch to link South Bay's own Swade with some of the greatest quarterbacks in NFL history, but George has become a legend in his own right. Swade, who was born in 1933 in Monessen, Pennsylvania, later became a District 3 NCAA first-team quarterback in 1959 and 1960 at California Polytechnic State University–Pomona and one of the most popular and successful high school and community college coaches in South Bay history.

From 1963 to 1968, Swade had a record of 44-23 and two league championships at Bishop Montgomery High School in Torrance. He then went on to coach three different times at Harbor College in Wilmington, amassing a record of 57-45-1. This included a 9-1 season in 2009 in which he was named California Community Colleges' Mountain Conference Coach of the Year while serving as both coach and athletic director at age seventy-six!

Besides coaching, the popular Swade dabbled in real estate, taught classes in high school and college and also served a few years as athletic director at Harbor. And in the late '80s and early '90s, Swade spent a year coaching pro football in Finland and three years in Italy. Whew! How in the heck did he accomplish all this?

George laughed. "I enjoy teaching young men how to do things successfully and what it takes to be successful—then watch the results," he said. "That's the pay for coaching."

Swade took a circuitous route to the top. He said he was on a single-wing team in high school and mostly played linebacker on defense and tight end and even second-string running back on offense. After high school, he joined the air force, where he played football and basketball while learning to be a jet mechanic. After he got out of the service, he said he went to Lockheed and was offered a job immediately. "I stood on the street corner figuring out what I wanted to do, and I decided to go to college," he said. He received a recruiting letter in the mail and went out for San Bernardino Valley College in 1956 after having married his sweetheart, Judith, in 1955. (They have seven kids and many grandchildren.)

George said he was blindsided at a practice in college and missed his entire first year. When he showed the coach that he could throw the ball, he went in during the second half of a game and threw three touchdown passes. Coach Don Warhurst of Cal Poly Pomona saw him and invited him to Pomona, where he warmed the bench until becoming a starter his second and third years and was eventually named District 3 NCAA first-string quarterback.

After college, and having a family to support, he went to work for the California Youth Authority, where he began coaching. "I was in charge of 50 wards of the court known as Company D," said George. "I had a variety of inmates and only a few with any football experience because the leaders of Section A and B took all the guys with experience. I started teaching them fundamentals—these guys were tough—and we excelled on defense, won four games and ended up playing for the championship, which we won 7–0."

Swade then took a job at Pomona Catholic (now Damian) and soon applied at Bishop Montgomery in Torrance, where he took over an ailing program (only four wins in three years). He went 5-4 in both 1963 and 1964 before turning the program completely around by going 8-1 in 1965 and winning the Camino Real championship in 1966 at 11-1. "That was probably the best team I ever had," said Swade of the '66 team. "It was led by players like Danny Graham, Chuck Bongard, Eddie Gilles, Charlie Reade, Mike and Mark Leamy, John Sullivan, Dan Miller, Greg Collins and Bob Jamison."

In high school, Swade said that he taught many things, "like being on time to all team activities, the importance of training, getting your school work done and keeping your nose clean." After Bishop, he landed a job with Seattle of the Continental Football League and helped the team to a 12-4 record as offensive coordinator. He was defense recognition coach at Long Beach State in 1970 and became an assistant at Harbor College in the early '70s before taking over the program in 1978. After going 3-6-1, 3-6 and 4-6 in his first three years, Swade went 8-3 in 1981 and 1982 and 6-3 in 1986. He returned to Harbor again in 1995 and 1996 and once more in 2009, when he was also athletic director.

"In college," George said, "if one wants to get a scholarship he must do the job in the classroom and on field, and I will get him placed accordingly. We have always preached being educated." He said one has to learn the "ability to listen, seek others' opinions, gather as much information as possible and make your own decisions. Football is a contact sport, and unless one has the basic fundamentals and conditioning, he will not last very long."

The year 2009 turned out to be an incredible one for Swade, as his team went 9-1 and he was also named Coach of the Year by the California

George Swade (right, with his son) coached Bishop Montgomery from 1963 through 1968 and remains the winningest coach in Knights history. *Courtesy of the Torrance Historical Society.*

Community College Football Coaches Association Region IV. Some of the great players he coached include David Williams, who is in the College Football Hall of Fame, as well as Keith Wright, Richard Johnson and Glen Walker, all of whom played in the NFL.

One of Swade's proudest achievements was starting the Lions South Bay All-Star Football Game in 1964; he served as chairman for the game in January 2014.

Swade concluded by saying, "Coaching is a very tough job with many inequities. Some schools have all the talent year in and year out, and many do a great job with what they have."

George Swade did that in spades.

CHAPTER 4

CARSON HIGH SCHOOL COLTS

Carson High School came into being in 1962—and so did its football team, which would become a California powerhouse on the gridiron. Since then, Colts have won 433 games, lost 179 and tied 5 for a .706 winning percentage and an average of 8.1 wins a season. That's bad, as the kids would say. Real bad!

Gene Vollnogle was the school's first and best coach, winning 236 games in twenty-eight years, an average of 8.4 a year. Nobody else comes close in terms of victories and longevity.

After Vollnogle's memorable year of 11-0 in 1966 (see accompanying story), the team went a not-too-shabby 7-1 in 1967. The 1970 team went 8-4 behind quarterback Joe Paura, tackle Meki Solomno, linebacker George Markulis, guard Peter Minko and fullback Junior Tupuela.

The rest of the decade was not exactly shabby, either, as the Colts won between six and eleven games every year. Then Carson won eleven games in 1981, '82 and '83. The 1983 team was led by quarterback Dan Acosta and players like James Barrett, Dwayne Smith, Allen Goree and Jaime Williams.

The year 1984 was another good one, with the Colts going 10-2. They beat San Fernando 39–32, Gardena 24–20 and Banning 33–20. Melvin Smith, Greg Ephrom, Derek Hill, Kevin Tate and Renaldo Caceres were instrumental players. The same went for 1985, as the Colts again went 10-2. In 1986, they finished 11-1 with wins in the playoffs over Cleveland (45–7), Granada Hills (56–14) and Banning (21–11). Running back Alvin Goree gained 2,345 yards rushing while captain Edwin Ulufanua had 104 tackles. All-League players included kicker Luis Solorio; defensive backs Michael

Left: John Calas Jr., son of John Calas, founder of the Carson Chamber of Commerce, and Kay Calas, longtime Carson city councilwoman, was an offensive lineman on the Carson team that lost only one game in 1967. *Courtesy of Carson High School.*

Below: Veteran South Bay coach Mike Christiansen (third row from bottom, middle) had three outstanding years at Carson: 2006 (9-4), 2009 (10-3) and 2007 (11-3). *Courtesy of Carson High School.*

Woodson, Sheldon Jones and Robert Ward; and defensive end Alan Wilson. More of the same (11-1) came in 1987, as the Colts lost only to Granada Hills, 27–14, after shutting out five opponents and allowing just forty-one points in eight games.

In 1988, it was another championship and another 12-1 season, with the only loss coming against Bishop Amat, 17–13. In the playoffs, Carson dismantled Kennedy and Banning, 53–0 and 55–77, respectively, and edged Dorsey 14–13. Errol Sapp was the South Bay Player of the Year and All-

City, while lineman Morris Unutoa, back Nkosi Littleton, Moheni Toiloto, Howard McCowan and Peter Hunt received All-City honors.

Then Vollnogle had his incredible last year and retired from Carson after the 1990 season. Marty Blankenship took the Colts to a nice 9-4-1 season in 1992, and then David Williams took over in 1993, going 10-4 and acquiring another city championship. In the playoffs, the Colts took care of El Camino Real 19–6, annihilated Garfield 61–14, edged Sylmar 22–21 and trumped Dorsey 26–0.

Then John Aguirre took over in 1999, leading the Colts to another city championship and a 12-2 season. Aguirre had a great six years, winning seventy games and losing only eighteen for an incredible .795 percentage. In 1999, the Colts beat Crenshaw 20–10 to win the championship behind such great players as Rique McNiel, Valentino Tofaeono, Taelenuu Tua'ua, Kevin Lindsey, Mike Moton and Ronnie Faavae. One good year after another followed.

In 2001, Aguirre went 9-2, beating Granada Hills 35–28 in the playoffs before losing to Taft of Woodland Hills, 17–14. In 2002, the Colts were 8-3, beating Jordan of Long Beach 32–22, Kennedy of LA 30–6 and Gardena 43–26 before losing to Jefferson of LA (48–28) in the playoffs. Aguirre won another city championship in 2003, going 11-3 and beating Taft 21–6, Grant of Van Nuys 27–24, Dorsey 19–18 and Venice 30–20.

Then veteran coach Mike Christiansen showed up with three strong years and twenty-five victories. In 2006, the Colts went 9-4, Dominique Blackman passed for 1,673 yards and fourteen touchdowns and Jack Sula rushed for 1,834 yards. They manhandled San Fernando (39–6) and Dorsey (38–20) in the playoffs before losing to San Pedro, 21–14.

Carson won eleven and lost three in 2007 behind Christiansen. The Colts beat Westchester 28–8, Banning 27–12 and Dorsey 6–0 in the playoffs before losing to Birmingham, 41–6. Wide receiver Chris Cockrell and Kennan Smith were helped by Blackman and Sula.

In 2009, Christiansen finished his tenure by going 10-3 and beating Santee 49–0 and Locke 31–7 in the playoffs before losing to Narbonne, 42–38. Quarterback Daniel Torres, receiver Brett Scott, defensive back Karon Walker and tackle Mckenzie Falo were all outstanding.

The last great year came under Elijah Asante in 2010, as the Colts beat Sylmar 42–6, Garfield 29–13 and Taft 40–21 before losing to Crenshaw, 45–7, in the finals. Quarterback Justin Alo passed for 2,534 yards and eighteen touchdowns, while Dion Willis rushed for 1,430 yards. On defense, Trevor Gagau and David Alevedo were outstanding.

It does not hurt that Carson High seems to produce outstanding athletes year after year. There is no reason that this pyramid of success will not continue.

Carson Win-Loss Records

1963: 2-6, Gene Vollnogle
1964: 2-6, Vollnogle
1965: 3-5, Vollnogle
1966: 11-0, Vollnogle
1967: 7-1, Vollnogle
1968: 3-5, Vollnogle
1969: 6-3, Vollnogle
1970: 8-4, Vollnogle
1971: 12-0, Vollnogle
1972: 12-0, Vollnogle
1973: 8-3-1, Vollnogle
1974: 6-4, Vollnogle
1975: 9-2, Vollnogle
1976: 7-4, Vollnogle
1977: 8-3, Vollnogle
1978: 11-1, Vollnogle
1979: 7-3, Vollnogle
1980: 8-3, Vollnogle
1981: 11-1, Vollnogle
1982: 11-1, Vollnogle
1983: 11-1, Vollnogle
1984: 10-2, Vollnogle
1985: 10-2, Vollnogle
1986: 11-1, Vollnogle
1987: 11-1, Vollnogle
1988: 12-1, Vollnogle

1989: 7-2, Vollnogle
1990: 12-1, Vollnogle
1991: 6-5-1, Mary Blankenship
1992: 9-4-1, Blankenship
1993: 10-4, David Williams
1994: 7-6, Williams
1995: 2-8, Mike Sakurai
1996: 4-7, Sakurai
1997: 6-6-2, Sakurai
1998: 5-6, Sakurai
1999: 12-2, John Aguirre
2000: 10-4, Aguirre
2001: 9-2, Aguirre
2002: 8-3, Aguirre
2003: 11-3, Aguirre
2004: 7-5, Rowen Tupuivao
2005: 3-8, Tupuivao
2006: 9-4, Mike Christiansen
2007: 11-3, Christiansen
2008: 5-6, Christiansen
2009: 10-3, Christiansen
2010: 12-3, Elijah Asante
2011: 8-5, Asante
2012: 6-7, Jimmy Nolan
2013: 7-6, Kevin McCall

Coaches' Records

1. Gene Vollnogle: 236-66-1 (.781)
2. John Aguirre: 70-18 (.795)
3. Mike Christiansen: 35-15 (.700)
4. Elijah Asante: 20-8 (.714)
5. David Williams: 17-10 (.630)

6. Mike Sakurai: 17-27-2 (.378)
7. Marty Blankenship: 15-9-2 (.615)
8. Rowen Tupuivao: 10-13 (.435)
9. Kevin McCall: 7-6 (.538)
10. Jimmy Nolan: 6-7 (.462)

Total: 433-179-5 (.706)

COACH GENE VOLLNOGLE

Gene Vollnogle of Carson High was undoubtedly the greatest—not one of the greatest—football coach in the history of the South Bay.

Tim Finney, statistician and former teacher at Carson High, claimed that Vollnogle, who died in his sleep at age eighty-one in 2012, had 384 wins, 91 losses and 1 tie in forty-seven years for an unbelievable percentage of .808. Vollnogle coached at Banning High School, Carson High and Los Alamitos High. But at Carson, where he was head coach from 1963 through 1990, he was a god, winning 236 games, losing only 66 and tying 1 for a .781 percentage.

Vollnogle had three undefeated seasons, eight seasons with only one loss and eight city championships. He developed many players who went on to the NFL, including wide receivers Mike Wilson (1976) for San Francisco, Bryan Reeves (1987) for Arizona and Wesley Walker (1972) for the New York Jets; quarterback Perry Klein (1989) for Atlanta; Laterio Rachel (1990) for Oakland; Arnold Ale (1988) for San Diego; L. David Aupiu Sr. (1979) for the Los Angeles Rams; Anthony Caldwell (1979) for the LA Raiders; Samoa Samoa (1974) for Cincinnati; Rick Baska (1970) for Denver; Wendell Cason (1981) for Atlanta; and Brian Treggs (1988) for Seattle.

"The hard part for Carson coaches today is living up to the gold standards that Coach Vollnogle set," said Carlos Ruis, who played under Vollnogle and later coached at Carson, in a 2012 article in the *Daily Breeze* newspaper. "People don't want to settle for anything less than what he stood for: personal accountability, teamwork and championships."

One of the school's great rivalries was with Banning High School in Wilmington, coached by Chris Ferragamo, who had played for Vollnogle at Banning. "It tore me up when I heard [of Gene's death]," Ferragamo said

South Bay coaching icon Gene Vollnogle teases Carson High running back Gary Miller in 1982. The Colts finished 11-1 that year and won the LA city championship. *Courtesy of Carson High School.*

to Tony Ciniglio of the *Breeze*. "He was my high school football coach, and I learned everything I know from him. He was the epitome of coaching. I respected him so much. I followed in his footsteps. Everything I've done is from him."

Vollnogle is missed by his family and friends as much as former coaches and players. He was married to his wife, Lucille, now eighty-three (2014), and had two children, Gary Gene and Teri; five grandchildren; and one great-grandchild.

"He was a man of integrity," Teri Vollnogle Hargreaves, Gene's daughter, said to Ciniglio. "He didn't cuss. He played everyone. He was a good person. Every player has said what a great coach he was and that he was a good individual."

Vollnogle, born in Los Angeles in 1930, attended Freemont High and Pepperdine. Coach Paul Huebner gave twenty-three-year-old Vollnogle his first coaching job in 1953, directing the Pilots' B team. He then named him co-coach of the varsity team in 1957. Vollnogle helped Huebner win two city titles for Banning before he moved on to coach Carson, where he went 2-6 in 1963 and 1964 and 3-5 in 1965 before going undefeated (11-0) and winning the city championship in 1966. That year, the Colts beat Jefferson 7–0, Reseda 28–0 and San Fernando 27–13 to win the championship. They were led by running back and Player of the Year Bob Bartlett, quarterback Jimmy Sander, lineman Joe Dymerski, guards Frank Gutierrez and Larry Costello, end Ron Carver and running back Dick Cross. The big event of the year was beating Banning 40–21 in front of twelve thousand fans at El Camino Stadium. The Colts blasted San Pedro 66–12, Jordan 45–0 and Roosevelt 39–0.

The team did all right in 1969, going 7-1, but had a 12-0 record in 1971 and 1972. In the playoffs in 1971, the Colts manhandled Venice 48–7 and also beat Dorsey (21–6), Cleveland (40–14) and Monroe (41–20) for the city championship. All-League players included linebacker Brad Vaughn, tackle Meki Solomona, guard Peter Minko, Co-Player of the Year running back Mike McClure and end Willie Guillory. Other victories were over Locke (43–0), San Pedro (46–0) and Narbonne (40–6).

Wesley Walker, who would go on to be a great receiver in the NFL, was on the team in 1972, leading the Colts to wins in the playoffs over Cleveland, Crenshaw, Wilson and Bell. All-League players included flanker Joe Shipp, center Kenny Gibson and tackle Larry Castagnola.

Vic Resendez, who played on the undefeated 12-0 Carson team in 1972, told the *Los Angeles Times* that Vollnogle "was the best. It was an honor to have played football for him…and yes, I learned to keep working hard, keep getting up the next day and getting at it."

Phil Collin, in the *Daily Breeze* in 2012, pointed out that the movie *Remember the Titans*, the story of T.C. Williams High in Virginia, struck a chord with Kise Fitatoa, a member of the 1972 team. Kise noted that Williams High finished number two in the nation—behind Carson.

"Coach Vollnogle was open-minded about some of those things," George Malauulu, quarterback of the 1987 team, said. "That's why he was such a great, great coach. It takes those kinds of coaches to show the humility part of coaching. He was ahead of his time."

Vollnogle continued on his winning roll, going 11-1 in 1982, 10-2 in 1984, 11-1 in 1986, 12-1 in 1988 and 12-1 in 1990, all accompanied by city championships.

After winning the 1988 title by routing Banning at the LA Coliseum, Phil Collin of the *Daily Breeze* reported that Vollnogle said he enjoyed picking up huge chunks of yardage with his two quarterbacks, Perry Klein and Fred Gatlin, and the running of Errol Sapp. "It was zap, zap, zap, then zap 'em with Sapp," Vollnogle said, chuckling at his own words.

Daughter Hargreaves said, "Coaching to him was fun, and he always said that playing football had to be fun. He had a great sense of humor."

And Vollnogle was instrumental in helping the huge Samoan community in Wilmington. "He gave us the opportunity," Malauulu told Collin. "He opened the door. He allowed us to kind of be who we wanted to be at that point in time...I wouldn't be a man if it wasn't for that man."

"He was a coach who always worked harder than everyone else and always stressed discipline," Coach Paul Huebner, who is now retired and living in Santa Barbara, told the *Los Angeles Times* in 1989.

Vollnogle seemed puzzled when he heard he was perceived as intimidating. "I just try to be honest and treat everyone fairly," he said, adding that he patterned his coaching style after Lefty Goodhue, the Banning coach from 1950 through 1956. "I compliment players when they do something right and correct them when they are wrong."

After he retired from Carson, Vollnogle spent ten years as an assistant coach at Los Alamitos High. "He was an incredible football mind," Los Alamitos coach John Barnes told the *Times* in 2012. "He'd watch film and get more out of it than 10 guys in the room. He's truly a high school football legend."

Fittingly, Vollnogle finished his career at Carson in 1990, going 12-1 and winning another city championship. Key wins were 56–12 over Washington, 47–0 over San Pedro and 56–0 over Gardena. Outstanding players included defensive end Bob Tuitan, running back Abdul Mohammad, quarterback John Walsh, wide receiver Laterio Rachal, linebacker Frank Padilla and defenseman Shawn Parnell.

Gene Vollnogle left an indelible mark on South Bay football that probably will never be equaled.

CHAPTER 5
CHADWICK SCHOOL DOLPHINS

Chadwick School on the Palos Verdes Peninsula has a very interesting history. It was founded in 1935 in San Pedro by Margaret Lee Chadwick and Commander Joseph Chadwick and moved to Palos Verdes in 1938. In the beginning, it was an open-air day and boarding school for 75 students. Today, there are 360 students in the high school portion of this independent, nonsectarian, K–12 education system. The school apparently began playing football in 1941—first six-man football, then eight-man and finally the eleven-man game of today.

The first coach was the legendary Edwin Ellis. He served as head football coach from 1941 through 1965, posting eighty-nine wins with just thirty-one losses. He had two undefeated seasons in 1961 and 1964.

Sid Grant was the next coach to have a legendary record, winning fifty-four games alone and another eleven games with Jim Drennan from 1986 through 2002. His tenure included the only undefeated team in history. The 1980 Dolphins won the CIF small school championship with a 10-0 record, defeating Rio Hondo Preparatory 43–20. The team was led by CIF Player of the Year Jeff Kaufman, who was assisted by a defense led by Todd Dalton, Greg Burrell and Fred Clark.

Other top players during Grant's siege were quarterback Jeff Karnes in 1988, running back Shawn Tucker and linebacker Chris Carasgoes in 1990, Todd Gordon and Rob Barnes in 1994 and Kunle Williams and Danny Oliphant in 1996.

Gary Willison, the current coach, started in 2003 and has a record of 73-39-2 for a .649 percentage. In 2004, Willison's Dolphins went 7-3-1, beating

Chudi Iregbulum was a running back on the great Chadwick team that went 11-2 in 2009. *Courtesy of Peninsula Library Archives.*

Rio Hondo Prep 48–12 before losing to Brentwood School, 41–7. Outstanding players included Daniel Kohl, who passed for almost 2,000 yards; Chris Kim, who rushed for over 1,200; and Austin Norris, who excelled on defense.

In 2006, the Dolphins were 8-3 with great wins over Webb Schools of Claremont (30–7) and Viewpoint of Calabasas (21–0). Leading players were Andy Magee, who passed for over 2,800 yards; Joseph Cioffi, who had seventy-three receptions; and Garrett Wymore, who had fifty-four tackles. But Willison's big year was 2009, when the Dolphins went 11-2 and downed Bloomington Christian and South High of Boron before losing to Linfield Christian of Temecula, 35–0. Outstanding in their field were Jordan Agnew, who passed for almost 1,500 yards; Kidd Harrison, who had thirty-three receptions; and Hank Trumbull, who had six sacks.

Chadwick has a very fine overall record of 275-195-6, with thirteen years unaccounted for. One thing is for sure: Chadwick remains competitive year after year, and the Dolphins keep on going—even if it is upstream sometimes.

Chadwick Win-Loss Records

1941: 5-2, Edwin Ellis
1942: 4-6, Ellis
1943: no football
1944: no football
1945: no football
1946: 1-1, Coach Blackman
1947: no record
1948: 0-2, Coach Connett
1949: 6-3, Ellis
1950: no record
1951: no record
1952: 3-3, Ellis
1953: 3-3, Ellis
1954: 0-5, Ellis
1955: 4-1, Ellis
1956: 5-2, Ellis
1957: no record
1958: 5-1, Ellis
1959: 3-4, Ellis
1960: 7-1, Ellis
1961: 6-0, Ellis
1962: 5-1, Ellis
1963: 5-1, Ellis
1964: 6-0, Ellis
1965: 2-5, Ellis
1966: 3-5, U.G. Smith
1967: 3-5, Smith
1968: no record
1969: 5-2-1, Smith
1970: 8-2, Smith
1971: no record
1972: no record
1973: 5-3, J.O. Owens
1974: no record
1975: 5-3, Owens
1976: no record
1977: no record

1978: no record
1979: 5-4, Steve Hare
1980: 3-6, Hare
1981: 5-4, Hare
1982: no record
1983: no record
1984: no record
1985: 7-3, Jim Drennan
1986: 10-0, Sid Grant
1987: 3-5-1, Grant
1988: 4-1, Grant and Drennan
1989: 4-5, Grant
1990: 4-4, Grant
1991: 5-3, Grant
1992: 4-5, Grant
1993: 8-2, Grant
1994: 4-5, Grant
1995: 4-7, Grant
1996: 4-4-1, Grant
1997: 4-4-1, Grant
1998: 2-8, Jim Drennan and Grant
1999: 3-7, Drennan and Grant
2000: 4-6, Drennan and Grant
2001: 1-9, Drennan and Grant
2002: 4-4-1, Drennan and Grant
2003: 4-6-1, Gary Willison
2004: 7-3-1, Willison
2005: 3-6-1, Willison
2006: 8-3, Willison
2007: 7-4, Willison
2008: 6-4, Willison
2009: 11-2, Willison
2010: 9-3, Willison
2011: 6-5, Willison
2012: 5-5, Willison
2013: 7-4, Willison

Coaches' Records

1. Edwin Ellis: 81-39 (.675)
2. Gary Willison: 73-39-2 (.649)
3. Sid Grant: 54-44-3 (.535)
4. Jim Drennan and Sid Grant: 14-34-1 (.296)
5. J.O. Owens: 14-8 (.636)
6. Steve Hare: 13-14 (.481)
7. Jim Drennan: 7-3 (.700)
8. U.G. Smith: 19-14-1 (.375)

Totals: 275-195-6 (.584)
(thirteen years unaccounted for)

CHAPTER 6

EL SEGUNDO HIGH SCHOOL EAGLES

The El Segundo High School Eagles have not done too badly in football since 1929, accumulating fifteen seasons of outstanding winning records. The best year the Eagles ever had was in 1988, when they finished 10-1 under Coach Steve Newell. They also won 10 games in 2002 and 2008 under Steve Shevlin, who has coached for the past twenty years and accumulated 105 wins, easily outdistancing his closest rival, Newell, who won 48 games in twelve years. In third is the school's first football coach, Harvey Hazeltine (who has the football field named after him), with 46 wins, and Clyde "Ike" Dougherty comes in fourth with 33.

Matt Engle (2000–03) was probably the most outstanding Eagle football player of all time. He passed for 8,634 yards and ninety-five touchdowns from 2000 to 2002. He completed 218 passes in one season and 35 in one game. He had 493 yards passing for seven touchdowns in a game against South Torrance in 2002. Engle was All-State and an honorable mention All-American at El Camino College in 2003. He later played for the University of California–Davis.

Receiver Brad Franks had a meteoric career at the same time. He has had the most receptions (173) and yards (2,553) in Eagle history. He also caught thirty-seven touchdown passes.

Kris Atmore is the leading rusher of all time, having garnered 2,816 yards in 2004–05. He gained 2,005 yards in 2005 alone and is second in scoring, with 240 points. Casey Gardner was an outstanding field goal kicker in 2000, kicking field goals of fifty-three and fifty yards.

Leading the defense over the years were players like Austin Brashear, Gage Morteson and Jerry Dillon. Jimmy Quiones had six interceptions in three consecutive seasons from 2007 to 2009, while Paul Wilk had ten fumble recoveries in his career (1980–82).

Steve Obradovich was one of El Segundo High's greatest football and volleyball players in the 1970s. He played quarterback for the Eagles and walked on at USC, where he played two years and won a ring with the national championship team in 1977. Later, Obradovich established himself as one of the premier players on the volleyball circuit. His older brother, Jim, was also an El Segundo standout at end and played six years in the NFL, mostly for Tampa Bay. Joe Caravello was an outstanding end in 1980 who went on to play at Tulane University and later with the San Diego Chargers and Washington Redskins.

Quarterback Jack Hawley went on to play at Los Angeles Harbor College, where he set many records and passed for 5,031 yards and forty-six touchdowns in his two seasons there.

El Segundo High's first traceable football record was in 1929, when the Eagles finished a great 8-1 under Coach Harvey S. Hazeltine. Unfortunately, the records through 1937 are missing, but Hazeltine had more good teams in 1938 (6-1-1), 1940 (6-1-1) and 1942 (6-2). In 1948, Bob Van Hosen was an All-League first-team center. But it was Frank Craven who carried the Eagles to their best record in over 120 years when El Segundo went 8-2 in 1951. The Eagles lost to Ventura in the CIF playoffs but had a great year behind linemen Bob Smith and Steve Bowls. Other outstanding players included Roger Peterson, Roger Martz and Glenn Judd behind the team's MVP quarterback, Ron Heusser. The season included great wins over Puente (12–0), Harvard (30–13), Downey (47–13), Hawthorne (27–13) and Mira Costa (32–0).

Things were pretty tame until 1957, when Ike Dougherty led the Eagles to a 6-3 record with quality wins over San Gabriel (21–18), Beverly Hills (26–0) and Culver City (25–6). A gaggle of players made All-League, including halfbacks Tom Matlock, Jim Bell and Sam Molinaro; quarterback Mike Giannini; tackle Fred Crook; end Dave Mordache; center Chuck Rausch; and guard John Anderson.

The team followed that up with a 7-1 record in 1958 behind none other than Pete Beathard, the quarterback who would go on to lead USC to a national championship in 1962 and play pro football for a dozen years. As a junior in 1958, Pete was All-League, as was end Jim Myers, halfback Carl Moore and tackle Norman Smotony. The Eagles' victims included

Inglewood (18–13), Torrance (19–13), San Gabriel (20–6) and Beverly Hills (39–0).

Pete repeated his great feats in 1959, as El Segundo went 6-1-1 with Beathard being named to the All-League first team and All-CIF second team. Center Tim Whipple, end Cliff Pleggenkuhle and running back Bob Brode were also All-League. El Segundo manhandled Mira Costa (19–13), Palmdale (26–6), Aviation (12–0) and Beverly Hills (19–6), among others.

New coach John McHargue helped the team to a 6-3 record in 1962, but the Eagles blossomed under George Hartman in 1964 and '65. He was an El Segundo coach for just two years but led the Eagles to records of 7-3 and 7-2. The '64 team is renowned for boasting the first famous Brett brother of professional sports. Ken "Kemer" Brett was an outstanding halfback his junior year. Even though he broke his ankle, he was an All-League running back along with lineman Terry Brown, linebacker David Stokley and end Bill Sligar. The Eagles went to the CIF playoffs, where they lost 14–0 to La Canada. Before that, however, they had shutouts over St. Monica (12–0) and Aviation (31–0) and also beat St. Bernard (14–6) and Torrance (33–6).

Ken, who at an early age was regarded as an even better prospect than his Hall of Fame brother, George (also an El Segundo football standout), played four years in big-league baseball. He won eighty-three games, carried a no-hitter into the ninth inning twice and holds the record for most consecutive games with a home run by a pitcher—four in 1973.

In 1965, Hartman led the team to a 7-2 record with wins over Culver City (21–14), Lennox (21–0), West Torrance (6–0) and Aviation (7–6). All-League players included quarterback Jerry Filson, tackle Richard Standage, center Jom Hough, guard Alan L'Hommedieu and end Bill Sligar.

El Segundo had another good year in 1966 behind new head coach Philbert Santia, who led the team to a 6-1-2 record. Big wins were over Beverly Hills (26–0) and West Torrance (20–13). Outstanding players included quarterback Marty Endquist, halfback Corey LaMar, fullback Randy Hayes, defensive end Curt Whitney, linebacker Jack Pancoast, guard David Peterson and tackle Cid Stolper.

The 1970 season was renowned for three reasons: the most wins in history, George Brett and Jim Obradovich.

Coach Doug Minner led the Eagles to a 9-1-1 record that year and was named South Bay Coach of the Year. That great season featured shutouts of Lawndale (14–0), Miraleste (8–0) and Bloomington (21–0). It didn't hurt that the even more famous Brett brother, George, was an All-League first-team running back, while Obradovich, who went on to play in the

Pete Beathard was a great quarterback for El Segundo High School in 1959 before he went on to stardom at the University of Southern California. He played for four NFL clubs, including the Kansas City Chiefs and Houston Oilers. *Courtesy of El Segundo High School.*

NFL, was All-League on defense. (Also All-League were quarterback Frank Judge and Mike Kistler, Bob Lourey and Eric Bimber on defense.)

George was a great Eagle running back but, of course, became more famous as a baseball player, earning a spot in the Hall of Fame with a lifetime batting average of .305. He also had 3,154 hits, 317 home runs and 1,596 RBIs. George is arguably the greatest sports achiever ever to come out of the South Bay.

Obradovich, who played at USC, spent nine years in the NFL and holds the Tampa Bay record for most tackles (eighty) on kickoff coverage. His brother, Steve, was also a great player at El Segundo in the 1970s before going on to USC.

In 1973, former USC star Damon Bame guided the Eagles to a 6-4 record behind All-Leaguers Tom Soto at quarterback and Bryan Smith on both offense and defense. Other outstanding players were running back Tim Cargill and wide receivers Alan Walker, Ben Beaird and Jeff Hancock. The Eagles made it to the CIF playoffs, only to lose 14–13 to Neff of La Mirada.

Steve Newell made his debut in 1974, leading El Segundo to a 7-3 record. The Eagles had three great shutouts against St. Bernard (9–0), Cerritos (17–0) and Harvard (20–0) but lost to Agoura, 40–0, in the CIF playoffs. First team All-League were nose guard Jorge Gigena, cornerback Joe Purvis, safety Ron Jellison, defensive end Jim Berggren, tackle Keith Keenum,

Ken (Kemer) Brett was a backfield star for El Segundo High School in 1964 before he went on to win eighty-three games in fourteen years as a pitcher in the major leagues. *Courtesy of El Segundo High School.*

George Brett (no. 83), a Hall of Fame baseball player for the Kansas City Royals, was also a backfield star for El Segundo High in 1969. Jim Obradovich (no. 32) played nine years at tight end in the NFL. *Courtesy of El Segundo High School.*

linebacker-center John Stroh, end Hoe Purvis and halfback Jim Buckingham. In 1980, Joe Caravello, who later played with the San Diego Chargers and Washington Redskins, was an outstanding player.

After a down period, El Segundo returned with a 9-4 record in 1987 under Newell. The Eagles beat Lompoc 20–8 and Monrovia 20–19 in the CIF playoffs before losing to Burroughs of Burbank, 26–16. Having outstanding years were quarterback Joe Montanyez; wide receivers David Lubs, Dan Brown and Donovan Gallatin; running backs Erik Evans and Heath Jones; and linemen Phillip Delk, Rob White, Sean Douglas and Keith Griego.

But in 1988, the Eagles turned in the best record of all time, going 10-1 under Newell. The highlight was a 41–0 washing of Mira Costa. The team was led by quarterback Matt Wise; running back Erik Evans; receivers Jeremy Carr, Roric Ruegsegger and Eric Stevens; and linemen Jason Whip, Rob Croxall, Dan Irvin and Ken Talenoa.

1991 was another good year, as the Eagles beat St. Francis 10–7 in the CIF playoffs. All-League selections included Brett Chauncey, Chris Feeny, Mike Fransz, Toby Hale, Hauss Hancock, Jim Hurley, David Scanlon (back of the year and first team All-South Bay), Sam Ward and Landon Wilson.

Steve Shevlin took over as coach in 1994 and has led the team to a record 101 wins. (See adjoining coach's profile.) And with another 10 wins in 2013, things are only looking up for the high-flying Eagles.

El Segundo Win-Loss Records

1929: 8-1, Harvey S. Hazeltine
1930–36: no records
1937: 5-3, Hazeltine
1938: 6-1-1, Hazeltine
1939: no record
1940: 6-2, Hazeltine
1941: 6-2, Hazeltine
1942: 6-2, Hazeltine
1943: 4-2, Hazeltine
1944: 3-3, Hazeltine
1945: 1-3-1, Hazeltine
1946: 2-5-1, Hazeltine
1947: 2-5-1, Hazeltine
1948: 0-8, Frank Craven
1949: 1-8, Craven
1951: 8-2, Craven
1952: 4-3-1, Craven
1953: 4-3-1, Craven
1954: 2-7, Craven
1955: 3-3, Clyde "Ike" Dougherty
1956: 3-5, Dougherty

1957: 6-3, Dougherty
1958: 7-1, Dougherty
1959: 6-1-1, Dougherty
1960: 4-4, Dougherty
1961: 3-6, Dougherty
1962: 6-3, John McHargue
1963: 5-4, McHargue
1964: 7-3, George Hartman
1965: 7-2, Hartman
1966: 6-1-2, Phil Santia
1967: 0-9, Santia
1968: no record
1969: 3-5-1, Doug Minner
1970: 9-1, Minner
1971: 2-6, Carter
1972: 2-7, Damon Bame
1973: 6-4, Bame
1974: 7-3, Steve Newell
1975: 5-4, Newell
1976: 4-4-1, Newell
1977: 4-3-2, Newell

1978: 3-6, Dougherty
1979: 2-6-2, Dougherty
1980: 2-8, Newell
1981: 2-8, Newell
1982: 5-6, Newell
1983: 4-6, Newell
1984: 2-6-1, Newell
1985: 3-7, Newell
1986: 4-6, Newell
1987: 9-4, Newell
1988: 10-1, Newell
1989: 5-6, Newell
1990: 5-5-1, Newell
1991: 8-3, Newell
1992: 4-6, Craig Cousins
1993: 3-7, Cousins
1994: 2-8, Steve Shevlin
1995: 1-9, Shevlin
1996: 5-5, Shevlin

1997: 6-4, Shevlin
1998: 2-7-1, Shevlin
1999: 4-6, Shevlin
2000: 4-4-2, Shevlin
2001: 5-4, Shevlin
2002: 10-2, Shevlin
2003: 6-5, Shevlin
2004: 5-5-1, Shevlin
2005: 4-5-1, Shevlin
2006: 6-5, Shevlin
2007: 5-5, Shevlin
2008: 10-3, Shevlin
2009: 7-5, Shevlin
2010: 6-5, Shevlin
2011: 6-5, Shevlin
2012: 7-5, Shevlin
2013: 10-4, Shevlin

Coaches' Records

1. Steve Shevlin: 101-97-10 (.510)
2. Steve Newell: 48-43-6 (.526)
3. Harvey Hazeltine: 46-27-5 (.622)
4. Clyde (Ike) Dougherty: 37-35-3 (.527)
5. Frank Craven: 19-24-2 (.444)
6. George Hartman: 14-5 (.737)
7. Damon Bame: 13-7 (.650)
8. Doug Minner: 12-6-1 (.694)
9. John McHargue: 11-7 (.611)
10. Craig Cousins: 7-13 (.350)
11. Phil Santia: 6-10-2 (.389)
13. Coach Carter: 2-6 (.250)

Totals: 317-281-29 (.529)
(eight years unaccounted for)

COACH STEVE SHEVLIN

Steve Shevlin is another football coach who has become a legend in the South Bay. Shevlin, who has a record of 111-105-5, has been head coach at El Segundo High School since 1994. While Steve has not had an incredible record, he has had his moments, including going 10-2 in 2003, 10-3 in 2008 and 10-4 in 2013 and some great wins in the CIF playoffs.

In 2002, the Eagles beat Rio Hondo 38–22 in the playoffs. In 2008, they handled Santa Clara 42–0 and St. Joseph's of Santa Maria 24–20. In 2009, they manhandled Nordhoff of Ojai 24–7. In 2012, they beat LaPuente 31–7, and in 2013, they really rolled, beating Santa Paula 35–28, Carpenteria 45–31 and Oak Park 59–40.

"I think if everything we did in high school was for win/loss record, the importance of impacting young men's lives gets lost," Shevlin said. "If you want to be a great winner or leader, you have to learn about loss and defeat. That makes success that much more humbling and respected. I think if kids buy into your program and understand the big picture, wins and losses are all teachable moments."

And a lot of great players have helped. "In 2002," Shevlin said, "Matt Engle was the state player of the year for the Medium Schools Division and broke all El Segundo career and season passing records and went on to play at UC Davis." Engle threw for 8,634 yards and ninety-five touchdowns in three years. "In 2008, Gage Mortesen, running back and linebacker, was second-team all-state and the catalyst for a team that tied for the league championship and took Serra to the brink in a 35–28 loss in the CIF semifinals." In his three years, Mortesen ran for 2,031 yards, averaging 6.1 yards a carry, and scored twenty-five touchdowns. "In 2013," Shevlin continued, "wide receiver Jamie Stewart was first-team all-state and broke all the receiving records for El Segundo. He put the team on his back and carried us to the CIF championship game." Quarterback Lars Nootbar was also incredible, passing for 2,864 yards and thirty-three touchdowns.

"I enjoy impacting young kids' lives," Shevlin said. "Football is the greatest sport in the world that requires the ultimate teamwork concepts. It's a sport many kids will not play past high school, and the experience they get in high school can have a positive impact for the rest of their lives."

Those mentioned above were not his only good years. Shevlin took over in 1994 and by 1997 had a competitive program, going 6-4. Scipio Stubbs led the South Bay in rushing with 1,338 yards and sixteen touchdowns that year.

Steve Shevlin (pictured here in 2013) was a running back and safety at Culver City High School and has directed El Segundo High to 101 wins in twenty years. *Photo by Robert Casillas; courtesy of the* Daily Breeze.

Bobby Gaines led the South Bay in touchdown receptions, with eleven, and quarterback Derek Ernest passed for 2,152 yards and twenty touchdowns.

In 2009, the team went 7-5, including a 24–7 win over Nordhoff of Jai in the CIF playoffs. They then lost to St. Joseph of Santa Maria, 34–11. But season highlights included Michael Bundy passing for 2,642 yards and twenty-three touchdowns and Grant Palmer catching forty-seven passes for four touchdowns.

And 2012 wasn't shabby either, as the Eagles went to the playoffs once more, beating La Puente 31–7 before losing to Centennial, 14–10. Quarterback Lars Nootbar started his two-year rampage with 1,428 yards passing, while Austin Brasher rushed for 619 yards.

Shevlin, who was born in Inglewood in 1962, played football at Culver City High School, where he was a starter for two years as wide receiver and defensive back. Culver City won the Ocean League championship his junior year.

A 1987 graduate of Long Beach State, Shevlin has a degree in English and a master's from Azusa Pacific. He taught English for seven years and physical education for two years, has coached football at El Segundo for twenty years and has been the athletic director for the past fifteen years. "My greatest football influence was Gene Engle, offensive coordinator at El Camino College," said Shevlin. "He volunteered his time and energy and taught me about perseverance, faith and the x's and o's of offensive football. He is the single greatest reason our program is as competitive as it has been since 1999."

Steve and his wife, April, have two children: Cassidy, seventeen, who plays water polo and swims, and C.J., fifteen, who is a football and baseball player. He also has over one thousand other kids whose lives are affected positively by his leadership and influence.

CHAPTER 7

FERMIN LASUEN HIGH SCHOOL PADRES

Fermin Lasuen High School was in existence for just ten years but obviously was a prime player in the Camino Real League, winning the championship five times under great Coach Bob Baiz, who had a 59-28-1 record for a .676 percentage.

Fermin Lasuen Win-Loss Records

1961: 5-3-1, Bob Baiz
1962: 12-0, Baiz (Camino Real champions and CIF AA champions)
1963: 9-2, Baiz (Camino Real champions)
1964: 7-4, Baiz (Camino Real champions)
1965: 5-4, Baiz
1966: 7-2, Baiz (Camino Real champions)
1967: 2-6, Baiz
1968: 4-5, Baiz
1969: 8-2, Baiz (Camino Real champions)
1970: 5-4, Mike Tedesco

Coaches' Records

1. Bob Baiz: 59-28-1 (.676)
2. Mike Tedesco: 5-4 (.556)

Total: 64-33-5 (.652)

CHAPTER 8

GARDENA HIGH SCHOOL PANTHERS

Gardena High School, which opened in 1907, moved into its current home in 1956. And the school's football program has a storied history, winning 359 games. Some of its great players who have gone on to significant careers in the NFL include tackle Ernie Smith, starting in 1935 for Green Bay; back Lowell Wagner for the New York Yankees (1946); quarterback Don Horn for Green Bay (1967); running back Charlie Evans for the New York Giants (1971); wide receiver Steve Holden for Cleveland (1973); defensive back Nesby Glasgow for Baltimore (1979); defensive back Keith Lee for New England (1981); the first George Farmer, wide receiver for the Los Angeles Rams (1981); and running back Gaston Green for the Rams (1988).

The first mention of football came in the 1913 yearbook, which notes, "Pat Sheehy, three quarters, known as the best booter of the team, won fame for his famous long drives at Monrovia and Compton." That was about it until a coach by the name of Norton took the team to a 1-4-1 season in 1916. And it was in 1926–28 that the team had its first great success under Coaches George Freeman and William McGinnis, going 4-1, 6-1 and 6-1. Great players included Gaile Parsons, Al Boehlert, Ernest Smith and George Bateman in 1927 and Bill Darnell and Harry Ulrich in 1928. Quarterback Russell White was All-Marine in 1930, and the Panthers tied for the league championship in 1931 with a 5-1 record under Loren Peak.

Peak led the team to an outstanding season in 1934, going 5-1-1. First-team All-League were tackle Howard Flint, center Morgan Moser, guard Dick Grace and quarterback Ira Van Riper. 1937 was even better, as the

Panthers finished 7-0-1 behind Peak. Great players included quarterback Louis Zaharia, halfback Marwood Kolyski, tackle Al Mardis and center Jack Stephens.

There were no records during the war years, and then Peak returned to lead the team to 8-1 in 1948. Quarterback Don Bahrman, fullback Jim Charles, center John Erbe, guard Jack Hammond and tackle Don Jackson were outstanding.

Then Stan Smith, the winningest coach in Gardena history, came on the scene in 1951 and proceeded to lead the Panthers to fifty-seven wins on his own and another twenty-four with Dick Enright. The team went undefeated in 1952 (4-0-1) and 6-1-1 in 1962. But from 1962 through 1975, the Panthers had their most successful era in history, going an incredible 113-25-2.

In 1963, all-time great quarterback Steve Sogge (later a USC star) and fullback Jim Lewis led the team, which also included end Danny Carr, lineman Pete Taculog and halfback Bobby Meyers. But Sogge was even more efficient in 1964, leading the team to a 9-2 record and receiving All-City and Player of the Year honors.

Things just kept getting better. Dick Enright joined Smith to lead the team to consecutive years of 8-2, 7-1 and 9-1, and then Enright, on his own, was 9-1 in 1968 and 11-1 in 1969.

Back Charlie Evans and end Tenny Warren were All-City in 1965. The 1966 team went 7-1 and featured All-Marine quarterback Greg Briner, All-City running backs Charles Evans and Mike Jeter and tackle Mike Baumgarner. Halfback Dick Sakai was also All-Marine.

In the great year of 1967 (9-1), the Panthers' only loss was to Westchester, 19–14, in the city finals. Great players included lineman Art Serrano, Donivan Hall, backs David Moch and Dick Sakai and quarterback Briner.

In 1968, the Panthers' only loss was to Canoga Park, 7–6, in the finals. But the beat went on. Gardena was an incredible 11-1 in 1969 with four shutouts over league rivals: Carson (21–0), Narbonne (21–0), Banning (39–0) and San Pedro (40–0). Fullback Greg Herd was the Marine Player of the Year, and kicker Glenn Walker, linebacker Larry Dean, guard Russell Stephen and defensive back Reedy Hall were all great.

Then Coach Ralph Vidal took over, leading the team to a great 40-10-1 record over the next five years. The Panthers had nineteen consecutive wins through 1970 before finally losing to Manual Arts, 6–0. All-City players that year included center Tom Surface, tackle Lonnie Graffel and defensive back Dave Robinson.

All-everything quarterback Steve Sogge led Gardena to a 9-2 record in 1964 and then led USC to a national title in 1967. He was also the catcher on the USC baseball team that won the College World Series in 1968. *Courtesy of Gardena High School.*

Then came the greatest year in the school's history, 1973, when Vidal led the team to the city championship and a 11-0-1 season. Vidal was named Coach of the Year, and Gardena outscored its opponents 294–53. Running back Kevin Cole, who gained 1,606 yards and scored seventeen touchdowns, was the City Player of the Year, while All-City players included linebacker Ricky Orange, lineman Michael Allen and end Brian Lee. All-Marine players included defenseman Craig Lancaster, fullback Raymond Cryer and quarterback Scott Nishikuni.

The following year was not bad either, as the team went 10-2, losing to Palisades, 6–0, in the finals. Player of the Year Ken Smith was aided by All-Marine lineman Dennis Malumaleumu, back Raymond Cryer and defensive players Antowaine Richardson and Nesby Glasgow.

In 1975, new coaches Bob Sugino and Jerry Case took over the team and led it to a 6-4 record. Defensive tackle Michael Jackson was All-South Bay, while end Seth Williams, tailback George Farmer and quarterback Keith Lee were All-Marine.

Bill Partridge led the team to three good years in 1980 (6-2-1), 1981 (7-4) and 1982 (7-4). Future UCLA great Gaston Green was on the 1982 team and was All-City along with linebacker Merkle Williams, while guard Doug Wood was All-League.

Then it took Coach Marshall Jones to bring some respectability back to the program as he proceeded to win forty-six games from 1999 through 2008. In 1999, Michael Henderson, Tyon Gilmore, Lorenzo Bailey and Milton Grimes helped lead the team to a 9-4-1 record before losing a critical game to Banning, 40–32. And in 2002, the Panthers had a fine 9-4 season before losing to Birmingham of Van Nuys, 34–20.

The team has not fared that well since 2004, winning only thirty-four games. But the tradition at Gardena is strong, and current coach Deon Toliver will try to bring them back to the top.

Above: Gardena, a powerhouse in the Marine League in the 1960s, was led by All-Marine quarterback Greg Briner in 1966. The Mohicans won seventy games from 1961 to 1969. *Courtesy of Gardena High School.*

Opposite, top: Fullback Greg Herd was the Marine Player of the Year in 1969, leading the Gardena Mohicans to an 11-1 record. *Courtesy of Gardena High School.*

Opposite, bottom: Coach Ralph Vidal (left) won forty games for Gardena from 1970 to 1974. His teams finished 11-0-1 in '73 and 10-2 in '74. *Courtesy of Gardena High School.*

Gardena High Win-Loss Records

1912: "Pat Sheehy, three quarters, known as the best booter on the team won fame by his famous long drives at Monrovia and Compton." —1913 yearbook
1916: 1-4-1, Norton
1918: no record
1919: no record
1920: 1-3, Nordahl and Phee
1921: 3-3, Leonard
1922: 3-1, Leonard
1923: 2-4, Leonard
1924: 2-3, Wheedon
1925: 2-0-3, Clark
1926: 4-1, George Freeman
1927: 6-1, Freeman
1928: 6-1, Freeman and William McGinnis
1929: 4-3, Freeman and McGinnis
1930: 3-3, Freeman and McGinnis
1931: 5-1, Loren Peak
1932: 0-4-1, Peak
1933: 2-2-1, Peak
1934: 5-1-1, Peak
1935: no record
1936: no record
1937: 7-1, Peak
1938: no record
1939: 2-1-1, Peak
1940: no record
1941: no record
1942: no record
1943: no record
1944: no record
1945: no record
1946: no record
1947: no record
1948: 8-1, Peak
1949: 0-3-3, Peak
1950: 0-8, Maggard
1951: 4-4, Stan Smith
1952: 4-0-1, Smith
1953: 4-4, Smith
1954: 4-4, Smith
1955: 4-4, Smith
1956: 2-6, Smith
1957: 1-7, Smith
1958: 2-6, Smith
1959: 3-3-1, Smith
1960: 3-3-2, Smith
1961: 3-5, Smith
1962: 6-1-1, Smith
1963: 8-2, Smith
1964: 9-2, Smith
1965: 8-2, Dick Enright and Smith
1966: 7-1, Enright and Smith
1967: 9-1, Enright and Smith
1968: 9-1, Enright
1969: 11-1, Enright
1970: 8-1, Ralph Vidal
1971: 4-4, Vidal
1972: 7-3, Vidal
1973: 11-0-1, Vidal
1974: 10-2, Vidal
1975: 6-4, Bob Sugino and Jerry Case
1976: 5-4, Sugino
1977: 5-5, Sugino
1978: 5-4, Sugino
1979: 4-5, Bill Partridge and Stanley Wilson
1980: 6-2-1, Partridge
1981: 7-4, Partridge
1982: 7-4, Partridge

1983: 5-4-1, Partridge
1984: 5-6, Partridge
1985: 4-5, Partridge
1986: 3-4, Dale Hirayama
1987: 5-4, Hirayama
1988: 4-8, Partridge
1989: 5-7, Mike Sakurai
1990: 4-7, Sakurai
1991: 4-6, Sakurai
1992: 1-8, Sakurai
1993: 0-10, Don Threatt
1994: 3-6-1, Threatt
1995: 2-8, Threatt
1996: 2-8, Threatt
1997: 1-9, Nate Howard and
   Gerald Gillard
1998: 2-7, Marshall Jones

1999: 9-4-1, Jones
2000: 10-4, Jones
2001: 5-5, Jones
2002: 9-4, Jones
2003: 7-4, Jones
2004: 6-5, Jones
2005: 5-6, Jones
2006: 3-7, Jones
2007: 0-10, Jones
2008: 2-8, Jones
2009: 5-5, Ed Lalau
2010: 2-9, Lalau
2011: 3-8, Eric Fitzpatrick and
   Ed Lalau
2012: 7-4, Deon Toliver
2013: 1-9, Toliver

Coaches' Records

1. Stan Smith: 57-48-5 (.541)
2. Marshall Jones: 46-46-1 (.500)
3. Ralph Vidal: 40-10-1 (.794)
4. Partridge: 38-33-2 (.534)
5. Stan Smith and Dick Enright: 24-4 (.857)
6. Loren Peak: 24-14-7 (.611)
7. Mike Sakurai: 14-28 (.333)
8. Enright: 20-2 (.910)
9. Bob Sugino: 15-14 (.517)
10. George Freeman and William McGinnis: 13-7 (.650)
11. Freeman: 10-2 (.833)
12. Leonard: 8-8 (.500)
13. Dale Hirayama: 8-8 (.500)
14. Deon Toliver: 8-13 (.381)
15. Ed Lalau: 7-14 (.333)
16. Don Threatt: 7-32-1 (.188)
17. Bob Sugino and Jerry Case: 6-4 (.600)
18. Bill Partridge and Stanley Wilson: 4-5 (.444)
19. Eric Fitzpatrick and Lalau: 3-8 (.278)

20. Clark: 2-0-3 (.700)
21. Wheedon: 2-3 (.400)
22. Nordahl and Phee: 1-3 (.250)
23. Norton: 1-4-1 (.250)
24. Nate Howard and Gerald Gillard: 1-9 (.100)
25. Maggard: 0-8 (.000)

Totals: 359-317-21 (.530)
(fifteen years unaccounted for)

CHAPTER 9

HAWTHORNE HIGH SCHOOL COUGARS

Hawthorne High School opened in 1951, with the first football team coinciding with the first graduating class in 1954. And guess what? The Cougars went 9-1—one of the greatest starts in secondary school history. Under the tutelage of Hal Chauncey and Dave Capelouto, the Cougars beat Carpenteria 18–0 in the playoffs before eventually losing to Paso Robles, 47–34, their only loss of the year. Other victims that year included Mira Costa (25–7), El Segundo (33–13) and Morningside (44–6).

Incredibly, the following year was even better, as the Cougars went 10-0-1, beating Harvard Westlake 41–0 and St. John Bosco 39–13 before tying Morningside 13–13. During the year, the Cougars beat El Segundo 26–13, Mira Costa 26–7 and Culver City 21–6. What a start, huh?

They weren't bad in 1956, either, finishing 6-1-1 and defeating North 33–6 and El Segundo 20–13. Future Hall of Famer tackle Ron Mix was a great player on the 1950s teams. There are no records for 1957, but 1958 was another good season under the C and C duo, with the Cougars going 5-1.

Then Chauncey, on his own, led Hawthorne to an incredible 10-1 season in 1960 as the Cougars beat El Rancho 25–10 and Glendale 9–7 before losing to Long Beach Poly, 42–10, in the CIF playoffs.

New coach Otto Plum arrived in 1961 for the start of a great career. In his first two years, the team finished 5-2-1 and 6-1-1. Morningside (27–0), Mira Costa (27–6) and South Torrance (42–20) all fell by the wayside. Chauncey returned in 1966–67 for another eight wins. The 1966 team (6-3) featured

Coach Hal Chauncey's first two years at Hawthorne High were an incredible 9-1 in 1954 and 10-0-1 in 1955. *Courtesy of Hawthorne Historical Society.*

MVP Harry Wolverton, lineman Frank Lucio, running back Pat Aldrich and co-captains Rob Latta and Herb Lewis.

In 1969, new coach Jim Bunyard led the Cougars to another good year (6-2-1). This '69 team featured Scott Laidlaw at quarterback, the same guy who later starred at Stanford and played at fullback for the Dallas Cowboys in three Super Bowls. Laidlaw was assisted by guard Tim Powers, running back Dan Rice, end Greg Bailey, tackles Ed Crowell and Bart Hale and center Daryl Lortiz.

The Cougars were kind of quiet until a resurrected Otto Plum took them to an 8-3 record in 1972. They beat Pacifica of Garden Grove 28–21 before losing to LaHabra, 15–14, in the CIF playoffs. Outstanding players included defensive back and MVP Tom Deuel, linebacker Chris Shaner, Ocean League co-MVP Terry Howse, defensive back Ken McAllister and tackles Mike Huhn and Frank Elroy. The 1973 team went 7-4 behind quarterback George Hunter, halfback McAllister and defensive end Bill Whitehorse.

Otto continued his reign in 1975, going 8-4. "We think attitude makes the difference," Plum said in a Hawthorne yearbook. "And our approach at Hawthorne is that we are going to have a good time." And a good time was had by all as the Cougars beat Palos Verdes 13–7, South 40–20 and even upended number-one Loyola. Tom Fowler, Robert Ambruster, Dennis Gonsalves, Steve Coogan, Dan Rael and Leo LaSala all contributed to the team's success. In 1975, they were even better, recording eight wins and four losses. In the CIF playoffs, they beat Hueneme 14–7 and Loyola 10–7 before losing to South Hills of West Covina, 28–6.

Things cooled down for a while until Coach Larry Reed came on the scene and led Hawthorne to a great 11-0-1 season in 1985. The Cougars were on a roll until the CIF finals, where they totally outclassed Antelope Valley but lost! They outgained the Antelopes 243 yards to 157 and held star running back Eric Mortensen to 62 yards on sixteen carries. But penalties and misplays resulted in a 13–12 loss in

Otto Plum coached the Hawthorne High Cougars on two different occasions. His best years were 1962 (6-1-1) and 1975 (8-4). *Courtesy of Hawthorne Historical Society.*

their third-greatest season of all time. Lending talent to the festivities were quarterback Alonzo Young, running back Richard Harrison, Andre Jackson and tackle Earnest Horn.

Reed had another good year in 1986 (8-3), but it was really Coach Goy Casillas who came to the rescue. Casillas took over as head coach in 1987, leading the team to four consecutive seasons of 9-1-1, 9-2-1, 9-2 and 10-3. Even though it lost to San Marcos, 33–26, in the playoffs, the 1989 team was really outstanding, particularly All-American quarterback Curtis Conway, who, after starring at USC, went on to play a dozen great years in the NFL as a wide receiver. Casillas also lauded the play of running back Chris Alexander and especially his two outstanding linebackers, Sione Mahe and Anthony Smith.

Casillas, who resigned at the end of the 1990 season, closed out his great Hawthorne career with his most wins, ten. The team went to the playoffs, beating Loara 17–9 before losing big to St. Paul, 31–0.

But Dan Robbins, the sophomore coach, took over in 1991 and led the Cougars to unprecedented glory with eighty-one wins in just ten seasons. He started off in 1991 with a 9-2 record, losing to Los Alamitos, 20–14, in the CIF playoffs. In 1992, the Cougars went 12-2, beating Bell Gardens 14–6 for the championship behind the legendary Tevita Moala. The story is sad for Moala, who died in 2013 at age thirty-seven after a five-year battle with cancer, leaving a wife and six children. However, in 1992, Moala set a school record with 175 tackles, had three pass deflections, caused four fumbles and recovered two. In the final game against Bell Gardens, Moala, who had a bad dislocated shoulder, went into the game injured and scored on a seventy-one-yard touchdown run and a sixty-five-yard scoring run to seal the victory. "If Tevita Moala is not around, we lose that game 6–0," Coach Dan Robbins told the *Daily Breeze* in April 2013. "It's amazing! It's a movie."

Hawthorne almost duplicated the feat in 1992, going 12-2 again but losing in the finals to Newbury Park, 22–14. Wide receiver Travis Hannah went on to play two years in the NFL. Robbins followed these epics with fine years of 8-2, 6-4, 7-3 and 8-4.

Several coaches have taken over for more than the decade following. The most notable player was a running back with the great name of Adimchinobe Echemandu, who played five years in the NFL.

Now a new coach, Donald Paysinger, hopes to help the Cougars to roar again.

Hawthorne Win-Loss Records

1954: 9-1, Hal Chauncey and Dave Capelouto

1955: 10-0-1, Chauncey and Capelouto

1956: 6-1-1, Chauncey and Capelouto

1957: 1-0, Chauncey and Capelouto

1958: 5-1, Chauncey and Capelouto

1959: 1-6-1, Chauncey and Capelouto

1960: 10-1, Chauncey

1961: 5-2-1, Otto Plum

1962: 6-1-1, Plum

1963: 5-3-1, Plum

1964: 1-6-2, Plum
1965: 4-3-2, Plum
1966: 6-3, Chauncey
1967: no record
1968: 2-6, Jim Bunyard
1969: 6-2-1, Bunyard
1970: no record
1971: 5-4, Bunyard
1972: no record
1973: 7-4, Plum
1974: 3-6, Plum
1975: 8-4, Plum
1976: 2-7, Plum
1977: 2-7, Plum
1978: no record
1979: 1-8, Plum
1980: 1-6, Kye Courtney
1981: no record
1982: 5-5-2, Fred Boehm
1983: 4-6, Boehm
1984: 5-4-1, Larry Reed
1985: 11-1-1, Reed
1986: 8-3, Reed
1987: 9-1-1, Goy Casillas
1988: 9-2-1, Casillas

1989: 9-2, Casillas
1990: 10-3, Casillas
1991: 9-2, Dan Robbins
1992: 12-2, Robbins
1993: 12-2, Robbins
1994: 7-4, Robbins
1995: 8-2, Robbins
1996: 6-4, Robbins
1997: 7-3, Robbins
1998: 8-4, Robbins
1999: 3-7, Robbins
2000: 5-6, Robbins
2001: 4-6, Robbins
2002: 0-10, Unknown
2003: 2-9, Daryl Brown
2004: 7-4-1, Art Houghtaling
2005: 2-8, Houghtaling
2006: 0-10, James Swain
2007: 0-10, Swain
2008: 0-10, Swain
2009: 0-10, Swain
2010: 2-8, Joe Kanach
2011: 5-5, Kanach
2012: 1-9, Swain
2013: 3-7, Donald Paysinger

Coaches' Records

1. Dan Robbins: 81-42 (.659)
2. Otto Plum: 44-51-7 (.466)
3. Goy Casillas: 37-8-2 (.809)
4. Hal Chauncey and Dave Capelouto: 32-10-3 (.744)
5. Larry Reed: 24-8-2 (.735)
6. Chauncey: 16-4 (.800)
7. Jim Bunyard: 13-12-1 (.519)
8. Fred Boehm: 9-11-2 (.455)
9. Art Houghtaling: 9-12-1 (.432)
10. Joe Kanach: 5-5 (.500)
11. Donald Paysinger: 3-7 (.300)

12. Daryl Brown: 2-9 (.189)
13. Kye Courtney: 1-6 (.143)
14. James Swain: 1-49 (.020)
15. Unknown: 0-10 (.000)

Total: 275-234-18 (.539)
(five years unaccounted for)

CHAPTER 10

INGLEWOOD HIGH SCHOOL SENTINELS

Inglewood High School started under Leuzinger High (see Leuzinger chapter), and its greatest moments came early in its existence. In 1932 and 1933, the Sentinels were named state champs, going 9-0 and beating Santa Ana 14–0 in '32 and going 8-0-1 and beating San Diego 7–0 in '33. Other great years were 1952 (7-1) and 1953 (8-1), both under Marty Ernaga, and 2000, when the team went 13-1 under Charles Nash.

Inglewood High School Win-Loss Records

1913: 1-4, A.H. Bodenoch
1914: no record
1915: 3-1, Bodenoch
1916: 1-4, Bodenoch
1917: 7-3, Bodenoch
1918: 2-1, C.E. Broderson
1919: 3-3, Bodenoch
1920: 3-4, Bodenoch
1921: 2-3, Bodenoch
1922: 2-3, Bodenoch
1923: 2-3, Bodenoch
1924: 1-5-1, Bodenoch
1925: 3-3, Bodenoch
1926: 7-4-1, Bodenoch

1927: 1-5, Bodenoch
1928: 3-4, Bodenoch
1929: 1-4-2, Bodenoch
1930: 3-2, Bodenoch
1931: 1-5, Dick Arnett
1932: 9-0, Arnett
1933: 8-0-1, Arnett
1934: 3-1-1, Bodenoch
1935: no record
1936: 5-2-2, Arnett
1937: 2-5-1, Arnett
1938: 4-5-1, Arnett
1939: 6-4, Bodenoch
1940: no record

1941: 6-3-1, Bodenoch
1942: no record
1943: no record
1944: no record
1945: no record
1946: 6-2-1, Bodenoch
1947: 3-6, Bodenoch
1948: 5-4, Marty Ernaga
1949: 4-1, Ernaga
1950: 4-1, Arnett
1951: no record
1952: 7-1, Ernaga
1953: 8-1, Ernaga
1954: 2-7, Paul Manahan
1955: 4-3-2, Manahan
1956: no record
1957: 2-3, Manahan
1958: 3-6, Manahan
1959: 5-4, Bill Peters
1960: 7-4, Peters
1961: 1-7-1, Peters
1962: no record
1963: no record
1964: no record
1965: 4-5, William Benjamin
1966–76: no records
1977: 3-6, Blayne Wallis
1978: no record
1979: no record
1980: 3-6-1, Bob Hunter
1981: 7-5, Hunter

1983: 6-4-1, Hunter
1984: 5-4-1, Bill Lapes
1985: 0-10, Rick Amedio
1986: 2-8, Billy Mills
1987: 3-7, Mills
1988: 0-9, Mills
1989: 0-9, Orville Echols
1990: 1-8-1, Echols
1991: 5-5, Echols
1992: 3-7, Angelo Jackson
1993: 1-9, Jackson
1994: 2-8, Jackson
1995: 7-4, Rico Perez
1996: 3-7, Bob Sharpe
1997: 5-5, Sharpe
1998: 2-8, Sharpe
1999: 1-8-1, Charles Nash
2000: 13-1, Nash
2001: 10-3, Nash
2002: 5-5, Nash
2003: 5-4-1, James Durk
2004: 0-10, Durk
2005: 3-7, Charles Mincy
2006: 7-3, Mincy
2007: 4-6, Mincy
2008: 5-5, Mincy
2009: 7-4, Mincy
2010: 9-3, Stephen Thomas
2011: 5-6, Thomas
2012: 7-4, Thomas
2013: 4-6, Tony Reid

Coaches' Records

1. H. Bodenoch: 67-71-7 (.486)*
2. Charles Nash: 29-10 (.686)
3. Dick Arnett: 29-17-5 (.618)*
4. Charles Mincy: 26-25 (.510)
5. Marty Ernaga: 24-7 (.774)*

6. Stephen Thomas: 21-13 (.618)
7. Bob Hunter: 16-15-1 (.515)
8. Bill Peters: 13-15-1 (.466)
9. Paul Manahan: 11-19-2 (.375)*
10. Bob Sharpe: 10-20 (.333)
11. Rico Perez: 7-4 (.636)
12. Orville Echols: 6-22-1 (.224)*
13. Angelo Jackson: 6-24 (.200)*
14. Bill Lapes: 5-4-1 (.550)
15. James Durk: 5-14-1 (.275)
16. Billy Mills: 5-24-1 (.183)*
17. William Benjamin: 4-5 (.444)
18. Tony Reid: 4-6 (.400)
19. Blayne Wallis: 3-6 (.333)
20. C.E. Broderson: 2-1 (.667)
21. Rick Amedio: 0-10 (.000)

* incomplete record

Total: 297-333-20 (.472)
(twenty-five years unaccounted for)

CHAPTER 11

LAWNDALE HIGH SCHOOL CARDINALS

Lawndale came into being in 1905 when a man named Charles B. Hooper subdivided it and named it after a Chicago suburb. In 1959, it was incorporated as a city in the county of Los Angeles, and at the same time, Lawndale High School and Friday night lights under Coach Richie Braunbeck were born. The first recorded football season was 1962, but the program's best year quickly followed.

The highlight of Lawndale's gridiron exploits was undoubtedly 1966, when the Cardinals became CIF champs after beating Eisenhower 26–15, Santa Clara 13–6 and Victor Valley 19–7, closing out the season with eight straight wins under Coach Braunbeck. Other great wins included a 33–6 victory over Aviation and a 47–0 pasting of Palos Verdes High. Outstanding players included ends Steve Carnes and Dave Freeman, tackle Wayne Chenault, guard Steve Lumley, quarterback Jim Coleman, halfback Jeff Freeman and center Danny Felix.

In 1962, the Cardinals were 2-6-1 before leapfrogging to a great 7-1-1 record in 1963. Great wins were 14–0 over Lennox, 37–13 over West High, 21–7 over El Segundo and 21–6 over Torrance. This was followed by an even better campaign in 1964, when Lawndale went 8-2. The Cardinals' major loss was to Loara High in the CIF playoffs, 18–14. Otherwise, they beat Leuzinger 19–12, Bishop Montgomery 32–7 and Torrance 38–6. Honors went to quarterback Mike Battle, the Centinela Player of the Year; guard Luigi DiFelice, All-Centinela Valley first team; and end Tom Duncan, All-

Pioneer first team. Fred Dryer, a defensive end on that team, went on to great stardom at El Camino College, where he was a 1966 Junior All-American, followed by thirteen years in the NFL, mostly with the Los Angeles Rams. Battle, after a great career at USC, played two years as defensive back for the New York Jets.

Even though their record was only 5-5-1 in 1965, the Cardinals made it into the CIF playoffs, where they beat Thousand Oaks 26–19 before losing to Palos Verdes, 35–20. Great players included quarterback Jim Coleman, guard Sam Garcia, end Phil Hampton, fullback Bob Caputo, halfback Jeff Freeman and center Jerry Nott. Lawndale handily took care of Beverly Hills (20–6), Aviation (18–0) and Lennox (20–6).

Then there was a flurry of great seasons, including 1966 (9-2-1), 1967 (8-1) and 1968 (7-2). The Cardinals' only loss in 1967 was to West Torrance, 27–12, as they beat Bishop Montgomery 13–7, Lennox 45–21 and Palos Verdes 20–0. Outstanding players included guard Joe Szalai, end Tom Mattera, quarterback Gary Granville, fullback Mike Ernagg, tackle Mike Donnelly and flanker Bud Bernard.

And in 1968, behind halfback Jim Daughtery and tackles Bob Duncan and Dave Rudiwitz, the Braunbeck gang had another good year (7-2) and beat Palos Verdes 12–6, Miraleste 39–0 and El Segundo 25–20.

Roy Benstead took over in 1969 and proceeded to win thirty-five games in seven years. The Cardinals were 9-3 in '69, beating Bellflower 14–7 and Daniel Murphy 20–6 before losing 21–18 in the CIF playoffs. Great players were tackles Tom Gonsales and John Holliday, fullback Dave Harness, quarterback Bryce Falk, fullback Ed Lopez and guard Richard Pierce. Other victims included El Segundo (34–12), Beverly Hills (24–18) and Miraleste (18–12).

The Cardinals finished 5-3-1 in 1970, beating St. Monica 39–13 and Daniel Murphy 29–14 behind Willie Salmon and Steve Garcia. Their next good years were 6-4 in 1973 and 7-4 in 1974. In '73, they lost to Antelope Valley, 33–14, in the CIF but beat Miraleste 19–14, El Segundo 35–8 and Lennox 17–15. Back of the year was Paul Feurborn, while Craig Sides was lineman of the year. Also outstanding were end Mike Reece, center Dave Brown, defensive back Rich Laraba, guard Tony Chavez and tackle Lee Graveson. In 1974, the Cards beat Pater Noster of Los Angeles 32–9 in the playoffs before losing to Neff High of La Mirada, 35–0. Fullback Timo Vamanrav was all-everything, while end Dave Robinson, guard Craig Sides, linebacker Dave Jackman, quarterback

Richard Laraba, guard Tony Chavez and linebacker Steve McGee were all outstanding.

In 1977, Coach Fred Boehm led Lawndale to a 7-2-1 record. Kory Dickinson was Pioneer defensive MVP, while back Jim Keys, guard Robert Suka and tackle Alan McCaw all had good years.

Roy Benstead returned in 1980, the Cardinals' last year before closing until 2004, to lead them to a 7-4 record. They beat Agoura 44–31 in the CIF before losing to Baldwin Park. All-League were Ron Ewing, Charlie Loynd, Paul Mattacks, Larry Wilson, Chad Whelen, Ken Bagsby, Frank Guitterez and Craig Scaringi.

Things have been kind of quiet since Lawndale returned to action in 2004. Mando Padilla helped the Cards win nine games in three years, while Mark Gomez led the team to a decent fourteen victories. Rick Mathieson, current coach, won eight games in 2012 and 2013.

But whatever they are asked to do, it seems the Lawndale Cardinals have a tradition to never give up.

Lawndale Win-Loss Records

1960: no record, Richie Braunbeck
1961: 4-4, Braunbeck
1962: 2-6-1, Braunbeck
1963: 7-1-1, Braunbeck
1964: 8-2, Braunbeck
1965: 5-5-1, Braunbeck
1966: 9-2-1, Braunbeck
1967: 8-1, Braunbeck
1968: 7-2, Braunbeck
1969: 9-3, Roy Benstead
1970: 5-3-1, Benstead
1971: 2-7, Benstead
1972: 1-8, Benstead
1973: 6-4, Benstead
1974: 7-4, Benstead
1975: 5-0, Benstead
1976: 1-6, Fred Boehm

1977: 7-2-1, Boehm
1978: 4-4-1, Boehm
1979: no record, Steve Carnes
1980: 7-4, Benstead
1981–2003: closed
2004: 4-6, Mando Padilla
2005: 1-9, Padilla
2006: 4-6, Padilla
2007: 4-6, Mark Gomez
2008: 5-5, Gomez
2009: 5-6, Gomez
2010: 1-9, John Guilfoyle
2011: 1-9, Guilfoyle
2012: 3-7, Rick Mathieson
2013: 5-5, Mathieson

Coaches' Records

1. Richie Braunbeck: 46-19-4 (.667)
2. Roy Benstead: 42-33 (.560)
3. Fred Boehm: 12-12-2 (.500)
4. Mando Padilla: 9-21 (.300)
5. Mark Gomez: 14-16 (.467)
6. Rick Mathieson: 8-12 (.400)
5. John Guilfoyle: 2-18 (.100)

Totals: 133-131-6 (.504)
(two years unaccounted for)

CHAPTER 12

LENNOX HIGH SCHOOL LANCERS

The Lennox High School Lancers played football from 1957 to 1983. Here is a partial record of their success. Names of coaches and some records are unaccounted for.

Lennox Win-Loss Records

1957: 5-2	1971: no scores recorded
1958: 4-4	1972: 2-1 (no other scores recorded)
1959: 3-5	1973: 2-8
1960: 3-5	1974: 4-2
1961: 3-6	1975: 4-2
1962: 2-7	1976: 7-3
1963: 4-5	1977: 1-3 (no other scores recorded)
1964: 3-6	1978: 1-8
1965: 0-8-1, Don Young	1979: 0-7
1966: 1-8	1980: 3-6
1967: 2-7	1981: 1-9
1968: 5-4	1982: 1-9
1969: 3-6	1983: 0-6-1 (final year)
1970: 10-1	

Totals: 74-138-2 (.350)

CHAPTER 13

LEUZINGER HIGH SCHOOL OLYMPIANS

Have you ever heard of Marvcus Patton? This graduate of Leuzinger High School in Lawndale was a six-foot-two, 239-pound linebacker who played thirteen years in the NFL for Buffalo, Washington and Kansas City. The guy was a marvelous athlete and obviously one of the greatest to come out of Leuzinger.

Patton was just nine years old when his father, an undercover detective in Los Angeles, was shot and killed in the line of duty. His mother, Barbara Patton, a former Women's National Football League player with the Los Angeles Dandelions, taught Patton about football. Mother and son both played middle linebacker, with Barbara once breaking an opposing player's helmet. "I thought it was really cool to tell my friends that my mom was a linebacker," Patton once said.

Besides being raised by a football-playing single mother, Patton is a living example of what a person can accomplish in spite of adversarial conditions. Today, he and his wife, Ina, own sports-themed restaurants in northern Virginia.

Patton is only one example of what this high school in Lawndale has accomplished. Starting out as Inglewood Union High School from 1915 to 1931, the school won thirty-eight football games before it evolved into Leuzinger High in 1932 and became the heart of Lawndale.

The first remarkable coach was A.H. Bodenoch, who led his team to twenty-eight victories. Dick Arnett took over in 1929, taking the Inglewood team to a perfect 9-0 record. Leuzinger opened in 1932, when the Olympics were hosted by Los Angeles, and the Lawndale school fittingly became the Olympians. Coach Bill Smith led the team to a 2-3-1 record that first year, with players Bob Allen, George Allison and Allen Harris all helping out.

Smith proceeded to coach six more years, compiling a record of 20-27-4. But it was only the start of things to come. George Thompson took over in 1939 and proceeded to win eighteen games. Dave Rebd came into the picture in 1947 and promptly won the first Bay League championship in 1949 with an 8-2 record. All-Bay League players included Bill Angel and Ed Schmidt. One of the Olympians' biggest victories was taking care of Santa Monica by a 26–19 score in front of seven thousand fans.

The team struggled in the 1950s, but Bob Isaacson and Ron Fletcher took over in 1960 and soon had two of the greatest years in Olympian history, going 9-0 in 1963 and 8-0 in 1964. The Sky League champs of 1963 featured MVP John Swoboda, who received help from Dave Rabuse, Albert Jones and Don Delano. Dan Green was MVP of the 1964 team, which included Lance Stewart and Randy McMichael. Wins that year included a 39–7 bashing of South Torrance, a 21–0 victory over Torrance, a 26–0 shutout against Morningside and a 21–0 pasting of North. One of Leuzinger's great players was defensive back Jason Simmons, who went on to play seven years in the NFL.

The 1965 season was also impressive, as the Olympians went 6-3 behind MVP end Gwen Cooper, halfback Rick Galloway, quarterback Sal Bommarito, halfback Ron Ross and center Larry Neville.

The next big year was 1972, under Coach Art Linden. The Olympians dismantled Gahr 28–0 and also beat Beverly Hills 35–13 and El Segundo 21–6. Back Gary Balo was All-CIF, while guard John Canulli, tackle Matt Robinson, wide receiver Gary Vacchio, linebacker Richard Martin, tackle Dean Peterson and end Ron Zuther were All-Sky League.

Things were quiet until 1979, when Pat Scuderi took over and went 8-2. The Olympians beat Bellflower 28–17 and Mission Viejo 27–14 before losing to Esperanza, 15–13, in the CIF semifinals.

In 1980, Scuderi brought his team to a fine 7-3 record, beating Mira Costa 27–25, Inglewood 21–0 and Lennox 34–6 before losing to Burroughs of Burbank, 23–20, in the CIF playoffs. Quarterback Frank Harrington, guard Troy Christensen and halfback Derek Linton were aided by Earl Gibson, Takeshi Yogi and Mike Martin on defense.

Coach Steve Carnes took over in 1984, and in 1985, Leuzinger had its greatest year, going 12-1-1. The Olympians were Desert Mountain

Conference champs, having throttled Bell-Jefferson 41–20, Agoura 22–13, St. Genevieve 16–14 and Harvard 39–17. Running back Mike Reddington was the CIF Player of the Year.

Carnes had more outstanding years in 1986 (6-3-1), 1988 (9-2-1) and 1990 (8-4). Defensive back Therrian Fontenot later played two years in the NFL. Fred Boehm took over and went 9-1-1 in 1994, after which Bobby Greer had some poor years before Don Markham led the team to a 10-3 record in 1999.

Mike Whitt had a good record in 2004, going 7-4, and Deon Toliver won six games each year from 2006 to 2009. Reginald Grant had less success, winning only one game in 2010 and 2011. However, Ronald Jenkins, who is a teacher at the school, took over in 2012 with high hopes. "I'm very excited," Jenkins said in a 2012 *Daily Breeze* article by Tony Ciniglio. "It's a tough challenge, but I'm excited. I understand the culture and the history."

Unfortunately, things did not turn out better for the Olympians, who have won only one game in the past two years. The new coach for 2014 will be Dameon Porter, former offensive coordinator for Crespi High School in Encino. It's now up to Coach Porter to try to rekindle the proud tradition of the Olympians.

Leuzinger Win-Loss Records

1932: 2-3-1, Bill Smith
1933: 3-3, Smith
1934: 2-6, Smith
1935: 1-7-1, Smith
1936: 4-4-1, Smith
1937: 4-5, Smith
1938: 4-5-1, Smith
1939: 0-3-2, George Thompson
1940: 3-4, Thompson
1941: 2-7, Thompson
1942: 4-5, Thompson
1943: 1-5, Thompson
1944: 4-2-1, Thompson
1945: 4-4, Thompson
1946: 0-9, Thompson
1947: 0-9, Dave Rebd

1948: 2-7, Rebd
1949: 8-2, Rebd
1950: 4-5, Bill Hoyt
1951: 2-6, Hoyt
1952: 2-6, Hoyt
1953: 1-6-1, Hoyt
1954: 1-4, Hoyt
1955: 2-7, Gus Braun
1956: 3-3-2, Braun
1957: no record
1958: 4-5, Jim Chadwick
1959: 1-7, unknown
1960: 0-8, Bob Isaacson and
    Ron Fletcher
1961: 0-9, Isaacson and Fletcher
1962: 5-4, Isaacson and Fletcher
1963: 9-0, Isaacson and Fletcher

1964: 8-0, Isaacson and Fletcher
1965: 6-3, Bob Isaacson
1966: 3-1, Isaacson
1967: 44-1, Isaacson
1968: 2-7, Isaacson
1969: 1-8, Isaacson
1970: 2-7, Art Linden
1971: 2-7, Linden
1972: 7-3, Linden
1973: 5-4, Linden
1974: no record, Linden
1975: no record, Linden
1976: 3-6, Linden
1977: no record
1978: no record
1979: 8-2, Pat Scuderi
1980: 7-3, Scuderi
1981: no record, Scuderi
1982: 5-4-1, Scuderi
1983: no record, Scuderi
1984: 4-4, Steve Carnes
1985: 12-1-1, Carnes
1986: 6-3-1, Carnes
1987: 9-2-1, Carnes
1988: 9-2-1, Carnes

1989: 8-3-1, Carnes
1990: 8-4, Carnes
1991: 4-6, Carnes
1992: 6-5, Carnes
1993: 5-6, Fred Boehm
1994: 9-1-1, Boehm
1995: 4-5, Bobby Greer
1996: 5-5, Greer
1997: 2-8, Greer
1998: 2-8, Greer
1999: 10-3, Don Markham
2000: 6-5, Mike Whitt
2001: 5-5-1, Whitt
2002: 4-6, Whitt
2003: 3-7, Whitt
2004: 3-7, Whitt
2005: 7-4, Whitt
2006: 6-5, Deon Toliver
2007: 6-5, Toliver
2008: 6-4, Toliver
2009: 6-4, Toliver
2010: 1-9, Reginald Grant
2011: 0-10, Grant
2012: 1-9, Ronald Jenkins
2013: 0-10, Jenkins

Coaches' Records

1. Steve Carnes: 66-30-5 (.678)
2. Mike Whitt: 28-34-1 (.452)
3. Deon Toliver: 24-18 (.571)
4. Bob Isaacson and Ron Fletcher: 22-21 (.512)
5. Pat Scuderi: 20-9-1 (.683)*
6. Bill Smith: 20-33-4 (.386)
7. Art Linden: 19-27 (.413)*
8. George Thompson: 18-35 (.340)
9. Bob Isaacson: 16-25-2 (.395)
10. Fred Boehm: 14-7-1 (.659)
11. Bobby Greer: 13-26 (.333)

12. Don Markham: 10-3 (.769)
13. Dave Rebd: 10-18 (.357)
14. Bill Hoyt: 10-27-1 (.362)
15. Gus Braun: 5-10-2 (.353)
16. Jim Chadwick: 4-5 (.444)
17. Reginald Grant: 1-19 (.050)
18. Ronald Jenkins: 1-19 (.050)

* incomplete record

Total: 306-366-17 (.456)
(seven years unaccounted for)

CHAPTER 14

MARY STAR OF THE SEA HIGH SCHOOL STARS

In 1960, Mary Star of the Sea had a storybook season—a tiny school with just sixty-one boys almost won a CIF championship. The Stars beat Fallbrook 32–0 and then managed to beat Brea Olinda 20–14 on a last-minute play before finally losing in the finals to San Luis Obispo, 13–6.

It was hard to believe they had gone that far. "The Stars dressed, but beneath all this silence and heartbreak, I was very proud of them," Coach Nick Trani wrote in a novel, *Thin Ice on the Gridiron*, in 1966. "There were no alibis, no complaints—just a realization that destiny evaded them."

Wow! It was still a heck of a year. The Stars lost their first game and their last. In between, however, they wiped out Harvard Prep 41–6 and shut out St. John Vianney 21–0, St. Monica 20–0 and Alemany 32–0. And to top it off, this was a culmination of a two-year odyssey in which the Stars won seventeen games and lost just three.

The little Catholic school in San Pedro, today with a little over five hundred students, entered Southern California football in 1951 under the same Nick Trani. Some of their players included Gennara DiLeva at right end, Richard Spires at right tackle, Bob Marques at quarterback, Dick Lopez at fullback and Bill Caldwell at left end. The team went 0-7 that first year but had representative games against San Gabriel Mission, losing 9–6, and St. Francis of La Canada, losing 13–0.

In 1952, the Stars turned their program around, going a marvelous 6-1-2 under Trani. The team still had DiLeva at end, and Ernie Martinez, Ray Martin and John Pirozzi were outstanding at tackles, as was Arky Pierce at quarterback. Big wins included a 42–0 rout of St. Francis of Riverside, a 45–6 victory over St. Agnes of Los Angeles and a 34–0 shutout of San Gabriel Mission.

In 1953, the Stars won only five and lost four under Coach Phil Cantwell but had outstanding wins against Bell-Jefferson of Los Angeles (14–0), Mater Dei of Santa Ana (33–0) and St. Agnes (20–0).

Their next great year was 1958, when Cantwell led them to a 7-2 record with wins over San Luis Obispo (20–14), Bishop Gorman of Nevada (21–6), St. Paul of Santa Fe Springs (21–6) and St. John Vianney of Los Angeles (13–0). This was the start of a great run, the highlight being the 1959 season, when the Stars finished 9-1 under Cantwell. Their only loss was in the playoffs to Brea Olinda, 14–13. Victims during the year included Bishop Montgomery (34–6) and Alemany of Mission Hills (12–6). Then came 1960 and the almost storybook-ending season under Trani, who returned as coach.

But then Fermin Lasuen, a boys' school, opened as a complement to Mary Star, which became an all-girls school. That lasted through the 1971 year, when, due to low enrollment, the Los Angeles Archdiocese decided to close Fermin. So in 1972, the Stars returned to football, this time under Coach Tom Schmidt, and went 2-6. Players included linebackers Andy Simon, Lee Wilkensen and Jeff Becker and a backfield of Don Jarrin, John Hatwan and Eddie Sullivan.

Dino Andrie, a former player, took over as head coach in 1994, leading the Stars to a great 11-2 record. The biggest disappointment of the year was losing in the CIF semifinals to Paraclete of Lancaster. Andrie, a running back in 1977–78, had set the school's single-game rushing record with 315 yards and had been named to the All-Santa Fe League team.

The Stars returned to the firmament in 1977, when Coach John Radisich led them to a 10-2 record. They beat Lawndale 3–0 and El Dorado 21–8 in the playoffs before losing to Norwalk, 25–8. Outstanding players included end Tim Wrightman, fullback Tim Rossin and future coach Andrie. The team had an incredible run of seven shutouts, including a 40–0 pasting of Paraclete and a 29–0 victory over Cathedral. Wrightman might be Mary Star's most famous football player, as he would go on to spend two years in the NFL with the Chicago Bears.

The Stars finished 9-3 in 1978, 7-3 in 1979, 7-2-1 in 1980 and 7-4 in 1982, all under Radisich. Outstanding players included All-CIF Tony Gioiello, quarterback Duane Martinez, running back Dino Andrie (the future coach), lineman Mark Montoya and, of course, Wrightman, who was named the South Bay Player of the Year.

In 1999, the Stars had another outstanding season, going 7-3. But 2001 was a landmark year as the team reached the CIF semifinals, beating Marshall of Pasadena 40–19 and High Desert of Edwards Air Force Base 21–15 before losing to Paraclete of Lancaster, 20–0. Other victims included El Segundo (29–28), LaSalle of Pasadena (28–21) and St. Anthony of Long Beach (41–8).

In 2002, the Stars finished 6-4 under Andrie and advanced to the playoffs, only to lose to Montclair Prep of Van Nuys, 48–14. The following season was a great one, as the Stars went 8-3, although they lost to Twenty-nine Palms, 17–14, in the playoffs. During the year, they beat Salesian of Los Angeles 40–16, St. Anthony of Long Beach 49–0 and Aquinas of San Bernardino 34–0.

None of the seasons from 2004 through 2012 were particularly outstanding, but the Stars continued to make the playoffs. In 2004, they finished 4-7 and lost to Village Christian of Sun Valley, 42–7. Jeff Mihaljevich threw for 1,438 yards, Bradford Andrews rushed for 1,268 and Travis Gooden was in on sixty-eight tackles.

In 2005, the Stars finished 3-6-2 but still made the playoffs, losing to Valley Christian of Cerritos, 37–21. In subsequent years, the playoffs went like this:

2006: Recording a 4-7 season, the Stars beat Vasquez of Acton but lost to Village Christian, 49–30.

2007: Mary Star lost to Bishop Diego of Santa Barbara, settling for a 5-6 season.

2008: Cathedral upended the Stars 56–21 in the playoffs, and Mary Star finished with a 5-6 record.

2010: Morro Bay defeated Mary Star in the playoffs, and the Stars finished with a 4-7 record.

2012: Mary Star lost to Gladstone of Covina, 54–17, after recording a 4-6 season.

Coach Andrie stepped down after the 2012 season, saying he wanted to spend more time with his family. Principal Rita Dever lauded his commitment to the Stars on Mary Star's website: "Over the years, his greatest achievement was his ability to help mold boys into responsible young men. He is such a great family man and does so much for our school. He truly is a great example for his player, coaches, alumni and colleagues." In his fifteen years at the helm, Andrie had qualified for the CIF playoffs thirteen times and reached the semifinals twice.

Mike Marinkovich, a former Mary Star player and current vice-principal, took over as coach in 2013 after having already served as coach from 1989 to 1993. "The kids are familiar with me," Marinkovich said on the same website. "I'm a known quantity. They know what to expect from me, and I feel I can make any changes that are necessary to take us into the next year and beyond."

One thing is for sure at Mary Star: the team is always competitive, and the young men coming out of the program seem ready for life—and sometimes more football at another level.

Mary Star of the Sea Win-Loss Records

1951: 0-7, Nick Trani

1952: 6-1-2, Trani

1953: 5-4, Trani

1954: 6-3-1, Phil Cantwell

1955: 3-5-1, Cantwell

1956: 2-6, Cantwell

1957: 4-3-1, Cantwell

1958: 7-2, Cantwell

1959: 9-1, Cantwell

1960: 8-2, Trani

1961–71: all-girls school

1972: 2-6, Tom Schmidt

1973: no record, Schmidt

1974: no record, John Radisich

1975: no record, Radisich

1976: no record, Radisich

1977: 10-2, Radisich

1978: 9-3, Radisich

1979: 7-3, Radisich

1980: 7-2-1, Radisich

1981: 7-4, Radisich

1982: 3-6, Radisich

1983: 7-4-1, Radisich

1984: 4-6, John Tousseau

1985: 3-6-1, Tousseau

1986: 2-7-1, Gerry Duffy

1987: 3-7, Jerry Aguilar

1988: 6-5, Aguilar

1989: 7-4, Mike Marinkovich

1990: 7-4, Marinkovich

1991: 1-8, Marinkovich

1992: 0-10, Marinkovich

1993: 1-9, Marinkovich

1994: 11-2, Dino Andrie

1995: 4-6, Andrie

1996: 5-5, Andrie

1997: 9-3, Aguirre

1998: no record, Aguirre

1999: 7-3, Andrie

2000: 4-5, Andrie

2001: 9-3, Andrie

2002: 6-4, Andrie

2003: 8-3, Andrie

2004: 4-7, Andrie

2005: 3-6-2, Andrie

2006: 4-7, Andrie

2007: 5-6, Andrie

2008: 3-7, Andrie

2009: 5-6, Andrie

2010: 4-7, Andrie

2011: 0-10, Marinkovich

2012: 4-6, Marinkovich

2013: 4-6, Marinkovich

Coaches' Records

1. Dino Andrie: 91-80-2 (.532)*
2. John Radisich: 50-25-1 (.664)*
3. Phil Cantwell: 31-20-3 (.602)
4. Mike Marinkovich: 24-57 (.296)
5. Nick Trani: 19-14-2 (.571)
6. Tom Schmidt: 4-10 (.286)

* incomplete record

Totals: 222-206-8 (.518)
(five years unaccounted for)

CHAPTER 15

MIRA COSTA HIGH SCHOOL MUSTANGS

Mira Costa High School has been an important player in South Bay high school football since its first years at the start of the 1950s. The Mustangs, under coach Walter Jacobsmeyer, were 5-2-1 in 1952 and 6-3 in 1953. In 1954, they were 5-3-1 under Don Cogswell. That was a heck of a way to start a program. Fullbacks Jim Arlney and Norton Enger, quarterback Dick Craig, center Pat Roberts, guard Paul MacDowell and tackle Tony Brubaker were all outstanding players in 1953. In 1954, Jim Linsay, LeRoy Vardeman, Bob Keene and Bob Gay led the team.

The year 1956 was another good one under Cogswell, as the team manhandled Inglewood 38–7 and Torrance 13–0 and finished 5-2-2. Trent Castricone, Nick Comitas, Joe Silk, Dave Hudson, Chris Bader and Jeff Plough all had good years.

Pete Austin took over the program from 1961 through 1966, winning twenty-one games in that span. His best year was 5-2-2 in 1963, and players on that team included Steve Verry, Mike Fairless, Ralph Gambin, Barry Winkler and Mike Moore.

In 1967, Bill Cooper was coach, leading the team to a nice 6-3 record. Highlights included a 49–7 win over Redondo Beach, and outstanding players were Dan Wooley, Rich Jarrette, Pat Moore, John Sain and Chuck Nunnelly. In 1970, Cooper led the Mustangs to their first Bay League title with a 6-2-1 record. Guard Dave Boice, tackle Bill Flaherty, tight end John Taylor and back Tom Sain were All-League on offense, while end Pat Harvey, cornerback Steve Thomas, tackle Nate Garner and linebacker Boice were All-League on defense.

The next good year came in 1976 under Steve Andersen's watch, as the Mustangs finished 8-2. Making first-team All-Ocean were Derrel Lyon, the defensive player of the year; linebacker Jeff Rohrer; lineman Mike Ambriz; back Mike Elliot; and end Bill Dougher. Rohrer went on to play six years at linebacker with the Dallas Cowboys.

The Mustangs finished just 5-4-2 in 1980 but still earned a trip to the CIF playoffs, where they lost to La Canada, 14–7. Leading players that year included guard Tim Roth, running back Tim Leonard and wide receiver Leif Johanssen.

Coach Herb Hinsche arrived in 1982 and promptly led the team to a 7-3-1 record in '83. The Mustangs lost to Oak Park, 13–8 in the playoffs, but had big wins over El Segundo (45–0), Lennox (35–12) and Torrance (21–13).

Then things were kind of quiet until the now-legendary Don Morrow took over in 1993, promptly going 13-1 and winning the CIF championship. (See accompanying story on Morrow.)

Don had a few "down" years as the Mustangs went 8-4 in 1995, 8-2 in 1997, 6-4 in 1998, 5-4-1 in 1999, 5-5-1 in 2004, 6-6 in 2006, 3-7 in 2007 and 4-7 in 2011. Even the great ones lose sometime—just not very often. The rest of those years were mostly ten to thirteen wins.

Sonny Byrd, who went on to play running back at USC, was on the 1995 team along with Mike Desanto, Lyle Huff, Albion Yi, Eric Valere and Maurice Russell. Quarterback Robert Hodge led the 1997 team along with running back Hussein Meadows and defensive back Mike Enos. Running back Chris Salazar, defensive lineman Matt Schafer and quarterback Dane McConnaughy were outstanding in 1998.

Quarterback Sean Kelly, running backs Adrien Dotson and Chris Loatman, receiver Greg Gelb and defensive stalwart Eric Mueller all stood out in 2006 even though they ended with a 6-6 record. The 2012 and 2013 seasons had similar records of 8-4.

It seems that the Mustangs are always chomping at the bit, ready to unleash another season of immortality.

Mira Costa Win-Loss Records

1951: no record, Walter Jacobsmeyer

1952: 5-2-1, Jacobsmeyer

1953: 6-3, Don Cogswell

1954: 5-3-1, Cogswell

1955: no record

1956: 5-2-2, Cogswell

1957: no record

1958: 1-6-2, Cogswell

1959: 2-6-1, Cogswell

1960: 3-6, Cogswell
1961: 2-7, Pete Austin
1962: 5-4, Austin
1963: 5-2-2, Austin
1964: 5-4, Austin
1965: 4-4-1, Austin
1966: 0-9, Austin
1967: 6-3, William Cooper
1968: 3-4, Cooper
1969: 3-6, Cooper
1970: 6-2-1, Cooper
1971: 1-9, Cooper
1972: 2-6-1, Cooper
1973: 4-5, Cooper
1974: 2-5-2, Steve Andersen
1975: 2-7, Andersen
1976: 8-2, Andersen
1977: 2-7, Andersen
1978: 1-8, Steve Verry
1979: 5-5, Bob Hunter
1980: 5-4-2, Hunter
1981: 0-10, Hunter
1982: 4-6, Herb Hinsche
1983: 7-3-1, Hinsche
1984: 1-8-1, Hinsche
1985: 1-8-1, Hinsche
1986: 0-10, Hinsche

1987: 3-6, Hinsche
1988: 1-9, Dan Brown
1989: 6-5, Larry Petril
1990: 6-5-1, Petril
1991: 4-6, Petril
1992: 4-5-1, Petril
1993: 13-1, Don Morrow
1994: 12-2, Morrow
1995: 8-4, Morrow
1996: 10-4, Morrow
1997: 8-2, Morrow
1998: 6-4, Morrow
1999: 5-4-1, Morrow
2000: 12-1, Morrow
2001: 12-1, Morrow
2002: 13-1, Morrow
2003: 12-1, Morrow
2004: 5-5-1, Morrow
2005: 10-2, Morrow
2006: 6-6, Morrow
2007: 2-7-1, Morrow
2008: 10-4, Morrow
2009: 12-2, Morrow
2010: 7-4, Morrow
2011: 4-7, Morrow
2012: 8-4, Morrow
2013: 8-4, Morrow

Coaches' Records

1. Don Morrow: 183-71-2 (.719)
2. William Cooper: 25-35-2 (.419)
3. Pete Austin: 21-30-3 (.417)
4. Larry Petril: 20-21-2 (.488)
5. Don Cogswell: 16-26-6 (.396)
6. Herb Hinsche: 16-41-3 (.292)
7. Steve Andersen: 14-21-2 (.405)
8. Bob Hunter: 10-19-2 (.355)

9. Walter Jacobsmeyer: 5-2-1 (.688)
10. Steve Verry: 1-8 (.111)
11. Dan Brown: 1-9 (.100)

Total: 312-283-24 (.523)
(three years unaccounted for)

COACH DON MORROW

Don Morrow, a South Bayan born and bred, has made his mark as one of the outstanding coaches in South Bay history. Morrow's record at Mira Costa High School is 183-71-2 for an outstanding percentage of .719.

Morrow came to Mira Costa in 1993 and quickly took the Mustangs to an incredible 13-1 record after the team had gone 4-5-1 the previous year. In October 1993, Morrow told the *Los Angeles Times*, "We've looked at our schedule closely, and we feel we can play with most teams. If we take them one at a time, we feel we're going to have a pretty nice season."

A nice season? That would prove to be the understatement of the year. The team went on to become CIF champions, beating Pomona, Lompoc, Kennedy of La Palma and finally Rancho Alamitos, 29–17, in the finals. Outstanding players on that team included Dino Rosi, Miquel Prieto and wide receiver Matt Guerrero, all led by quarterback Ryan Barnes and tailback Ronnie Hand. "We definitely owe this season's success to Coach Morrow," Joe Byrd said.

The 1994 season was not far behind. Mira Costa finished 12-2, beating Buena Park, South Hills and Lompoc in the CIF before losing to Arroyo Grande, 16–0. Morrow always got the best out of his players. Running back Mike Fikes gained 2,700 yards, while Isaac Mario, Julio Rosales, Matt Guerrero, Eric Miller and Jason Hughes were all outstanding.

From 2000 to 2004, the Mustangs won forty-nine games and lost just four under Morrow. In 2000, the team finished 12-1, beating Valencia 20–14 and Notre Dame 41–38 before losing 34–11 to Hart of Newhall in the finals. The team was led by running back Michael Okwo, quarterback J.R. Martinez, wide receiver Morgan Ralls and tight end Nick Wynand. In 2001, it was much of the same as Morrow led his team to another 12-1 year, beating Saugus 30–21 and St. Francis of La Canada 24–21 before again losing to

Coach Don Morrow, shown here in 2003, is one of the greatest coaches in South Bay history. He won 183 games at Mira Costa in Manhattan Beach from 1993 to 2013. *Photo by Brad Graverson; courtesy of the* Daily Breeze.

Tailback Ronnie Hand was an important part of Mira Costa's 13-1 season in 1993. *Courtesy of Manhattan Beach Historical Society.*

Michael Okwo was a star running back for the Mira Costa High team that went 13-1 in 2002. *Courtesy of Manhattan Beach Historical Society.*

Hart, 35–6. Running back Okwo led a team that included Peter Dobush, David Enos, Tyler Caldwell and Greg Sabo.

Morrow kept up the pace in 2002, as the team finished 13-1, the only loss coming to Notre Dame of Sherman Oaks in the championship, 20–17. Also in the CIF playoffs, the Mustangs annihilated Crescenta Valley 68–34, edged St. Paul of Santa Fe Springs 21–17 and wiped out Antelope Valley of Lancaster 31–12. During the regular season, victims included Hawthorne (75–6) and Peninsula (42–0). That great team was again led by quarterback Pete Dobush and running back Michael Okwo, assisted by running back Nick Haley and offensive lineman Kasy Stichler.

Morrow concluded this fantastic run in 2003, going 12-1 again. This time the Mustangs beat Paramount 49–6 and Chaminade of West Hills 52–24 before losing to Notre Dame—again—21–13. Quarterback Brian Seidenstricker, running back Tyler Pringle, linemen Andy Oldfield, Spencer Smith and Kevin Fox were all outstanding.

This all came about naturally. Morrow was raised in Manhattan Beach and attended Aviation High School, where he was an All-CIF quarterback for the Falcons. After playing football, baseball and basketball at Aviation, Morrow became an All-Conference quarterback at El Camino and then a starter at Cal State Northridge for two years. He earned a degree in chemistry and became a science teacher and football coach. Morrow became head coach at South High School in Torrance, going 5-3 his first year. He spent four years at South, finishing his last two seasons with excellent 8-3 records.

Morrow's teams have been in the CIF finals eight times, winning three championships: 1993, 1997 and 2009. The 2009 season was particularly memorable, as the Mustangs went 12-2 and in the CIF playoffs beat Quartz Hill 42–6, Chaminade of West Hills 41–19 and Palmdale of Lancaster 51–27 before edging Alemany of Mission Hills 24–21 to take the championship. The team was led by quarterback Kyle Demarco, who passed for 1,857 yards and seventeen touchdowns, while Morgan Reece rushed for 1,026 yards and Kyle Nunn had fifty-one receptions and fourteen touchdowns.

One of the highlights of Morrow's career was having three sons in his football program: Taylor in 2007 at wide receiver, Jackson in 2010 as a linebacker and Harrison in 2014 at wide receiver. In a January 2014 article in the *Daily Breeze* newspaper by Dave Thorpe, Morrow said his experience coaching his sons was something he wouldn't trade for anything. "It's been awesome," he said. "There's been a couple of difficult times, but the way they've handled everything has been fantastic. They committed themselves to football and have a love for the sport like I do. And they are true Costa guys."

Harrison relished having his father as his coach, Thorpe reported. "We had more opportunities to talk football; there is no disconnect between us," Harrison said. "We can always communicate."

Coaching one's own sons is an interesting proposition.

"In the earlier parts of my career, I was not athletic," Harrison said. "And he (his father) was always pushing me to get out of the house and exercise. He motivated me to do it."

"Harry's improvement from his junior to senior year was one of the all-time improvements I've seen in our program," Morrow said. "His junior year, he caught like one ball. His senior year, he caught 50 or so and went from 175 pounds to 190 to 195 pounds."

For Morrow, coaching his own sons has not always been easy, Thorpe reported.

In 2007, Morrow said, "Taylor was our quarterback our first few games his senior year and we switched to Sean Kelly, and then Taylor did a tremendous job at wide receiver. We knew we needed to make a move, and he handled it beautifully…It's the hardest thing ever to have to tell any kid that, much less your own son."

"It's been amazing to have this opportunity to play for my father," Harrison said. "I think he builds a special relationship with every player on our team."

Obviously, Don Morrow has built a football program that produces outstanding young men, and that bodes well for the future.

CHAPTER 16

MIRALESTE HIGH SCHOOL MARAUDERS

The Miraleste High School Marauders had some impressive years in their brief 1968–90 tenure.

Wilbur Lucas, the school's first coach from 1968 through 1976, had a very good year in 1971. The Marauders went 11-1 and beat South Pasadena 24–14 and Riverside North 24–3 before losing to St. John Bosco of Bellflower, 21–12, in the CIF playoffs. Led by the Player of the Year running back Dave Tenn, the team also featured All-CIF quarterback Steve Doran, All-League guards Steve Burns and Dave Fauchaid, running back Larry Hoover, tackle Rick Mileham, All-CIF linebacker Tom Papadakis and wide receiver Kevin Butler. Outstanding wins were over Rolling Hills (22–7), Palos Verdes High (26–0), Lawndale (28–7) and El Segundo (48–12).

Lucas had another good year in 1972, when the Marauders went 6-2-2 and made the playoffs, where they lost to Santa Paula, 14–13. Some of their great players that year were defensive tackle Bob Whitaker, linebacker Jon Jackson, guard Craig Nash and Player of the Year Mark Doran at running back.

South Bay coaching icon Gary Kimbrell started his career at Miraleste in 1977 with a 7-2 record, beating Brea 14–7 in the CIF playoffs before losing to Neff of La Mirada, 7–6. Outstanding players included quarterback Bob Martin, running back Guy Grant and defensive players Steve Armen, Mort Hansen and Anthony Misetich. Big wins came over El Segundo, Lawndale, Redondo and Leuzinger.

"Mark Gray, a center and defensive player in 1977, '78 and '79, practiced and played with more intensity than anyone I ever coached," Kimbrell said.

Top: Wayne Lucas won thirty-eight games at Miraleste High from 1968 through 1976. *Courtesy of Peninsula Library Archives.*

Bottom: Gary Kimbrell, future South Bay coaching icon, starred at tailback for the Miraleste team that finished 10-3 in 1984. *Courtesy of the Peninsula Library Archives.*

Kimbrell had several more outstanding seasons. In 1981, the team finished 9-4 and defeated Bloomington (near Riverside), Notre Dame of Riverside and Atascadero before losing to Verbum Dei in the CIF playoffs. Offensive player of the year was Chris Ridout, who went on to graduate from Harvard and is now practicing law. Defensive player of the year was Craig Halverson. "Craig was a great athlete and tough," Kimbrell said. "He would have started on any team I've ever had." He played at quarterback and wide receiver in addition to defense.

Kimbrell went 7-4 in 1982, losing to Notre Dame of Riverside, 13–7, in the CIF playoffs. Great players included Kurt Schroeder, Tim Wahl, Dan Cray and Eric Norris.

In 1986, Kimbrell took the Marauders to a 6-3-2 record, losing to Temple City in the playoffs. The team was led by quarterback Todd Hollingshead and halfback Mike Silane.

Tom Graves took over the team in 1987 and went 1-9. The Marauders' sole win came against Morningside, 21–0, behind quarterback Lou Budde, linebacker Brad Barez, fullback Troy Jankovich and defensive back Jim Silane.

In 1988, coaches Todd DeAngelis and Darren Del Conte helped the team to a 4-5 record. Future coach Brett Peabody was a great all-around player, assisted by quarterback Mike Booth, running backs Ruben Pulido and Rick Galyean and Mark John on defense.

Miraleste's last two seasons were led by offensive lineman of the year Mark John, fullback Scott Courtney, quarterback Steve Cooper and running back Dan Sarner. The last year was memorable for Brett Ostergard kicking a fifty-seven-yard field goal and Danny Sarner rushing for over one thousand yards. Outstanding on defense were Ostergard, Steve Keesal and Matt Miladinovich.

After Miraleste and Palos Verdes High closed their doors because of low enrollment, undergraduates from Miraleste and Palos Verdes High School and Coach Kimbrell went on to Peninsula High School at the end of the 1990 season, closing a long chapter on some outstanding football in the South Bay.

Miraleste Win-Loss Records

1968: 0-5, Wilbur Lucas
1969: 4-5, Lucas
1970: 5-3-1, Lucas
1971: 11-1, Lucas
1972: 6-2-2, Lucas
1973: 3-6, Lucas
1974: 3-8, Lucas
1975: 3-7, Lucas
1976: 3-3-1, Lucas
1977: 8-3, Gary Kimbrell
1978: 6-4, Kimbrell
1979: 6-5, Kimbrell

1980: 10-3, Kimbrell
1981: 9-4, Kimbrell
1982: 7-4, Kimbrell
1983: 2-7, Kimbrell
1984: 10-3, Kimbrell
1985: 5-6, Kimbrell
1986: 6-3-2, Kimbrell
1987: 1-9, Tom Graves
1988: 4-5, Todd DeAngelis and
    Darren Del Conte
1989: 5-4, Tony Bantula
1990: 5-3, Bantula

Coaches' Records

1. Gary Kimbrell: 69-41-2 (.625)
2. Wilbur Lucas: 38-36-2 (.513)
3. Tony Bantula: 10-7 (.588)
4. Todd DeAngelis and Darren Del Conte: 4-5 (.444)
5. Tom Graves: 1-9 (.100)

Totals: 122-98-4 (.554)

CHAPTER 17

MORNINGSIDE HIGH SCHOOL MONARCHS

Morningside High School is not exactly a football power, but it has had its moments, including going 12-1 in 1966 and 10-1 in 1967, both under Leon Wheeler. Then in 2003, longtime coach Ron Tatum carried the Monarchs to a 12-2 record.

Morningside Win-Loss Records

1952: no record

1953: 1-3-1, coach unknown

1954: 3-5-1, Marty Ernaga

1955: no record

1956: 3-6, Howard Johnson

1957: 8-1, Johnson

1958: 8-1, Johnson

1959: no record

1960: 6-1-2, Johnson

1961: 4-4-1, Jay Roelen

1962: 2-6-1, Roelen

1963: 1-7-1, Roelen

1964: 1-8, Roelen

1965: 4-5, Roelen

1966: 12-1, Leon Wheeler

1967: 10-1-1, Wheeler

1968: 5-4, Wheeler

1969: 3-6, Wheeler

1970: 8-1-1, Wheeler

1971: 2-5-1, Dave Van Hoorebeke

1972: 3-5-1, Van Hoorebeke

1973: 8-3, Van Hoorebeke

1974: 7-2, Van Hoorebeke

1975: no record

1976: no record

1977: 6-3-1, John Rotella

1978: 8-3, Rotella

1979: no record

1980: no record

1981: 7-2, Ron Tatum

1982: no record

1983: no record

1984: 3-6-1, Tatum
1985: 1-9, Tatum
1986: 6-4, Tatum
1987: 2-6-1, Tatum
1988: 7-3, Tatum
1989: 8-3, Tatum
1990: 9-3, Tatum
1991: 9-2, Tatum
1992: 5-5, Tatum
1993: 0-9, Tatum
1994: 3-7, Tatum
1995: 0-10, Tatum
1996: 2-8, Tatum
1997: 0-10, Tatum
1998: 1-6-2, Tatum

1999: 0-10, Tatum
2000: 1-9, Tatum
2001: 1-8, Tatum
2002: 3-7, Tatum
2003: 12-2, Tatum
2004: 3-6-1, Lafayette Fletcher
2005: 1-9, Fletcher
2006: 6-5, Fletcher
2007: 4-6, Fletcher
2008: 3-7, Fletcher
2009: 2-8, Fletcher
2010: 1-9, Fletcher
2011: 4-6, Sheron M. Butler
2012: 5-5, Butler
2013: 6-5, Derwin Henderson

Coaches' Records

1. Ron Tatum: 79-129-4 (.377)
2. Leon Wheeler: 38-13-2 (.736)*
3. Howard Johnson: 25-3-2 (.850)*
4. Dave Van Hoorebeke: 20-15-2 (.568)
5. Lafayette Fletcher: 20-50-1 (.289)
6. Jay Roelen: 18-24-9 (.480)
7. John Rotella: 14-6-1 (.690)*
8. Sheron Butler: 9-11 (.450)
9. Derwin Henderson: 6-5 (.545)
10. Marty Ernaga: 3-5-1 (.389)

* incomplete record

Totals: 232-261-21 (.472)
(nine years unaccounted for)

CHAPTER 18

NARBONNE HIGH SCHOOL GAUCHOS

Nathaniel Narbonne High School is named after a sheep rancher whose land the school was built on in 1925. The school mascot is Gaucho, an Argentinean cowboy, and the school motto is *Domus Victorum*, which means "Home of the Victors."

And that's exactly what Narbonne has established on the football field under Coach Manuel Douglas—a home for the victors. Since he took over in 2002, the team has gone 107-49-1 for a winning percentage of .685. Not bad. And the Gauchos have had five city championships since 2000.

Narbonne also has had some legendary players who have gone on to the NFL, including linebacker Antwan Applegate with Carolina, cornerback Nnamdi Asomugha with Philadelphia, safety Dashon Golson with Tampa Bay, defensive end Patrick Goodpaster with Baltimore, linebacker Tom Graham with Denver, cornerback Roy Lewis with Seattle, tight end Brandon Manumaleuma with San Diego and running backs Marcus O'Keith and Jonathan McKenzi Smith with Kansas City.

The Gauchos played their first season in 1924 under Coach Victor Jones and went 2-3—not bad for a neophyte program without a home. They beat Sawtelle 6–0 and Torrance, an early whipping boy, 20–19.

In 1925, under new coach Ben Camrada, Narbonne went 2-2-1, beating Torrance again, 19–0.

But 1926 was incredible, as the Gauchos went 5-0 and outscored their opponents 85–0. Obviously, that never happened again. Their victims that year included Torrance, Jordan, Gardena, Wilmington and Bell. Outstanding players were Glenn and Harold Hammack, John Munger, Orel Perry, Jack Santich and Cortland Meyers. The Narbonne yearbook said, "Little but mighty Corky [Meyers] played some mighty fine games for Narbonne and was responsible for some of its wins."

The following year, 1927, was more of the same, as the Marine champs went 7-0. This time, however, they were scored on. Key wins came over Gardena (13–8) and Torrance (41–0). Captain George Wilkinson at tackle, guard-end John Powers, guard-fullback Harry Haslam and back Harry Morgison led this distinguished team.

This early winning tradition continued as Camrada led the Gauchos to an impressive record of 40-9-2 from 1928 through 1936, winning four more championships and tying for one as they went 6-1 in 1929, 5-1 in 1931, 6-0 in 1933, 5-1 in 1935 and 7-1 in 1936. Some pulverizing along the way included shutout wins over Banning (66–0), Torrance (26–0), Leuzinger (27–0), Gardena (19–0), El Segundo (31–0) and South Gate (32–0). Whew!

Great players? Many.

1929: Lineman Art Johnson, tackle Norman Robb and quarterback Darrell Wolverton

1932: Guard Ralph Allman, quarterback Homer Cheek, end Elmer Holman and tackle-guard Hall McEwen

1933: Guard Donald Davis, end Harry Townsend and quarterback Gordon Woods

1935: Fullback Warren Haslam, MVP halfback Clinton Powers, tackles Lee Savant and Bill Brians, guard Wallace Mayer and center Stanley Nietupski

Camrada didn't let down in his last year, as he went out with a 7-1 record and another championship. Halfback James Ammon, guard Swao Hirata, end Lloyd Powell and, again, tackle Bill Brians were all team leaders.

Then it was obviously time for some down years. World War II interrupted playtime, but Coaches Sheldon Louhborough and Walter Kuns brought the team back on track from 1944 through 1952. The 1949 season was particularly outstanding, as the Gauchos went 5-0-1, winning the city championship again behind Dale Atkeson, Harold Duncan, Bill Stits, Jimmie Timms and Jarvis Watson.

Times were a little tough until 1956, when Coach Gordon Wells took over and the Gauchos went 7-3. Wells proceeded to win nineteen games in his career. Outstanding players included Clary Banks, Carl Wada, Jim Kaul and

Bill Knocke in 1956; halfback George Mackey, quarterback Walter Prince, end Gary Stephen and tackle Jim Jones in 1957; halfback Ray Burleson and tackle Bob Nichols in 1959; and fullback George Mitchell and quarterback Ed Ferrante in 1960.

John Olafson coached for a few years before Jack Bobinette took over for the next eleven. His record wasn't great, but the team hung in there. The Gauchos went 5-3 in 1964 and had a remarkable seven players on the All-Marine team: Paul Orseth, Ron Lund, Clark Davis and Greg Gordon on offense, and Paul Russell, John Taylor and Richard Zacker on defense.

The year 1965 was also good for the Gauchos, who ended with a 5-3 record and had several first-team All-League players: quarterback Joe DiMassa, tackle Clark Davis, lineman Rod White and defensive back Jess Mota.

The 4-3-1 team in 1966 featured MVP defensive lineman Martin Nakazawa, offensive lineman Gary Bergen and back Lynn Hughes. MVP Tom Graham led the 4-4 1967 team, and quarterback Steve Mitchell was MVP for the 4-4 1968 team. Offensive lineman James Williams was MVP for the 1969 team, which went 5-4 and also featured quarterback Steve Cannon and running back Robert Crow. The 5-5 1970 team featured All-League wide receiver Ron Cheatham, running back Crow and tackle Mike Miller. In 1975, the Gauchos' record was 4-5, with Andy Gray, George Comfort, Jemes Peoples and Anthony Myles all having their moments.

The years from 1978 to 1983 were the Coach Jack Epstein years. And fine ones they were, as he led the team to a 32-25-3 record. Particularly outstanding was 1979, when the Gauchos went 9-2 and Epstein was named Coach of the Year. In the playoffs, they beat Jefferson 35–16, Marshall 35–3 and Van Nuys 21–12 before losing to Canoga Park, 22–21, in overtime. Offensive MVP was Mike DeCastro, while Pili Tutuvanu was defensive MVP. Defensive back George Mix had six interceptions.

In 1980, the Gauchos were co-champs of the 3A conference even though they had a 6-4-1 record. In the playoffs, they beat Monroe 7–6 and Locke 17–14 before tying Van Nuys, 14–14, for the city championship. Outstanding players included running back Brian Wiley, wide receiver John Walsh and defensive players Romalas Troupe, Manny and Moe Iosio, Bobby Brown and Curt Jepsen. Narbonne finished just 6-5 in 1981 but beat Hamilton 26–0 in the playoffs before losing to Canoa Park, 34–0.

Lee Haley took over from 1984 to 1986, winning six but losing twenty-one, and Lynn Hughes won only three games from 1987 to 1992 but didn't take it lying down. "If (other) schools had to play with kids that walked in their front door," Hughes told the *Los Angeles Times* in 1988, "they would get their ——

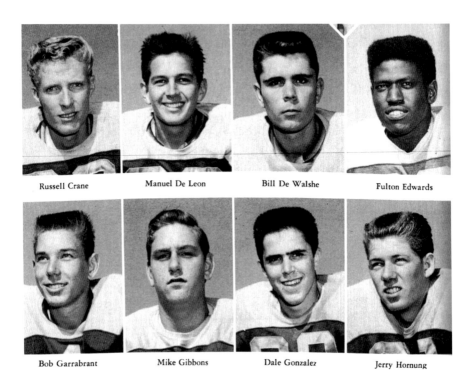

Russell Crane   Manuel De Leon   Bill De Walshe   Fulton Edwards

Bob Garrabrant   Mike Gibbons   Dale Gonzalez   Jerry Hornung

These members of the Narbonne High Gauchos led their team in the 1973 season. *Courtesy of Narbonne High School.*

kicked just like I am. They get a lot of kids from tougher areas, and there are no real tough areas here. It would be nice to see some buses come here." Jack Bobinette, who was athletic director then, said in the same article, "When it comes to the game, you can't make something out of nothing. If a team is faster than you, you cannot catch them…You have to be realistic."

But Leroy Wilson took over in 1993 and quickly led Narbonne to a great 10-2 record, beating Taft 49–21 and Sylmar 22–21 in the playoffs before losing the championship to San Pedro, 19–3. Wilson was Coach of the Year; Damion Rogers, Barry Yarbough and Cameron Taylor led an outstanding running game; and Kevin Jordan, Carl Servino, John Bailey and Antoine Armstrong were defensive stalwarts. Wilson had another good year in 1996 (7-5), but something incredible happened when Manuel Douglas took the program in hand in 2002. (See accompanying story.)

Since 2002, Narbonne has won the most games among the Los Angeles city schools in the South Bay. The Gauchos' record for that period is 107-49-

1; San Pedro is 103-40-1, Carson is 100-56, Gardena is 50-79 and Banning is last with a 43-83-1 record.

The power has shifted. For now, the Narbonne Gauchos reign supreme—tough guys or not.

Narbonne High Win-Loss Records

1924: 2-3, Victor Jones
1925: 2-2-1, Ben Camrada
1926: 5-0, Camrada
1927: 7-0, Camrada
1928: 4-2, Camrada
1929: 6-1, Camrada
1930: 4-1-1, Camrada
1931: 5-1, Camrada
1932: 2-0, Camrada
1933: 6-0, Camrada
1934: 1-2-1, Camrada
1935: 5-1, Camrada
1936: 7-1, Camrada
1937: 0-2-1, Phil Lieb
1938: 2-2-1, Lieb
1939: 3-0-1, Bill Sloan
1940: 3-3, Sloan
1941: 4-1, Sloan
1942: no record
1943: no record
1944: 3-1-1, Sheldon Loughborough
1945: 3-2-1, Walter G. Kuns
1946: 4-3-1, Loughborough
1947: 2-4, Loughborough and Kuns
1948: 3-4, Loughborough and Kuns
1949: 5-0-1, Loughborough and Kuns
1950: 2-3-2, Loughborough and Kuns
1951: no record
1952: 2-5, Loughborough
1953: no record

1954: 4-5, Kuns and Alex Mechikoff
1955: 1-7, Mechikoff
1956: 7-3, Gordon Wells
1957: 3-1-1, Wells
1958: 4-3, Wells
1959: 4-3-1, Wells
1960: 1-7, Wells
1961: no record, Wells
1962: no record, John Olafson
1963: 3-4-1, Olafson
1964: 5-3, Olafson
1965: 5-3, Olafson
1966: 4-3-1, Olafson
1967: 4-4, Jack Bobinette
1968: 4-4, Bobinette
1969: 5-4, Bobinette
1970: 5-5, Bobinette
1971: 0-8, Bobinette
1972: no record, Bobinette
1973: no record, Bobinette
1974: no record, Bobinette
1975: 4-5, Bobinette
1976: 1-8, Bobinette
1977: 1-8, Bobinette
1978: 2-5-2, Jack Epstein
1979: 9-2, Epstein
1980: 6-4-1, Epstein
1981: 6-5, Epstein
1982: 5-4, Epstein
1983: 6-5, Epstein
1984: 2-7, Lee Haley
1985: 2-7, Haley

1986: 2-7, Haley
1987: 0-9, Lynn Hughes
1988: 0-9, Hughes
1989: 1-8, Hughes
1990: 0-9, Hughes
1991: 1-8, Hughes
1992: 1-9, Hughes
1993: 3-7, Leroy Wilson
1994: 2-8, Wilson
1995: 10-2, Wilson
1996: 7-5, Wilson
1997: 5-6, Wilson
1998: 4-7, Wilson
1999: 5-5, J.R. Munoz

2000: 5-5, Munoz
2001: 8-5, Munoz
2002: 6-8, Manuel Douglas
2003: 6-6, Douglas
2004: 10-3, Douglas
2005: 7-3, Douglas
2006: 7-5, Douglas
2007: 10-2, Douglas
2008: 12-1-1, Douglas
2009: 8-6, Douglas
2010: 6-6, Douglas
2011: 11-3, Douglas
2012: 14-1, Douglas
2013: 11-3, Douglas

Coaches' Records

1. Manuel Douglas: 128-57-1 (.691)
2. Ben Camrada: 57-14-2 (.795)
3. Jack Epstein: 34-25 (.576)
4. Leroy Wilson: 31-35 (.470)
5. Jack Bobinette: 24-46 (.342)*
6. Gordon Wells: 19-17-2 (.526)*
7. John Olafson: 17-13-2 (.563)
8. Sheldon Loughborough and Walter Kuns: 12-11 (.522)*
9. Bill Sloan: 10-5 (.667)*
10. Sheldon Loughborough: 9-9-2 (.500)
11. Lee Haley: 6-21 (.286)
12. Walter Kuns and Alex Mechikoff: 4-5 (.444)
13. Lynn Hughes: 3-52 (.054)
14. Kuns: 3-2-1 (.583)
15. Victor Jones: 2-3 (.400)
16. Phil Lieb: 2-4-2 (.313)
17. Alex Mechikoff: 1-7 (.125)

* incomplete record
Totals: 262-307-12 (.461)
(nine years unaccounted for)

COACH MANUEL DOUGLAS

Manuel Douglas is the football surprise of the South Bay. Only Scott Altenberg of Serra High School surpasses his win total since 2002. Altenberg has guided Serra to 128 victories in that time, while Douglas has an impressive 107 wins at Narbonne. (Trailing close behind is Mike Walsh at San Pedro with 103 wins.)

Narbonne has been more than good in the past dozen years, as Douglas, a graduate of South Gate High School, has accumulated four city championships. The Gauchos were particularly tough this past year when they started off the playoffs by manhandling Camino Real 53–0. They also demolished Birmingham of Van Nuys 21–13 and Carson 40–12 before losing the city championship to Crenshaw, 20–13.

But nothing equals the 2012 season, when Douglas and Narbonne had their best year, going 14-1. Their victims included Long Beach Poly, the Pacific-5 Division champion; Mater Dei of Santa Ana, the Pac-5 runner-up; Serra of Gardena, the Western Division champion; Palos Verdes, the Northern Division champion; and Crenshaw, the city runner-up. Their only loss was to Corona Centennial, when they came back from a 27–8 halftime deficit, only to fall 41–34 in the last seconds of the game. "It was a bitter loss," Douglas told Eric Sondheimer of the *Los Angeles Times* in December 2012, "but I was glad our players showed who we were. Now everyone knows who Narbonne is, and it's a great legacy for our program."

In an earlier article in December, Douglas, with tears in his eyes, told Sondheimer how important the 25–0 victory over Crenshaw was. "I was thinking about those kids when they were 10th graders and Crenshaw blew us out (49–14)," he said. "14-0 is an incredible thing. I was thinking about my family. (He has a wife and three young children). Everything at once hit me. I don't get sentimental. I try to stay low-key and even keel. But that's the time to let it go because those moments don't come very often. Those two minutes were lots of years in the making."

It's funny because Douglas had nothing to prove. His team had already won the city championship outright in 2011 with an 11-3 record and tied San Pedro for the championship in 2008 with a 12-1-1 record.

Douglas, who became head coach in 2002, remembers his beginnings very well. The team won just two out of its first ten games but ended up winning the city championship. That run included wins over Eagle Rock (48–29), Westchester (39–14), Jordan (57–22) and Granada Hills (49–38).

Coach Manuel Douglas, who has won 107 games in twelve years at Narbonne High in Harbor City, celebrates a 48–32 win over Carson for the 2011 city championship. *Photo by Scott Varley; courtesy of the* Daily Breeze.

Incredibly, in 2003, Narbonne lost four of its first seven games but made it to the playoffs again and beat Birmingham 27–20 before losing to Sylmar, 27–24. But we hadn't seen anything yet.

The following year was just a harbinger of things to come. Douglas led the Gauchos to a 10-3 season, as they beat Chatsworth Charter, 38–21, and Carson, 31–14 in the CIF playoffs. But it was the following 21–0 loss to Birmingham of Lake Balboa that changed everything.

According to that same Sondheimer article, Douglas decided to study what Urban Meyer was doing at Florida. He abandoned his running game in favor of spread option attack with his quarterback in shotgun formation. He also studied what Corona Centennial was doing with a no-huddle formation, as well as the University of Oregon's fast-break offense. The results were spectacular, to say the least. Douglas said that he didn't remember why he let the running game dominate for so long. "This is so fun," he said of his new offensive strategy.

It took a couple good years (7-3 in 2005 and 7-5 in 2006) for Douglas and the team to get acclimated to the new style. That's when the great years of 10-2, 12-1-1, 11-3, 14-1 and 11-3 followed. And since then, the Gauchos' record against their archrivals is 5-2 against Carson and 6-1 over Banning, including consecutive blowouts of 64–6, 36–3, 54–7 and 53–2!

Other coaching possibilities have loomed large for Douglas, but he is still at Narbonne. He told Sondheimer that it is a struggle to maintain a good football team with demanding academics. "Our district continues to place barriers," he said. "Their focus is on advanced test scores and attendance rates, which are all important. Guys like us understand all those things intertwine with athletics."

Douglas points out that his greatest rewards are the players—kids who come back grateful for the time spent with him and Narbonne. One is Major Culbert, who rushed for over 1,900 yards and attended Nebraska. "To see that kid mature and grow up as an athlete…that kid was one of the hardest workers I've known," said Douglas in the Sondheimer article. "He didn't make to the NFL, but he says, 'Coach, I just want to thank you for everything you've done…you can trust I'm going to take care of Narbonne.' Those are the reasons you coach. The fact that he comes back when he never has to—those are the relationships that matter most and have kept me grounded and kept me within L.A. Unified."

And certainly the players, the school and the community are the lucky ones.

CHAPTER 19

NORTH HIGH SCHOOL SAXONS

In September 1955, North High School became the second high school in Torrance. The Saxons even fielded a football team under Coach Cliff Grayhbell, winning one and losing seven. Never fear. The team went 1-6-1 the following year.

And when Coach Bob Shoup came in 1957, the Saxons went 3-5 before winning their first league championship in 1958 at 6-3. The Saxons beat Mira Costa 6–0, manhandled Beverly Hills 47–13 and squashed El Segundo 26–7 before losing 19–13 in the CIF playoffs to mighty Long Beach Poly. Outstanding players included center George Morgan, halfbacks Hershel Lawson and Chuck Webb, quarterback Bill Hall and tackle Steve Harper.

The team slumped in 1959 before bouncing back with two good years in 1960 (5-2-1) and 1961 (7-2), winning Shoup's last league championship. MVP of the team, tackle Bob Martin; end Dan Claxton; quarterback Jeff Bell; and left half Joe Castorena were outstanding. Key wins were 20–13 over both Warren and Mira Costa and 29–26 over Morningside. The Saxons lost the first game of the playoffs to El Rancho, 16–0, having a ninety-five-yard return on the opening kickoff negated by a clipping penalty.

There was no letdown when Ed Levy took over the reins in 1962, as the team went 8-2. Quarterback Norm Dow (who would become famous for beating USC while he was at UCLA) led the team with assistance from linemen Carey Hubert and Richard Parker and end Paul Harnum. The mighty Saxons shut out six teams that year, including Mira Costa (6–0) and Morningside (33–0). North then beat Santa Barbara in the playoffs, 6–0, before losing 20–13 to Loyola.

1967 brought another league championship as Levy's team went 6-3 behind All-South Bay players Dan Hanswen, Rick Francis, Guy Sutryk and Rick Creighton. Then the Saxons lost to Santa Barbara, 48–7, in the playoffs.

1970 brought the beginning of two good years under new coach Howard Taylor: 6-3 in 1970 and 9-1 in 1971. All-South Bay quarterback Robbie Schmitz (Steve's brother) led an offense that included Chuck Hodge at center, Dennis Littlejohn at tight end, Denny Martindale at flanker, Ray Perkins at linebacker and Mark Windell at defensive back.

Schmitz was the third-greatest quarterback in the CIF, and Littlejohn and Hodge excelled again. Quality wins came over Palos Verdes (28–7), West (13–6) and Long Beach Jordan (20–8). Unfortunately, the Saxons lost the first game in the playoffs to Western of Anaheim, 20–7.

In 1973, Jim O'Brien went 8-3 in his second year, and the Saxons won the crown again. They beat Long Beach Millikan 18–7 in the playoffs but then lost to Anaheim, 7–0.

The school's twentieth year marked the team's ninth winning season—not bad for a neophyte program. Another new coach, Bill Cunerty, took the club to its seventh championship in 1974 with a 7-3 record marred by a first-round playoff loss to St. John Bosco of Bellflower, 29–9. The outstanding North team was led by quarterback Tom Olsen, wide receiver Brian Ragsdale, running back Kirk Bennett and linemen Jeff Goddard and Craig Wolfram.

Then the Steve Schmitz era began. A graduate of North, Schmitz took his team to eleven consecutive winning seasons. Everything started off in 1975 behind quarterback Steve Trankett and running back Bryan Brasel. Championships were recorded in 1978, 1979, 1980, 1982, 1983, 1984 and 1985. 1980 was a particularly strong year, as North beat Westlake 10–7 in the playoffs but lost to Long Beach Poly, 24–3.

But it was 1983 that turned out to be the greatest season in North history, as the Saxons went 13-1, their only loss coming to mighty Hart of Newhall in the playoffs, 29–16. Quarterback Neal Maeyama; running back Rodney Trammel; wide receiver Bernard Johns; Bay League Player of the Year Greg Clark, who excelled on both offense and defense; lineman of the year Mark Sager; kicker Bill Perkins; and All-Leaguers Jim Tulette and Craig Thomas were all instrumental in the team's great success. Clark went on to play four years in the NFL.

North had another great season in 1984, going 8-2-1 with another league championship before losing to St. Bernard in the CIF playoffs. Maeyama, with 1,786 yards passing, was named Ocean League back of the year.

Running back Rodney Trammel helped the North High Saxons to their best record in history, 13-1, in 1983. *Courtesy of the Torrance Historical Society.*

Schmitz closed out his career at North in 1985 with a 9-3 season and another championship. This time the Saxons beat Cabrillo but lost to Lompoc, 31–14, in the playoffs.

Their next big year was 1992, when Joe Austin took the Saxons to a 9-2 record and the league championship. Gary Duperon polished off four good seasons with a 10-1 record in 2000.

Then it was Todd Croce's turn, and make a mark he did. He has won more games than any coach in Saxon history, garnering a 95-62-2 record and five league championships since he arrived in 2001. His 2004 team was really impressive, as it lost only one game all season until being whipped by Crespi of Encino, 32–14, in the CIF finals. The Saxons had downed Bosco Tech of Rosemead 28–20, La Canada 28–23 and St. Joseph of Santa Maria 21–18 to reach the finals. The team was led by quarterback/ defensive end Lyle Moevao and running backs Ruddy Irving and Dionte Harvey, who made an incredible one-two punch and racked up 1,613 yards and 1,419 yards, respectively. Jason Juarez was a standout at defensive end and tight end, as was Chris Brown on the offensive line and at defensive end. Quality wins were over San Pedro (28–21), Palos Verdes (41–13) and Torrance (42–8).

Croce's winning ways continued with a 9-2 season in 2008 before losing 48–37 to Morro Bay in the first playoff game. The Saxons had several big wins that year, including a 28–21 victory over West, a 24–13 decision over Bishop Montgomery and a 30–7 thrashing of Redondo. This was followed by a 7-4 season in 2010 in which they lost to Santa Ynez in the CIF playoffs, 28–14.

Then 2012 was a landmark year, as North won the league and went all the way to the CIF finals before losing to Nordhoff of Ojai. On their way to the finals, the Saxons knocked off Oak Park 27–0, Gladstone of Covina 42–34 and Bishop Diego of Santa Barbara 28–14. Outstanding players included quarterback Jorge Hernandez, wide receiver/defensive end Trendell Gholar, wide receiver/defensive back Devonte Carter and linemen Joseph Franco, Louis Yepez and Anthony Ciombo.

Some of the great North players who went on to play for Division I colleges include Sam Elliott (1964) at Ohio State; John Rance (1964) at Michigan State; Bill Cunerty (1964) at USC; Dennis Littlejohn (1972), Denny Martindale (1972) and Mark Sager (1984) at USC; Bob Francis (1973), Barnard Johns (1984) and Greg Clark (1984) at Arizona State; Wally Leistner (1973) and Joe Gasser (1981) at UCLA; Joel Anderson (1975) at West Point; David Connor (1980) at Arizona; James Harder (1983) at Oregon; Anthony Cole (1989) at Nebraska; and Frank Ramirez (1992) at Virginia.

Croce returns for his fourteenth season in 2014 and undoubtedly will continue to produce outstanding young men and outstanding teams, with hopes for more championships. North has knocked on the door so many times that a CIF championship seems to be in the cards.

North Win-Loss Records

1955: 1-7, Cliff Grayhbell
1956: 1-6-1, Grayhbell
1957: 3-5, Bob Shoup
1958: 6-3, Shoup
1959: 1-6-1, Shoup
1960: 5-2-1, Shoup
1961: 7-2, Shoup
1962: 8-2, Ed Levy
1963: 6-2-1, Levy
1964: 5-4, Levy
1965: 4-5, Levy
1966: 4-5, Levy
1967: 6-3-1, Levy
1968: 4-4-1, Levy

1969: 2-5-2, Levy
1970: 6-3, Howard Taylor
1971: 9-1, Taylor
1972: 5-4, Jim O'Brien
1973: 8-3, O'Brien
1974: 7-3, Bill Cunerty
*1975: 6-3, Steve Schmitz
*1976: 6-3, Schmitz
*1977: 6-4, Schmitz
1978: 8-3, Schmitz
1979: 8-3-1, Schmitz
1980: 10-2, Schmitz
1981: 7-3, Schmitz
*1982: 7-4, Schmitz
1983: 13-1, Schmitz

*1984: 8-2-1, Schmitz
*1985: 9-3, Schmitz
1986: 1-9, Don Bohanon
1987: 5-6, Bohanon
1988: 6-5, Bohanon
1989: 1-9, Bohanon
1990: 2-8, Joe Austin
1991: 4-5-1, Austin
1992: 10-2, Austin
1993: 5-6, Tony Uruburu
1994: 0-10, Uruburu
1995: 2-8, Bud Kuhn
1996: 2-8, Kuhn
1997: 7-4, Gary Duperon
1998: 5-3, Duperon

1999: 6-3-1, Duperon
2000: 10-1, Duperon
2001: 6-3-1, Todd Croce
2002: 12-2, Croce
2003: 4-6, Croce
2004: 12-2, Croce
2005: 6-6, Croce
2006: 1-9, Croce
2007: 4-7, Croce
2008: 9-2, Croce
2009: 5-5, Croce
2010: 7-4, Croce
2011: 3-8, Croce
2012: 11-3, Croce
2013: 6-5, Croce

* If there were conflicting records, the coach's version was used.

Coaches' Records

1. Todd Croce: 95-62-2 (.604)
2. Steve Schmitz: 88-31-2 (.736)
3. Ed Levy: 39-30-5 (.561)
4. Gary Duperon: 28-11-2 (.707)
5. Bob Shoup: 22-18-2 (.548)
6. Joe Austin: 16-15-1 (.516)
7. Howard Taylor: 15-4 (.789)
8. Don Bohanon: 13-29 (.310)
9. Jim O'Brien: 13-7 (.650)
10. Bill Cunerty: 7-3 (.700)
11. Tony Uruburu: 5-16 (.238)
12. Bud Kuhn: 4-16 (.200)
13. Cliff Grayhbell: 2-13-1 (.156)

Totals: 347-258-19 (.571)

COACH STEVE SCHMITZ

Steve Schmitz is another name on a long list of iconic football coaches in the South Bay. Schmitz coached at North High School and El Camino and Harbor Colleges for almost forty years.

Schmitz, who also teaches, was head football coach at North High from 1975 through 1985, accumulating an outstanding record of 88-31-2 for a .736 winning percentage! He also coached eighteen years at El Camino College and five at Harbor. It was all worth it to Steve, especially "watching a player grow!" he said. "Helping them mature and the camaraderie" on the field and off are what he misses the most.

Born in Des Moines, Iowa, in 1947, Steve's family moved in 1950 to Sioux City, Iowa, where he attended grade school and played football and basketball and ran track. After the family moved to Torrance in 1962, Schmitz attended North High School, where he participated in football, basketball, wrestling, baseball and track.

He ended up at El Camino College, where he played football for two years before getting a ride to Weber State in Utah as a fullback. He played for Weber State in 1969 and 1970 and then, in the spring of 1970, started his coaching career as a graduate assistant at Arizona State with legendary head coach Frank Kush. In the fall of 1971, he moved back to Torrance and was hired at North High School. He was an assistant football coach for three years under Jim O'Brien and Bill Cunerty before taking over in 1975.

Steve's team went 6-3 in his first year, and he never looked back. The first thing he learned was that "we needed to get bigger and faster. I started the mandatory weight-training class and started coaching the track team." His ties to North were constant and unending, as he also coached baseball, basketball, wrestling, track and golf.

The Saxons went 8-3 in 1978 and 9-3 in 1980, when they beat Westlake 10–7 before losing to Long Beach Poly. But everything culminated in the 1983 season, North's best, when the Saxons won the league title and finished second in the CIF, losing only to the great Hart team of Newhall, 29–16. Coach Schmitz said, "We just had a lot of great players: Bay League Player of the Year Greg Clark, lineman of the year Mark Sager, defensive back Ryan Rasnick and quarterback Neal Maeyama, the Ocean League back of the year. We lost our starting quarterback with a broken collarbone in the first quarter on a sopping wet field. [The score was tied at the time,

Steve Schmitz (kneeling) was the second-winningest coach in North High history, compiling a record of 88-31-2 for a .736 percentage. *Courtesy of Torrance Historical Society.*

and North eventually lost by six points.] Our players were committed and expected to win every game. Our attitude changed from 'hope we win' to 'we expect to win every game.'"

"I have nothing but respect for the coaches nowadays," Schmitz continued, "as they have it much tougher than we did with all the fundraising and getting coaches."

And Schmitz will never forget all the great players he had the pleasure to coach, like Chris Farasoupolis, who went to Brigham Young and played for the New York Jets, and Greg Clark, who played for Arizona State and then Chicago, Washington, San Diego and Miami in the NFL.

And there were many more who went on to major colleges: running back James Harper (Oregon), tackle Mark Sager (USC), defensive back Joe Gasser (UCLA), linebacker Mike Fitzgerald (Washington State), Bob Francis (Arizona State) and defensive back John McGillivray and wide receiver Dave McGillivray (Michigan).

Schmitz, who probably will never retire completely, still coaches boys and girls golf at North and coaches in many boys football summer camps.

Football is obviously in his blood, and the South Bay students and community will continue to benefit from this.

COACH TODD CROCE

Todd Croce, forty-four, who took over football at North Torrance High School in 2001, is the winningest coach in the school's history, with a record of 95-62-2 through 2013.

Croce said he absolutely loves to help mold young high schoolers both on the field and off. "Building relationships with the kids and watching them grow into mature responsible young adults is what coaching at the high school level is all about," he said.

Croce, who was born in Torrance, graduated from Redondo Union High School in 1987, having played wide receiver for three years under Les Congelliere. (The Sea Hawks were Pioneer League champions in 1986 before losing to Santa Maria on the road.)

Croce said that was it as far as playing football. He went on to UCLA, where he decided "to focus on academics" rather than sports, majoring in economics. While Croce was still a student at UCLA, legendary South Bay coach Don Morrow "attained his first head coaching job at South in 1989 and asked me to help coach," Croce said. "I coached the freshman team the first year and then moved up to varsity the next season and became offensive coordinator while I still was a student at UCLA." He remained at South for six seasons before becoming an assistant at North, where he served first under Bud Kuhn and then Gary Duperon.

Croce took over at North in 2001, going 6-3-1 his first year and winning the league championship at 12-2 in 2004. "2001 was a special season filled with great competitors and plenty of talent," Croce remembered. "Quarterback Kenny Brown was selected at the *Daily Breeze* Player of the

Todd Croce has more wins (ninety-five) than any other coach in North Torrance High School history. *Courtesy of the* Daily Breeze.

Year. Steven Juarez went on to play linebacker at Michigan State, while Alex Ligon played defensive end at Colorado. And perhaps the best overall athlete, wide receiver Michael Bolio, went on to find success playing in Europe. Offensive tackle Robert Gustavis and wide receiver Jeff Gray were standout juniors who played at Arizona State."

North also went 12-2 in 2004, 9-2 in 2008 and 11-3 in 2012. "2004 and 2012 were also CIF finalist teams," Croce said. "The 2004 team was led by quarterback/defensive end Lyle Moevao, who later played at Oregon State and beat USC. Offensive tackle Pepa Letuli played college football at the University of Hawaii and signed with the Dallas Cowboys before being cut. This Saxon team had tremendous character and a remarkable work ethic. The 2012 team was led by quarterback BJ Denker, who just finished his career at the University of Arizona, who upset the University of Oregon. Another great player was Ryan McDaniel, who currently is a running back for the University of Washington."

Croce, who is married, teaches four classes of world history at North. He indicated that coaching high school kids is a remarkable life. "The record on the field says very little about the impact high school coaches have on the surrounding community," Croce said. "Football is truly a microcosm for life in general. Coaches have the opportunity to influence kids as they experience the highs and lows of their time in the high school world."

Amen.

CHAPTER 20

PALOS VERDES HIGH SCHOOL SEA KINGS

First you see the Palos Verdes High School—then you don't. P.V. High opened its doors at 600 Cloyden Road in Palos Verdes Estates in 1961 and closed at the end of the 1990 school year (due to low enrollment in the Palos Verdes Unified School District), only to be resurrected again in 2003.

Such is also the case for the Sea Kings football team. The players have gone through many ups and downs, but since 2009, they have been a part of one of South Bay's best football programs (winning forty-three games in five years) and won a CIF championship in 2012 under Coach Guy Gardner.

But that wasn't the first time the Sea Kings experienced phenomenal success. Under Coach Ron Terry in 1965, the team went 11-0-1 on its way to winning the CIF AA championship. Not only were halfback Bill Tapp and linebacker Mark Carpenter first-team All-CIF, but Terry was also named Pioneer League Coach of the Year. After great wins over Rolling Hills (28–7), West High School (27–7) and Lennox (31–0), the Sea Kings rolled in the CIF playoffs, beating Santa Paula 20–0, Lawndale 35–20 and Foothill 20–7 to win the championship. Other outstanding players included wingback Lloyd Miller, guard Rick Wheldon, fullback Gary Bilotti, linebacker Craig Bryan, tackle John Belloni and end Dick Ruppert.

Coach Terry won thirty-one games in seven years, not bad for an inaugural program. After starting at 1-7 in 1961, the Sea Kings won the

Palos Verdes High's first team was coached by Ron Terry and finished 1-7, beating Aviation 27–13. *Courtesy of Peninsula Library Archives.*

Bay League title in 1964, going 6-4 overall. Co-MVPS were quarterback Bruce Berger and running back Bill Tapp. Tackle John St. John was also first-team All-League, while other outstanding players included center Don Ballard, halfback Roger Riggs, tackle Tim Haendle and guard Mark Carpenter.

New coach Dick Jacobson had two good years in 1968 and 1969, going 5-3-1 and 7-2, respectively. In 1968, John Jacobson was an All-CIF center, while defensive end Greg Papke was All-League. Other outstanding players included fullback Roger Theisen, cornerback Jeff McGallian and quarterback Dennis Finne. Quality wins were 27–0 over Aviation, 14–0 over El Segundo and 25–13 over Leuzinger. The 1969 season was even better, as halfback Jeff Smith, tackle Brad Bush, guard Chris O'Brien, linebacker Gerald Peeke, guard Bob Pickard and wide receiver Don Gause were all All-League.

Bill Ludwig took over for the Kings in 1970. The team went just 4-5 but had some outstanding players like wide receiver Jeff Smith and kicker Bob McAllister. Key wins that year came over Aviation (17–6), Leuzinger (30–2) and Rolling Hills (24–20).

In 1971, the team's record was only 3-6 under Ludwig, but quarterback Scott Gregory and defensive back Bob McAllister were All-League. P.V. beat Redondo Union 22–20, Morningside 19–12 and Leuzinger 21–12.

But the Sea Kings turned things around, going 6-3-1 in 1972 and 7-2 in 1973. The big news in 1972 was Bill Gregori amassing 1,906 yards rushing.

Brian Sweeney, Tom Spillane, Hugh Taylor, Keith Von Zup, Ted O'Neill and Dean Rallis also had big years. Quality wins were 18–6 over Mira Costa and 33–14 over Culver City.

In 1973, the team went 7-2, and Tom Spillane, Blair Bush, Dave Kirk, Bernie Lyons and Pete Hathaway were all All-Ocean League. Outstanding center Bush went on to play six years in the NFL.

A new coach in 1974, Ken Russell, carried the team to a 6-3-1 record before losing to Orange in the CIF playoffs. Bernie Lyons, Tom Spillane and Scott Faust all had good years. In 1976, Russell went 6-2-1 before losing to South Hills in the playoffs. Big wins were over South (34–21) and Rolling Hills (37–34). In 1975, the Sea Kings were 5-4 behind quarterback Carl Levander, receivers Dennis Allen and Keith Stafford and halfbacks Steve Islava, Dana Tirada and Rick Von Zup. MVP was Scott Bechler.

Russell led the Sea Kings to a 6-2-1 record in 1976 and beat South Hills in the playoffs. Key players included Bill Lohmiller, Rick Von Zup, Hal Longley and Keith Peterman. A 27–26 upset of West Torrance was a big highlight.

The Sea Kings went 4-5 in 1977 as quarterback John Demerjian led a team that included Marc Mills, Brian Smith, Don Elmajan and Scott Rouse.

But Russell closed out his career in fine style. In 1978, the Sea Kings went 7-2 and beat Thousand Oaks in the CIF. Outstanding players included Andy Bask, Andy Goetz, Earl Wilson and Clay Eisenbrand behind quarterback Demerjian.

Palos Verdes finished 10-3 in 1979, beating Long Beach Jordan and San Marcos before losing to Compton in the semifinals. MVP was Clay Eisenbrand, with great play from quarterback Mike O'Hara and halfback Jim Mays as well. The team finished 9-3 in 1980, beating Compton 7–6 before losing to Santa Barbara in the quarterfinals.

Mike House took over the program in 1981, going 5-3-1, led by quarterback Greg Denham. The team fell to 2-7 in 1982; Bill Mashy, Bob Mueller, Bill Mulkey and Andy Markesano led the team.

New coach Bill Judy repeated the 2-7 year in 1983 but bounced back in 1984 with a 7-4 record, including going 5-1 in the Bay League. Blair Bush, an outstanding defensive back, was drafted by the San Francisco 49ers. The Sea Kings beat Mira Costa 28–0, South Torrance 34–15 and Westlake 31–26 before losing to Oxnard, 28–10, in the playoffs. Outstanding players included lineman Chris Steskal, halfback John Yoon, tackle Mark Stofile, defensive end Don Humphrey and tackle Howard Jensen.

The year 1989 was a big one, as Judy led the team to a 9-2 record before losing 19–9 to Newbury Park in the CIF playoffs. Quarterback Blake Andersen led a team that included punter Mark Antrobius, linemen Kyle Holderman and David Bohner and halfback George Felactu. But 1990 was an even bigger year, as the Sea Kings played the most games since their inception. In the playoffs, P.V. beat Santa Paula 45–18, Bloomington 21–7 and Cabrillo 21–7 before finally losing to Temecula, 29–7. Felactu was MVP on offense and Rich Radford MVP on defense.

P.V. High closed at the end of 1990, with students going to Peninsula High School. However, the school reopened in 2003, with Coach Pat Fresch leading the football program. "Pat Fresch was a true Sea King," said Guy Gardner, who became coach in 2009, "and we owe him a lot."

Fresch went just 2-8 in 2003 but featured some outstanding players, including quarterback Sam Dotts, running back Scott Lulejian, defensive back Nick Dahlen and center Scott Holh. Wins over Bishop Montgomery (27–19) and Centennial (41–14) highlighted the season.

2004 was a big year even though the team went just 4-6. Quarterback Andrew Trunowski threw for over 1,900 yards, and Jon Hart had over 950 receiving yards.

The Sea Kings went 6-5 in 2005 with great wins over El Segundo (38–21), Golden Valley (62–14) and West Torrance (35–20). Brendan Lamers, Joey Capellino and Jimmie Carmack led the team.

Fresch's best year came in 2007, when the Sea Kings went 8-3-1 and beat Santa Monica in the CIF playoffs, 34–20, before losing to Gahr of Cerritos, 24–21. Quarterback Marc Venning headed a good offense that included halfbacks Robert Gregorio and Joe Gonzalez. The defense was led by Jordan Capellino and Steve Pizella.

Then came the era of Guy Gardner, who took over the program in 2009, going 6-4 behind quarterback Max Baiz and running back Victor Mancusi, who rushed for 1,246 yards. Big wins were over Peninsula High School (42–3) and Mira Costa (21–7). Gardner's breakout year came in 2010, when the team went 10-2 and beat West Ranch in the playoffs, 48–10, before losing to Westlake, 49–28. Quarterback Zach Flixen had a good year, as did running back Marc Sasso, who rushed for 1,649 yards. David Davis and Joe Walker led the defense.

In 2011, the team started off with two losses, and then the Sea Kings won eight in a row before losing to Hart, 15–14, in the playoffs.

"Our homework launched us to the Bay League title," running back Zack Henkhaus said in the 2012 yearbook. The team, featuring quarterback Zack

Flixen and wide receiver Robby Kolanz, beat South 44–07, Peninsula 35–3 and Redondo Union 31–6.

In 2013, Gardner had his fifth good season in a row, finishing 9-3 and beating Rhigetti High of Santa Maria 63–16 before losing to Hart of Newhall, 33–12. Quarterback Daniel DiRocco, receivers Joey Chenoweth and Lance Brown and running back Tyler Moore led the offense, while Will Scolinas, Phil Bernard, Ryan Corcoran and Lucas Cooper excelled on defense.

With outstanding scholar-athletes both in the classroom and on the field, the future looks bright for Coach Guy Gardner and the Palos Verdes High Sea Kings.

Palos Verdes Win-Loss Records

1961: 1-7, Ron Terry

1962: 3-5-1, Terry

1963: 4-5, Terry

1964: 6-4, Terry

1965: 11-0-1, Terry

1966: 1-6-2, Terry

1967: 5-4, Terry

1968: 5-3-1, Dick Jacobson

1969: 7-2, Jacobson

1970: 4-5, Bill Ludwig

1971: 3-6, Ludwig

1972: 6-3-1, Ludwig

1973: 7-2, Ludwig

1974: 6-3, Ken Russell

1975: 5-4, Russell

1976: 6-2-1, Russell

1977: 4-5, Russell

1978: 4-5, Russell

1979: 10-3, Russell

1980: 9-3, Russell

1981: 5-3-1, Mike House

1982: 2-7, House

1983: 2-7, Bill Judy

1984: 7-4, Judy

1985: 3-7, Judy

1987: 6-5, Judy

1988: 6-4, Judy

1989: 9-2, Judy

1990: 8-6, Judy

1991–2002: school closed

2003: 2-8, Pat Fresch

2004: 4-6, Fresch

2005: 6-5, Fresch

2006: 5-5, Fresch

2007: 8-3-1, Fresch

2008: 2-8, Fresch

2009: 6-4, Guy Gardner

2010: 10-2, Gardner

2011: 8-3, Gardner

2012: 11-3, Gardner

2013: 9-3, Gardner

Coaches' Records

1. Guy Gardner: 44-15-1 (.742)
2. Ken Russell: 44-25-1 (.636)
3. Bill Judy: 39-35 (.527)
4. Ron Terry: 31-31-1 (.500)
5. Pat Fresch: 27-35-1 (.437)
6. Bill Ludwig: 20-16-1 (.554)
7. Dick Jacobson: 12-5-1 (.694)
8. Mike House: 7-10-1 (.417)

Totals: 224-172-7 (.565)

COACH GUY GARDNER

Guy Gardner, who has only coached Palos Verdes High Sea Kings since 2009, is easily the most successful football coach in the school's history. A native of Redondo Beach and a 1983 graduate of Mira Costa High School in Manhattan Beach, he has a record of 44-15 for a great percentage of .742.

Gardner, whose worst season (6-4) was his first one for the Sea Kings, says that he really likes coaching high school kids. "I have no intention of coaching at any other level," Gardner said. "I strive to get the boys to work hard so they can give more of themselves than they thought they could, and having that helps them in their future endeavors, whatever they choose to do."

Gardner's team progressed the farthest in 2012, when it went 11-3. It was a strange year because the team lost the first three games (including a 41–0 shellacking by Narbonne) but then never lost again. In the CIF playoffs, the Sea Kings beat Antelope Valley 49–13, Hart of Newhall 49–28 and Valencia 50–33 before polishing off West Torrance 34–14 to win the championship. "It will always be a special season for all kinds of reasons," Gardner said. "That team really went through a lot of adversity, as we lost four starters to injury—for the entire season—early on. We also began the season 0-3. We just kept doing what we do, getting better each week and working as hard as we could. Of course, we had very good players, but they played as a TEAM—everyone was unselfish. I was blessed to have a great staff that can get the most out of these kids. This 2012 team also benefited from learning from the teams before them and the great legacy of a great work ethic."

"Lopes carried our team through the season," said guard Jackson Waite in the 2012 school yearbook. "We just handed him the ball and blocked, and he piled up yards."

Gardner grew up in the South Bay playing football and baseball at Mira Costa. "I was an okay athlete," Gardner said modestly, with a sense of self-deprecation, "but I worked very hard. I was deceptively slow…they thought I was slow, but I was much slower than that."

Gardner said he started volunteering to coach flag football when he attended Arizona State University, where he did not play football because there were "not a lot of five-eleven quarterbacks who ran the 40-yard dash in two days!" He added, "I think I got into coaching because I liked sports and because I wanted those that I coached to have a good, positive experience they could look back on. Two great coaches who influenced me were Ron Gonser in Pop Warner and John Burgess in both Pop Warner and Little League." Gardner said they influenced not only his sporting life but also, and more importantly, his life. He still receives guidance from Coach Gonser, who today lives in Tennessee.

Gardner, who with his wife, Tina, has two children—Quinn and Cooper—said he started as an assistant at Mira Costa after former coach Herb Hinsche, who was a vice-principal there, got in touch with him. "I was an assistant there from 1989 to 1990 under Larry Petrill, Bill Lysle and Don Morrow," he said. "All these men taught me a lot about coaching and character. Coach Morrow is not only a close friend but also a great mentor today."

Gardner was head coach at Las Quinta High School in Westminster from 1999 to 2002 and then spent one year as an assistant to Pat Fresch at P.V. before becoming head coach at Pacifica High School in Garden Grove. But P.V. came calling again, and Gardner took over as head coach, going 6-4, 10-2, 8-3, 11-3 and 9-3 in his first years. Not bad.

Gardner, who also teaches social studies and health at Palos Verdes, said, "The goal is to win, but not at any cost. Winning is just a byproduct of hard work and doing the best you can and having fun doing it. If you win, even better. Building relationships is the thing that lasts."

"I have had the opportunity to coach some great players," Gardner said. "These guys could be great in terms of ability, or they can be great in terms of character and people or both. I have great admiration for all the kids that I have been blessed to coach. I can only hope that most of them have had a positive experience and will cherish the time spent in high school and in our football program."

Gardner has four players who are currently in Division I programs: Joe Walker (2011) is at the University of Oregon, Robby Kolanz (2012) is a walk-on at USC, David Davis (2011) is at Cal Berkeley and Matt Lopes (2013) is another walk-on at USC.

"I have been blessed to have some great coaches around me as well," Gardner said. "We are different personalities that share the same goals for these young men. I thank God that I have had an opportunity to try to positively impact young men and use football as a vehicle to do that."

And Palos Verdes High can thank God for Coach Guy Gardner.

CHAPTER 21
PENINSULA HIGH SCHOOL PANTHERS

Peninsula High School took Miraleste and Palos Verdes High under its wing in 1991 due to dwindling enrollment (Palos Verdes High reopened in 2003), and a new football dynasty was born.

At least it seemed like a dynasty under Coach Gary Kimbrell, who won seventy-four games in nine years for an average of 9.25 wins a year. His complete record was 74-16-1 when he retired at the end of the 1999 season to move to Hawaii.

Kimbrell's first year at the new school matched his worst record (1998) at Peninsula, 8-3. Wow! In the CIF, the Panthers beat Santa Monica 20–16 before losing to Schurr of Montebello. Outstanding players included Scott Gordon, Taso Papadakis, Smiley Sanchez and Rich Radford.

It didn't take the Panthers long to get into the swing of things and win the Bay League title in 1992 with an 8-2 record. They eventually lost in the second round to Bell Gardens, but during the year, they beat Leuzinger 29–9, Inglewood 28–3 and Redondo Union 38–9. The team was led by quarterback Scott Gordon, running backs Jens Fleming and Jimmy Durroh and fullback Taso Papadakis. In 1993, quarterback Peter Krogh, lineman Matt Redman and captains Keith Harter and Tony Perdichina led the way.

The great Petros Papadakis, who is now a sports talk show host in Los Angeles, was an outstanding fullback for the Panthers in 1994, helping them go 11-2 that year. Quarterback Peter Krogh rushed for 598 yards and had a lot of help from Clark Haggans, Chris Duffy and Jeremy Sparling. Haggans, who would go on to play at Colorado State, played thirteen years in the

Scott Huber (left), Petros Papadakis (current sports talk personality on 570 Fox Sports) and Peter Krogh were stars on the Peninsula Panthers from 1993 to 1997. *Courtesy of Gary Kimbrell.*

NFL, eight of those seasons with the Pittsburgh Steelers. Guard-tackle John Welbourn played eight years in the NFL.

Could things get better? Yes! Quarterback Damon Gourdine and running backs Marty Cheatham and Brady Facer helped the Panthers go 12-1 the following year.

This is getting old. The team "only" went 10-1 in 1996 behind running back Marty Cheatham, lineman Scott Jackson, quarterback Garret Smith, safety Scott McMorris, running backs James Gill and Dan Maloney and lineman Brad Hively. Victims included North (49–16), Leuzinger (41–8) and West (31–13).

The great 1997 year (see accompanying story on Kimbrell) was followed by a "mediocre" 8-3 in 1998 with such players as Chris Haines, Tom Swoboda, Rob Meissner, Tommy Bell and Tyler Clinton. The Panthers annihilated teams left and right, including Culver City (48–6), Leuzinger (40–0), Santa Monica (47–0) and Mira Costa (22–0). Then Kimbrell finished up in 1999 with a 12-1 record before retiring to Hawaii.

Peninsula did not slow down under new coach Tony Urburu, going 9-3. Quarterback Eric Meissner and running back Chris Beal were outstanding as the Panthers beat West 42–14, Beverly Hills 36–14 and Long Beach Wilson 27–3. Even when the Panthers went just 4-6 in 2001, they still made

Dwain Lyon (pictured here with running back Marty Cheatham in 1994) was coach of Rolling Hills High from 1964 to 1978 and was an assistant on Peninsula High in '94, when the Panthers went 11-2. *Courtesy of Peninsula Library Archives.*

the playoffs, beating Muir 43–18 before losing to Notre Dame of Sherman Oaks, 24–17. Quarterback Kyle Degener and offensive linemen Luke Pollock, Justin Santrose and Jamie Barth were all outstanding.

The Panthers were obviously hanging in there under Urburu as they finished 7-5 in 2002 and beat Muir of Pasadena 52–35 in the playoffs before losing again to Notre Dame, 27–14. (Tight end Craig Stevens is still playing with the Tennessee Titans.)

"The strength of this year's team was the attitude of the players," Urburu said in the 2003 Peninsula yearbook. Quarterback Richard Haynes, linebacker Blake Gillman and defensive players Mike Duran and Rashid El-Malik played important parts during the season.

Then the 2004 team took off, finishing 10-1-1 and winning the Bay League title. Quarterback Theo Nikolakopulos, running back Dane Morck, defensive lineman Jeremy Lawson and defensive end Brett Stevens all stood out. Another great year of 11-2 followed in 2005, when the Panthers beat Highland 35–9 and Chaminade 21–18 before losing to Dominguez, 24–15, in the playoffs. Running back Cyrus Shabzian, kicker Ben Bobit and defensive players Colin Baxter (who drafted into the NFL) and Derek Pavia were all excellent.

Things have cooled off a bit since 2005, as the Panthers have won just twenty-five games in eight years. They still had some outstanding players, though, including Ryan Solomon and Todd Huber in 2006; Harry Sherwood and Ryan Reese in 2007; Anthony Papadakis and Chris Sutherland in 2008; Fred Warner, Matt Roesga and Dylan Rushe in 2009; Josh McGuiness, Ryan Sawelson and Brock Dale in 2010; Matthew Imwalle in 2011; and Zach Riley, Jordan Gates and James Nelson in 2012. (Defensive end Eric Lorig is with the Tampa Bay Bucs.)

One thing is for sure: the program will be back. Veteran coach Mike Christensen is at the helm, and the Panthers will growl again.

Peninsula Win-Loss Records

1991: 8-3, Gary Kimbrell
1992: 9-3, Kimbrell
1993: 10-2, Kimbrell
1994: 11-2, Kimbrell
1995: 12-1, Kimbrell
1996: 10-1, Kimbrell
1997: 14-0, Kimbrell
1998: 8-3, Kimbrell
1999: 12-1, Kimbrell
2000: 9-3, Tony Urburu
2001: 4-6, Urburu
2002: 7-5, Urburu

2003: 5-3-3, Urburu
2004: 10-1-1, Urburu
2005: 11-2, Urburu
2006: 4-6, Urburu
2007: 4-6, Urburu
2008: 4-7, Adam Boyd and
  Kevin Moen
2009: 0-10, Boyd and Moen
2010: 2-8, Boyd and Moen
2011: 5-5, Boyd and Moen
2012: 2-8, Boyd and Moen
2013: 4-6, Mike Christensen

Coaches' Records

1. Gary Kimbrell: 94-16 (.855)
2. Tony Urburu: 54-32-4 (.622)
3. Adam Boyd and Kevin Moen: 13-38 (.224)
4. Mike Christensen: 4-6 (.400)

Totals: 165-92-4 (.642)

COACH GARY KIMBRELL

Gary Kimbrell, a South Bay high school football legend, had a lifetime record of 180-70-3 for a winning percentage of .717—that ain't chopped liver!

Kimbrell, who has since retired to Hawaii, is enjoying the good life, running and surfing, and has two children and four grandkids, although his wife of forty-seven years, Karen, died in 2006.

Kimbrell had an outstanding record of 69-41-2 at Miraleste High School, 17-13-1 at the now-defunct Rolling Hills High School and an incredible 94-16 at Peninsula High School before retiring after the 1999 season. Does he miss coaching? "I miss playing!" he laughed. "I wish there was a seventy-and-over league." Undoubtedly, Kimbrell would excel in that, too. The zenith of his career has to be 1997, when the Peninsula Panthers went 14-0 and clinched the CIF Division II championship with a 35–14 win over Ayala High of Chino Hills.

"Surprise!" Kimbrell laughed. "We had the smallest and most inexperienced line offensively in the school's short history. Our left tackle was a 175-pound sophomore and left guard a 165-pound junior. Our offensive line coach Dwaine Lyon did a great job." What an understatement! The year included wins over Lakewood (28–0), Narbonne (30–0), Inglewood (48–0), Leuzinger (55–0) and Santa Monica (56–0). Are you kidding me? Apparently the defense wasn't bad, either. "What I didn't realize was the excellent depth, talent and speed we had at the skilled positions," Kimbrell said. "The combination of quarterback Greg Beal and running backs Andy Peeke, Brad Durbin and Cabot Denny was unstoppable. We also had two Division I tight ends in Tom Swoboda and Scott Huber."

Kimbrell also led the Miraleste Marauders to league championships in 1977, 1980, 1981 and 1984 before taking Peninsula in 1992, 1994, 1995, 1996, 1997 and 1999. The Panthers didn't lose a single league game from 1994 to 1997.

Other great years for Kimbrell were 1995 and 1999, when his teams went 12-1 each year. The 1995 team was led by Damon Gourdine at quarterback and Marty Cheatham at running back. "Damon was undersized but a tremendous athlete," Kimbrell recalled. "He was quarterback and wide receiver at Peninsula and played a year at El Camino and three more at San Diego State, where he was a preseason All-American as a punt returner." Cheatham became an All-Ivy League fullback at Princeton, and Peter Krogh rushed for 598 yards.

Gary Kimbrell went 74-16-1 as coach of the Peninsula Panthers from 1991 through 1999. *Courtesy of Gary Kimbrell.*

The year 1999 was also outstanding as the team featured running backs Brandon Miyoshi and Chris Beal, quarterback Brian Smith and other players like Sydney Gordon, Brent Pollock, Sean Maier and Case Duhler.

Kimbrell, who was born in 1940 in St. Paul, Minnesota, lived with relatives in Oklahoma and California while his father was in World War II. After his dad got out of the air force, the family settled in Hawthorne, where Kimbrell played all sports, growing up with two younger sisters and a brother.

"My dad bought me boxing gloves when I was seven," Gary said, "and he taught me how to defend myself. The neighborhood bully left me alone after that. I had a passion for football all my life. I used to pretend I was a running back at USC like Frank Gifford, Jim Sears and Aramis Dandoy in my front yard."

Kimbrell, a running back, played varsity ball in 1956 and 1957 at Hawthorne High, helping the Cougars win the Pioneer League both years. After graduating, he played football one year at El Camino College under Coach Norm Verry, and by 1958, he knew he wanted to coach.

Gary married Karen in 1959 and was a walk-on at Pepperdine College. "USC was not recruiting 135-pound defensive backs," he laughed. "I earned a full scholarship [at Pepperdine] in two-a-days [practice], and by the third game, I was in the starting lineup. John Scolinas was the coach and a great human being. He taught me to reward effort."

"One humorous note," Kimbrell added, "was in a 1961 game against Long Beach State, when I put myself in the game in the fourth quarter and refused to come out. Pepperdine dropped football a couple of weeks later. Lucky for me that I didn't need a letter of recommendation," he laughed.

Kimbrell then taught physical education in middle schools in Los Angeles Unified before getting a job at Rolling Hills High School in 1967. He was an assistant coach there under Dwaine Lyon until 1977, when he was hired by Miraleste. He taught physical education and coached at Miraleste through 1986. "All my seasons at Miraleste were memorable," Kimbrell said. "I got the job two weeks before the season started in 1977," but the team went on to win the league and finish 8-3 his very first year. Other great years were going 11-3 in 1980 and 1981 and 10-3 in 1984.

"Most of the kids, especially at Miraleste, were overachievers," Kimbrell said, remembering such players as lineman Jimmy Winsten in 1977–78, lineman Jim Martin in 1980–81 and running back/defensive back Mike Silane and lineman Mark Comings in 1985–86.

In 1983, Kimbrell said, the team scored nine points in the last thirty seconds to win the league championship. "We had a long TD pass, recovered the onside kick and then Gavin Arthur kicked a fifty-three-yard field goal for the win," Kimbrell remembered.

Then in 1988, Kimbrell took over the head coaching job at the now-closed Rolling Hills High School, where his record for three years was 17-13-1. "The first thing I saw after being hired was the equipment room—it was a disaster," he laughed. "I was quoted saying the program was in shambles. I was referring to the equipment room, not the former coaching staff. I knew Coach John Brown. He was very knowledgeable, and he and his staff did a good job.

"In 1989 and '90, we had a talented running back named Robert Coutler. Tight end/linebacker Jim Rudberg (1989–90) and defensive back Mike Lemon were 100 percenters. I also made one of the biggest coaching blunders of my career by not moving Greg Schwartz to starting quarterback sooner."

When Rolling Hills High closed after the 1990 season, Kimbrell became the head coach at Peninsula High School. "The first two years were the toughest of my coaching career," Kimbrell said. "I had to make a lot of compromises for the good of the program. We had a roster of eighty, and over half were seniors. You have to have happy players to be successful, and you can only have eleven on the field at a time."

But Kimbrell wasted no time in leading his team to an 8-3 record in 1991, and they finished 9-3 in 1992 and shared the Bay League title. Then he went on an incredible run, winning ten, eleven, twelve, ten, fourteen, eight and twelve over the next seven seasons. "We ran a base 3-4 defense with many variations, depending on the opponent," Gary said. "We had smart kids, and that gave us a lot of flexibility. Offensively, we had multiple formations featuring a running game, option, trap and play-action passes."

At seventy-four, Kimbrell has had a great run and has no plans to return to coaching. "What I do miss the most, however, is the interaction with the players and the camaraderie with my staff and the coaches I coached against," he said. "Joe Austin at South is a good friend of mine who never got the recognition he deserved." He remembered that "Steve Carnes at Leuzinger hated playing day games. Dan Robbins of Hawthorne did a great job with his kids, while Donnie Morrow of Mira Costa is still kicking a— and taking names."

Gary Kimbrell will always be remembered as a great coach who gave back to his players, his staff, parents, the community and the school more than he ever received.

CHAPTER 22

REDONDO UNION HIGH SCHOOL SEA HAWKS

Redondo Union High School is one of the oldest high schools in the South Bay—with a gridiron pedigree to match. The school opened its doors with one teacher and ten pupils in 1905. It became an accredited high school in 1912 and fielded its first football team in 1915 under Coach A.L. Walton (0-4). The team then went 0-3 under Fred Seltzer in 1916 and 0-6 under Coach Mitchell in 1917.

But it did not take the Sea Hawks long to have some success. Coach Tom Wilson led them to a 3-4-1 record in 1919, and football became a Redondo staple. Then, after suffering fourteen years of mediocrity, Coach Lloyd Walker took the team to a 5-3-2 record in 1929 and an 8-3 mark in 1930. Some of the top players included Red Egerer, Melvin Seifert and George Kirk, who helped beat Covina 31–6, Santa Barbara 12–7, San Pedro 12–7 and Santa Monica 21–7. Walker also had a good record in 1931 (5-3-1), but it was Joe Day who led the Sea Hawks to their first great year, going 8-1 in 1934. Walt Neilson captained a team that beat George Washington 30–0, Inglewood 14–13, Compton 32–0 and Santa Monica 13–0.

In 1936, Russell Striff led the Sea Hawks to their first CIF win, 25–0 over Orange, before losing to Glendale, 6–0. John Colmer, George Pschaida and Clifford Donahue helped Redondo beat Santa Monica 6–0 and Compton 10–0. The team tied (6–6) a great Long Beach Poly team that went on to become the champions of Southern California.

The Sea Hawks marched on, starting a series of good years in 1940 by going 4-3-1 under Striff. Fullback Roy Cole was first-team All-League,

Harold Huff (no. 76) was a dominant running back for the Redondo Sea Hawks in the early 1940s. *Courtesy of Redondo Union High School Archives.*

while quarterback John Logan and guard Jack O'Connor made the second unit.

The Sea Hawks dominated Southern California football from 1942 to 1944. They won their first CIF championship in 1942, going 8-1-1 under Striff. They beat Pomona 19–13 and Alhambra 21–14. There were several All-Bay players, including guard Dick Hatfield and halfback Bob Teagle. Guard Oliver Coury and Roy Riley also contributed.

The Sea Hawks went undefeated in 1943 (6-0), led by versatile running back Harold Hatfield, and in 1944 (7-0 under Harold Grant). They beat Santa Monica 27–13 and were declared the unofficial CIF Southern Section champion for 1943. In 1944, the team went 7-0 and beat Santa Monica again (31–7) for its third straight CIF crown.

A 6-1 record followed in 1945 under Grant, and Russell Striff returned to lead the team to a 6-2 record in 1946 and a 6-2-1 mark in '47. Dick Null, Mike Torres, George Pappe and Rod Craig helped beat Santa Monica 50–7, Whittier 27–0 and Compton 21–0.

Coach Cal Rossi resuscitated the program with a 6-3 record in 1950, and Bob Cardona took over in 1952, going on to notch eighteen wins in six seasons. The 1956 season was particularly memorable, as the team went 7-1-1. Many players made All-League, including Louis Cook, Bruce Seifert and Tom McDonnell. Halfbacks Henry Fernandez and Gene McCann also contributed, as did Art Webb, Stan Santee and Tom Wilhite.

In 1960, Vince McCullough became coach and led the team to a 7-2 record. Outstanding players included end Carl Neiman, fullback Wayne Willis, halfback Ronnie Serrato, tackle Dennis Smith and guard Ray Gilman. The Sea Hawks annihilated Morningside 25–6, Hawthorne 26–0 and Leuzinger 34–0.

Lud Keehn came in 1962 and took the Sea Hawks to a 7-2 record, including key wins over Torrance (19–7) and North Torrance (19–16). All-Bay stars included running back Rich Eber, tackle Bill Nieman, Lindsay Hughes and Bob Johnson.

In 1963, Keehn had another good season (5-2-2), beating El Segundo 35–0, San Gabriel 12–0, South High 12–0, Palos Verdes 21–13 and Hawthorne 21–13. All-Bay players included tackles Nick Carollo and Jerry Taylor, end John Jones and halfback Bob Laurella. Then new coach Don Hay won thirteen games in two years, going 5-3-1 in 1964 and 8-1 in 1965.

The next few years were kind of quiet. Jim Archer won twelve games in five years, Jim Hold twelve in four years and Les Congelliere sixteen in five years. But Bob Paulson came on the scene in 1980, winning twenty-five games in four seasons. The 1980 Sea Hawks became the first Redondo Union team in thirty-seven years to win a CIF playoff game, as they beat Rio Mesa 14–6 before losing to Atascadero, 27–24. Outstanding players were K.C. Cullen on defense and Butch Seifert on offense, while Chris Johnson was MVP. The following year was even better, as the Sea Hawks went 8-4 and beat Calabasas in the CIF before losing to Verbum Dei. They beat El Segundo 20–0 and Lennox 21–0 and tied Miraleste for the league title.

Then Coach Congelliere came back to win twenty-nine games in six years, including an outstanding 9-3 season in 1986. In the CIF playoffs, the Sea Hawks beat Daniel Murphy 42–0 before bowing to Santa Maria, 20–14. Quarterback Scott Yessner threw for over 1,500 yards, while wide receivers Mike Stone and Todd Croce (the future coach); running backs Nat Muzik, Eric Craig and Jeff Stock; and defensemen Clint Mosley, Mark Wessel and Jason Neubauer were all outstanding.

Then Chris Hyduke won thirty-one games in six years. In just his second year, Hyduke went 7-5, with lineman Ryan Turner, running back John Hogrelius and tight end and free safety Jeremy Veasey among the All-League performers. The Sea Hawks made it to the playoffs in 1995, beating Pacific 21–7 before losing to Fullerton, 32–0. Quarterback Eddie Sanchez, running back Alfred Pressley, Jumah Blaylock, Justin Howard and Michah Borret all had great years.

Then it was Gene Simon time as the coach took the Sea Hawks to one hundred victories (see accompanying story) in sixteen years, with dozens of his players going on to Division I programs in college. Simon's teams put up

Running back Eric Craig helped the Redondo Sea Hawks to a 9-3 record in 1984. *Courtesy of Redondo Union High School Archives.*

a fight every year. In 1998, the Sea Hawks were 6-4-1, beating Morningside 48–6, Mira Costa 20–14 and Culver City 39–0. They were 6-4 in 2000, with significant wins over Torrance (35–7), Orange (42–15), Culver City (38–7) and North (25–6).

Even though the Sea Hawks did not have great seasons from 2008 through 2011, they made the playoffs every year. They lost to Palmdale, 28–14, in 2008. In 2009, they beat Knight of Palmdale 42–14 before losing to Dominguez of Compton, 48–21. In 2010 and 2011, the Sea Hawks lost to St. Bonaventure of Ventura, 44–14 and 19–10.

Matt Ballard took over the program in 2012, winning a decent eleven games in two years. And now he continues a tradition that began almost one hundred years ago.

Redondo Union Win-Loss Records

1915: 0-4, A.L. Walton
1916: 0-3, Fred Seltzer
1917: 0-6, Mr. Mitchell
1918: no games (flu epidemic)
1919: 3-4-1, Tom Wilson
1920: 3-4-1, Lee Cannon
1921: 0-1-1, Cannon
1922: no games
1923: 0-2-1, Cannon
1924: 2-5-1, Howard Schroeder
1925: 3-4-1, Schroeder
1926: 2-5-1, Cannon
1927: 1-4-2, Cannon
1928: 2-6-1, Hob Uhls
1929: 5-3-2, Lloyd Waller
1930: 8-3, Waller
1931: 5-3-1, Waller
1932: 3-4, Waller
1933: 2-5-1, Waller
1934: 8-1, Joe Day
1935: 5-2-1, Russell Striff
1936: 5-4-1, Striff
1937: 1-6-1, Striff
1938: 1-4-1, Striff
1939: 0-4-4, Striff
1940: 4-3-1, Striff
1941: 5-1-2, Striff
1942: 8-1-1, Striff

1943: 6-0, Harold Grant
1944: 7-0, Grant
1945: 6-1, Grant
1946: 6-2, Striff
1947: 6-2-1, Striff
1948: 4-5, Striff
1949: 5-4, Striff
1950: 6-3, Cal Rossi
1951: 4-4, Rossi
1952: 4-4, Bob Cardona
1953: 3-4, Cardona
1954: 2-6-1, Cardona
1955: 2-6-1, Cardona
1956: 7-1-1, Cardona
1957: 0-7-2, Cardona
1958: 2-6-1, Vince McCullough
1959: 5-4, McCullough
1960: 7-2, McCullough
1961: 4-4-1, McCullough
1962: 7-2, Lud Keehn
1963: 5-2-2, Keehn
1964: 5-3-1, Don Hay
1965: 8-1, Hay
1966: 6-2, Jim Archer
1967: 1-7, Archer
1968: 3-6, Archer
1969: 1-8, Archer
1970: 1-8, Archer

1971: 5-4, Jim Hold
1972: 3-5-1, Hold
1973: 0-9, Hold
1974: 4-5, Hold
1975: 2-7, Les Congelliere
1976: 4-5, Congelliere
1977: 2-5-2, Congelliere
1978: 3-5-1, Congelliere
1979: 5-5, Congelliere
1980: 7-5, Bob Paulson
1981: 8-4, Paulson
1982: 6-5, Paulson
1983: 4-5, Paulson
1984: 0-9-1, Congelliere
1985: 6-4, Congelliere
1986: 9-3, Congelliere
1987: 6-5, Congelliere
1988: 5-6, Congelliere
1989: 3-6-1, Congelliere
1990: 5-5, Chris Hyduke
1991: 7-5, Hyduke
1992: 5-5, Hyduke

1993: 4-7, Hyduke
1994: 4-6, Hyduke
1995: 6-6, Hyduke
1996: 2-8, Gene Simon
1997: 9-4, Simon
1998: 6-4-1, Simon
1999: 8-3-1, Simon
2000: 6-4, Simon
2001: 6-5, Simon
2002: 6-4-1, Simon
2003: 8-4, Simon
2004: 9-3, Simon
2005: 6-4, Simon
2006: 4-6, Simon
2007: 8-4, Simon
2008: 5-6, Simon
2009: 6-6, Simon
2010: 6-5, Simon
2011: 5-6, Simon
2012: 5-6, Matt Ballard
2013: 6-5, Ballard

Coaches' Records

1. Gene Simon: 100-76-3 (.567)
2. Russell Striff: 50-36-12 (.571)
3. Les Congelliere: 45-60-4 (.431)
4. Chris Hyduke: 31-29 (.517)
5. Lloyd Waller: 23-18-4 (.555)
6. Bob Paulson: 25-19 (.568)
7. Harold Grant: 19-1 (.950)
8. Vince McCullough: 18-16-2 (.543)
9. Bob Cardona: 18-27-5 (.410)
10. Don Hay: 13-4-1 (.750)
11. Jim Hold: 12-23-1 (.347)
12. Lud Keehn: 12-4-2 (.722)
13. Jim Archer: 12-31 (.279)
14. Matt Ballard: 11-11 (.500)

15. Cal Rossi: 10-7 (.588)
16. Lee Cannon: 6-16-6 (.321)
17. Howard Schroeder: 5-9-2 (.375)
18. Tom Wilson: 3-4-1 (.438)
19. Hob Uhls: 2-6-1 (.278)
20. A.L. Walton: 0-4 (.000)
21. Fred Seltzer: 0-3 (.000)

Totals: 415-404-44 (.506)

COACH GENE SIMON

Gene Simon, the most successful coach in Redondo Union High School history, is not content to rest on his laurels—or anything else.

Simon, who still teaches health at the high school, is now the running backs coach at the prestigious Loyola High School in Los Angeles. Simon had a record of 100-78-3 in sixteen years with the Sea Hawks, far outdistancing Russell Striff, who won fifty games from 1935 through 1949. Simon also won two Ocean League championships in 2002 and 2003 and the Bay League title in 2007. He sent twenty-eight players to four-year schools, and another five went to Division I schools on scholarships. Two players, brothers Keith and Kevin Ellison, landed in the NFL. Keith, who was the Bay League Defensive Player of the Year in 2002, played linebacker for the Buffalo Bills, and Kevin (All-Bay League MVP in 2004) was a safety for the San Diego Chargers.

Simon said that "teaching the game well enough for kids to love and respect it, and for them to then want to be a team willing to follow our plan through thick and thin," is what he enjoys most about coaching. "I love witnessing kids' and coaches' self-confidence grow while their respect for each other becomes obvious and then seeing kids move on in life using their football lessons to live."

Simon married Carolyn Ambrosi in 1980, and they have three children: Claire, twenty-two; Mary (Molly), twenty-one; and Robert, sixteen.

Simon, who was born in San Francisco in 1957 and raised in Gardena, is a graduate of Serra High School, where he played four years at quarterback. He also played football for Long Beach State before receiving a master's degree from Loyola University. He began his coaching career in 1976 for

Coach Gene Simon (shown here in 2002) led the Redondo Union High School Sea Hawks to one hundred wins from 1996 through 2011. *Photo by Sean Hiller; courtesy of the* Daily Breeze.

Serra junior varsity before becoming co–head coach at Serra in 1977. He was a varsity assistant at Bishop Montgomery from 1979 to 1981, a junior varsity assistant at Gardena High and also an assistant at Pierce Junior College and El Camino before becoming the head coach at Redondo Union in 1996.

When Simon came to Redondo, the team hadn't had a winning record since 1991, when the Sea Hawks were 7-5 under Chris Hyduke. Simon quickly carried the team to a 9-4 record his second year. "The 1997 team set the standard for future Redondo teams under my lead," Simon said. Running back/defensive back Dennis Jones and quarterback Troy Doran led a tough team that included fullback/linebacker Joby Zamarippa, defensive lineman Pauli Kaho, lineman Matt Dorn, wide receivers and defensive backs Chris Reno and Sydney Blue and wide receiver, defensive back and kicker Aaron Kogan. "That team started 5-0, finished league at 7-3 and then made Redondo history by beating No. 1 seed Atascadero, 32-29, breaking their forty-seven-game win streak in the first round," Simon said. The Sea Hawks then smashed Duarte 31–6 before losing to Mira Costa, 18–6, in a rainstorm. "This team wasn't a great team because it had more talent than all others, but the team did great things because players bought in and played for each other," he said. "This helped set the proper standard for all my succeeding Redondo teams, a very important achievement for the program from a coaching point of view."

The Sea Hawks won their first Ocean League title in 2002 behind league MVPs Chris Meadows and Kevin Ellison. "Meadows was a tremendous offensive weapon," Simon said, "but Kevin Ellison was probably the best I ever coached with his enormous and historic defensive contributions as a defensive back and linebacker and his huge offensive production as an outstanding tailback."

2007 was another championship year as the Sea Hawks finished 8-4. "Many of the players on this team had a gym rat mentality," Simon sighed. "They loved everything about sport…even pick-up basketball after our fall camp three-a-day workouts. We won the Bay League with that group because they had great heart. They would have done anything for each other, even talking smack the whole time they were doing it."

Simon never underplays the value and importance of coaches. "Coaching is a service to humanity—a ministry," he said. "I love believing I made a positive, significant contribution to thousands of young men." But he points out what a brutal job it can be—hiring and firing staff, developing assistants and handling fundraising, budgets, conditioning, facility repair, parent communication and practice preparation while balancing a full-time teaching schedule.

Simon says that a coach has to "have a philosophy and from it perspective enough to compartmentalize what he's going through and give it the proper emotional weight and attention. Once the dust settles, he later will determine how the situation really affects him, and the ideas that emerge will probably last for the rest of his life, good or bad."

Many coaches struggle on year after year without significantly winning records, but Simon says that "if their perspective is on building strong, committed and unselfish people, even losing years can be viewed as significantly successful when players approach their tasks as they were expected to and show themselves to be better young men from their football demands."

Simon abruptly resigned his position as head coach at the end of the 2011 season without much explanation. The *Easy Reader* newspaper reported that high school principal Nicole Wesley said that it was "in the school's best interest to seek new leadership for the football program."

Simon pointed out that despite all the work a football coach must do on his own, he isn't on contract and is subject to the "whim of his leaders and their 'expert' opinion of his performance, even though many have no experience in the sport or in coaching or what it really takes to do the job well." He adds, "I am proud of my players and coaches I worked with and sacrificed for without reservation over the sixteen years I was head coach at Redondo. I feel fortunate."

Simon said he thinks he helped bring out the best in his players on and off the field. "These principles produced an outstanding era of football at Redondo," he said. "The record shows kids competed successfully against top competition and were prepared daily to be champions."

Simon says, "Successful high school programs excel because average to above-average athletes all work their tails off for four years to make themselves into good to very good high school players. I tell kids they'll play for four years but that they will remember their experience for forty years. Many kids never play beyond high school but make significant contributions, have a great time, develop lifelong friendships, employ valuable character traits and build many memories to enjoy for a lifetime."

I could not say it any better.

CHAPTER 23

ROLLING HILLS HIGH SCHOOL TITANS

The Rolling Hills High School football team came into being in 1964, when Dwaine Lyon coached the Titans to a 3-5-1 record. Quarterback Marty Meagher and halfbacks Bob Cage, Jim Day and Jim Hooper were aided by such players as Carl Tomlinson, Bob Sedey and James Benefield. Two of their big wins in their inaugural year were 31–19 over Verbum Dei and 27–13 over Mt. Carmel.

But Lyon would prove to be the most outstanding coach in Rolling Hills history, posting seasons of 6-3, 10-2, 10-1, 9-2, 7-2, 6-3, 6-2-l and 9-1 over fifteen years for a total of 93-47-7 and a winning percentage of .656 (one year estimated).

In their second year, the Titans went only 4-5, but that included shutouts of Aviation (19–0) and Beverly Hills (35–0). The team was led by returning quarterback Marty Meagher; offensive linemen Bob Lynn and Marc Gentile, who played both ways; center Steve Graner; fullback Joe Juge; offensive linemen Kim Smith and Mike Mahaffey; and John Engelhardt on defense.

The Titans had their first good year in 1966, when they went 6-3 and beat Palos Verdes 26-7, Culver City 25-7, Beverly Hills 41–19 and West Torrance 18–0. Outstanding players included quarterback Jon Robertson, linebacker/fullback John Papadakis, defensive back Paul Fieri, tackle Jeff Ferguson and fullback Joe Juge.

The following year proved more of the same as Lyon's Titans posted a 5-1-3 record with big wins over Palos Verdes (25–0), Torrance (20–6) and Culver City (27–0). Defensive end Brian Butler, defensive back Paul Fieri, center

Dan McNeer and defensive tackle Dale Page joined fullback/linebacker John Papadakis, who was All-CIF.

Then 1968 was the year! The Titans were Sky League champs as they went 10-2, topping Bishop Montgomery and Laguna Beach before losing to Loara of Anaheim, 21–7, in the CIF playoffs. All-Sky League selections included guards Jeff Jackson and Dave Carter, tackle Larry Sander, end Barry Sullivan, halfback Daryl Arenstein, defensive end Brian Butler and, on special teams, Gianni Miglia. Lopsided wins included a 60–0 pasting of Duarte and 47–0 blowout of San Marcos.

History repeated itself in 1969 as the Titans again won the Sky League title, going 10-1. They beat Fermin Lasuen in the playoff, 27–21, before losing to Foothill of Santa Ana, 23–6. Guard Ross Catron and defensive end Bruce Sweany were All-CIF, while other outstanding players included guard Keith Parker, center Bill Barr, end Dave Ruehlman, tackle Ken McDonald, halfback Jim Conti and defensive back Rick Jacobs. Sweany was also a powerful running back.

Coach Lyon kept up the team's winning ways in 1970, going 9-2. The Titans made it to the CIF quarterfinals but lost to Edison of Huntington Beach, 41–8. All-League were Mark Ensinger at fullback and linebacker, fullback Dave Kraker and tackle Rick Lessel, while tackle Doug Posey was All-CIF.

Rolling Hills finished 7-2 in 1971, with Darrel Kreitz as MVP, and 6-3 in 1972, led by quarterback Mike Ongarato, halfback Kevin Kreitz and fullback Mike Adair. The next outstanding year was 1974, when the Titans finished 6-2-1 with quarterback Joe St. Geme, tight end Tom Mosich, halfback Lee Rosen, offensive lineman Rick Allen and defensive back Tim Dunckel.

Lyon's last year was one of his best, as the Titans went 9-1 and beat Dos Pueblos of Goleta 24–0 before losing to Long Beach Wilson, 14–0, in the CIF. The loss was odd because earlier in the year, R.H. had whipped Wilson 35–22. Quarterback Kevin Moen, tailback Don Mosich and running back John Speltz led the team.

Moen went on to fame as the player who scored a remarkable last-minute touchdown for California against archrival Stanford in 1982. Moen was playing strong safety for California when Stanford kicked a go-ahead field goal to lead 20–19 with only four seconds left. Stanford's Mark Harmon then squibbed the ensuing kick, and the ball bounced into the hands of Moen, who then lateraled the ball to Rodgers, who lateraled to Dwight Gardner, who threw the ball back to Rodgers, who threw the ball to Mariet Ford, who lateraled it back to Moen, who took off for the end zone and scored.

Nobody could believe it, but the touchdown counted, and Moen went down in history. Today, he works for Coldwell Banker on the Peninsula.

Coach John Oswald took over the program in 1979, going 5-5-1 with Ed St. Geme at quarterback, who was assisted by good players like John Speltz, Tom Sayer, Ted Pintar and Jon Trombley.

Dan Phillips became coach in 1982 and took the Titans to a 5-6 record and the playoffs, where they beat Centennial 19–14 in the first round before losing to Oxnard, 33–14. Quarterback Mike Kraft, halfback Mike Jarozs and defenseman John Schlatter led the team. "This year's Titan football team," reported the 1982 yearbook, "was a truly dedicated and determined squad. Evidence of this was exemplified by their awesome hairstyle and 'never quit' attitude." Okay.

The Titans slowed down until new coach Gary Kimbrell took over in 1988, but there were many outstanding players in that time. In 1983, linebacker Mike Jarosz and nose guard Robert Harris were All-Bay League. In 1984, quarterback Dan Speltz, receiver Kevin White, tailback Paul Moebius, tackle Bill Bartz and defensive back Chris Ahearn were outstanding. Dan Bellows excelled at quarterback in 1985 and 1986, as did offensive lineman Walter Cathey.

In 1988, Kimbrell, who had spent ten years at Miraleste, promptly went 5-5 with such players as Rick Judge, John Lee, Jeff Savich, Tim Wagner and Tom Tavoularis. But Kimbrell improved the team immediately, going 6-3-1 the following year with tailback Robert Coulter, quarterback Greg Schwartz, running back Isaac Brown and defenders Dan Beck and Jim Rudberg.

In 1990, the Titans' last year before being absorbed by Peninsula High, they went 6-5 and earned a trip to the playoffs but lost to Temecula in the first round. That year, Rolling Hills gave North (41–28), West (14–12), Redondo (34–6) and South (32–14) memorable goodbyes.

Peninsula High awaited, but at the same home at 27118 Silver Spur Road, Rolling Hills Estates.

Rolling Hills Win-Loss Records

1964: 3-5-1, Dwaine Lyon
1965: 4-5, Lyon
1966: 6-3, Lyon
1967: 5-1-3, Lyon
1968: 10-2, Lyon
1969: 10-1, Lyon

1970: 9-2, Lyon
1971: 7-2, Lyon
1972: 6-3, Lyon
1973: 4-5, Lyon
1974: 6-2-1, Lyon
1975: 5-4, Lyon

1976: 4-5, Lyon
1977: 5-5, Lyon
1978: 9-1, Lyon
1979: 5-5-1, John Oswald
1980: 5-5, Oswald
1981: 1-9, Oswald
1982: 5-6, Dan Phillips
1983: 3-6-1, Phillips

1984: 5-6, Phillips
1985: 1-9, John Mack Brown
1986: 1-9, Brown
1987: 3-6-1, Brown
1988: 5-5, Gary Kimbrell
1989: 6-3-1, Kimbrell
1990: 6-5, Kimbrell

Coaches' Records

1. Dwaine Lyon: 99-46-5 (.677)
2. Gary Kimbrell: 17-13-1 (.583)
3. Dan Phillips: 13-18-1 (.422)
4. John Oswald: 11-19-1 (.383)
5. John Mack Brown: 5-24-1 (.183)

Totals: 145-90-9 (.613)

CHAPTER 24

SAN PEDRO HIGH SCHOOL PIRATES

From 1914 to 1991, the San Pedro High School Pirates struggled mightily on the football field. However, they did have some success. In 1921, they went 9-1-1, and in 1930 under Manuel Lareta, they were 9-1. Their first undefeated season came in 1940 under Joe Barry, as they finished 6-0-1. In 1950, they went 7-1 under John Satschi. But it was not until 1992 under Coach Mike Walsh that winning became a real habit. The Pirates were 12-1-1 that year, and it was just the start of something big. They finished 13-1 the following year and an even more impressive 14-0 in 1996. Other outstanding seasons include 1997 (13-1), 2006 (12-2), 2008 (12-1-1) and 2011 (12-1).

San Pedro High School came into being in 1903 with twenty-three students, but it wasn't until 1914 that the school fielded a football team. The Pirates lost both games they played that year, giving up eighty-two points to Alhambra and sixty-two to Inglewood. The first real season was in 1916, when Coach Bill Haney led the team to its first victory, a 24–0 shutout of Redondo Union High School. They finished 2-5-1 that year. Bill was one of four sports brothers who grew up in San Pedro, the most successful being Fred Haney, who became a major-league manager and led his 1957 Milwaukee Braves to a World Series championship. Brother Karl became one of the Pirates' most successful coaches, leading the team to a 5-2 record in 1917. A flu epidemic canceled the 1918 football season, but the team was back in action in 1919, finishing 6-4. One of the Pirates' first great players was Herbert "Red" Ballinger, who later played for Navy. Ballinger kicked a field goal in the last quarter of a game against Princeton to tie the game and send Navy to the 1924 Rose Bowl. Two more prominent players in 1919 were George Kosonen and Ry Coover, who later owned a drugstore in San Pedro. Also, on October 1, 1919, the high school kids played a team from two USA battleships—and surprisingly won 6–0. That same year, principal Ralph C. Daniels, father of the current athletic field, died of peritonitis.

In 1920, the team went crazy under Karl Haney, scoring 103, 83 and 67 points in three games and finishing 8-2-1. In one famous game in 1920, the Pirates lost to Santa Monica High, a team supposedly filled with "ringers," older boys who did not attend school and were ineligible to play.

In 1921, the Pirates finished 9-1-1, beating two battleship teams—the USS *Oklahoma* (7–2) and the USS *New York* (12–0). Beeb Kirchner, a speedy back, ran wild, with gains of ninety, fifty, thirty-five and forty yards.

One of the big games of the 1920s happened in 1922, when the Pirates lost to Santa Monica High School, 10–7, in front of four thousand fans. Some of the outstanding players on that team included Frank Murdock, Jack Logan and Bud Parks. The Pirates had three more good years in the 1920s, going 7-2 in 1923, 7-1 in 1924 and 8-3-1 in 1928. Two of the team's leaders in 1927 were end Nick Felando and blocking back Vince Thomas, who later became an assemblyman and had a bridge named after him. The 1928 season also featured an astounding 24–0 victory over previously undefeated Compton, the number-one team in Southern California at the time.

In 1930, Coach Manuel Laraneta, then in his third season, had his best team. The Pirates went 9-1, led by backs Frank Patalano, Joe Tarango and Gene Metzger. The rest of the 1930s were pretty forgettable until Joe Berry came and led the team to a 5-3 season in 1939 and a 6-0-1 record in 1940. John Gligo was an outstanding back in 1940.

The early 1940s were pretty unremarkable. But things improved after the war when, in 1946, Nick Mosich drop-kicked an extra point in San Pedro's 32–0 victory over Narbonne.

In 1950, coach John Santschi took the Pirates to a 7-1 record, with halfbacks Jim Decker and Ralph Moreno leading the team. Santschi thought he had one of San Pedro's best teams in 1951 with Moreno at fullback, Bob Keith at blocking back and Lew Morales at right half, but the Pirates finished just 4-3. Coach Bob Tabing took the Pirates to a 6-2 year in 1954 before Bill Seixas took over in 1957, leading the team to outstanding seasons in '57 (5-2-1), '59 (6-1-1) and '61 (8-2).

Mel Mothershead took over in 1968, finishing 6-2 with a team led by David Garasic and Danny Bondon. The 1970s and '80s were unremarkable until Henry Pacheco had a good 8-2 team in 1985.

The 1921 San Pedro Pirates went 9-1-1 under coach Karl Haney. *Courtesy of San Pedro Bay Historical Society.*

John Gligo was a great running back for the San Pedro Pirates in 1940. *Courtesy of San Pedro Bay Historical Society.*

And then came Mike Walsh. The 1972 San Pedro High graduate, who was captain of his high school team in 1971 and later a lineman at Harbor College and Cal Poly Pomona, took over in grand style. In his very first year (1991), the Pirates finished 8-5. The following year was one of the best in Pirates history, as they finished 12-1-1 and beat Taft for their first city championship. The Pirates went 7-5 in 1994 and 10-5 in 1995 before having their best season in history in 1996, going 14-0. That year, San Pedro ranked fifth in Southern California and sixth in the state. Giuseppe Cracchiolo kicked a record fifty-yard field goal that season, and quarterback Melvin Yarbrough completed 119 of 193 passes for twenty-three touchdowns with only four interceptions. He also ran for

Sean Rittgers was a running back on the 1997 San Pedro Pirates, leading the team to a 13-1 record and the city championship. *Courtesy of San Pedro Bay Historical Society.*

seven touchdowns. Over his three-year career, Yarbrough passed for 5,077 yards, a school record. The Pirates beat Taft, also undefeated at the time, 22–20 to earn their first 4A championship.

There was no letdown in 1997, as the team won its first four games before losing to Washington High, 12–10, its only loss of the year. And 6,500 people showed up to see San Pedro beat Narbonne at El Camino Stadium. Tiger Reese, who had been announcing Pirate games since 1946, had his dream come true when he announced the championship game against Taft at the Los Angeles Coliseum. Again San Pedro came away victorious, beating Taft 24–9. San Pedro back Holmon Wiggins was named All-City and received a scholarship to the University of New Mexico. Five players were named to the L.A. Football Association's All-Academic team: Ryan Solomona, Tony Danelo, Mario Amalfitano, Eric Mendoza and Jon Marselis.

Big Dean Marconi, a longtime Pirates supporter who used to cook pregame meals for the team, died in 2000, but the Pirates also got a new six-thousand-seat stadium in 2000. Some of the great players in the early years of the decade included Kenny Taylor, Steve Taylor, Deon Bell, Darrell Bullock, Grant Thorne, Andrew Mortz, Zack Herberer, Devin Carter and Joseph Diaz. In 2005, Herberer, who went on to USC, was named first-team All-City, while Padilla and Carter were named to the second team. In 2006, the Pirates won eight straight games before losing to Narbonne, 9–6.

This was followed by a 28–10 win over Banning and three straight wins in the city playoffs—44–16 over Hamilton, 27–26 over Venice and 21–14 over Carson—before losing the championship to Birmingham, 45–7. The offense was led by running backs J'vone Hibbler, who gained 1,111 yards, and Marcelez Brooks, who had 769. Matt Navarette and Robert Franco led the defense with seventy-seven and sixty tackles, respectively.

The next big year was 2008, when the Pirates finished 12-1-1. They were 9-1 in the regular season, boasting one of the best defenses in the city. They started the season with six straight wins before losing a close game, 27–24, to Narbonne. The Pirates won the season's final three games before overwhelming their opponents in the playoffs 34–3 (Sylmar), 31–0 (Venice) and 27–7 (Taft). They faced Narbonne again in the city finals and came away with a 21–21 tie to share the city championship. Quarterback Barry Heads passed for 1,445 yards, while running back Joseph Deguchi gained 1,162 yards and Christian Farrow 743. Robert Franco was outstanding on defense, recording eighty-three tackles.

In 2011, the Pirates had another great season, finishing 12-1. They annihilated most of their opponents but lost to Carson in the section finals, 24–19. They beat Gardena 49–7 and Crenshaw 31–7 before losing to Venice, 27–24, in the championship game.

First-team All-City players since 1924 include Roy Provence in the 1930s; John Gligo in the 1940s; Jim Decker, Don Shinnick, Joe Herrera and Jim Zar in the 1950s; Ron Barber in the 1960s; Ernie Crow in the 1970s; Andrew Tuiasosopo, Lionel Robinson, Michael Ford, Traveon Adams, David Samperio, Joe Santos, Arnold Madrid and Corey Miller in the 1980s; thirty-six players in the 1990s; and a whole bunch in the 2000s.

Coaching records, of course, were dominated by Mike Walsh, whose record through 2012 was 209-75-2. Far behind were Karl Haney (42-16-2) and Manuel Laraneta (35-32-12).

San Pedro has many representatives in major colleges and the NFL. Robert Franco (2009) attended UCLA. Steve Smith (2003) played at Oregon. The late Mario Danelo (2002) was a kicker for USC. Anthony Banks (1998) played for the University of Arizona. Bromar Butler (1986) played at San Diego State. Shawn Jones (1981) played at the University of Illinois. Richard Johnson (1978) was at the University of Colorado. Steve Bozan (1971) played for Oregon State. Ronnie Barber Sr. (1963) was at Arizona State. And Jim Decker (1950s), Jim Trani (1943) and Ted Rafalovich (1932) all played for USC. Going on to play in the pros were wide receiver Steve Smith (2001) for Jacksonville, wide receiver Richard Johnson (1987–90) for Baltimore, defensive end Bob Petrich (1963–67) for the San Diego Chargers, kicker Ben Agajanian (1945–64) for eight teams in both the NFL and AFL, defensive back Dick Harris (1960–65) for the San Diego Chargers, linebacker Don Shinnick (1957–69) for the Baltimore Colts and running back Ed Smith (1948) for the Green Bay Packers.

San Pedro Win-Loss Records

1908: 1-0, unknown
1909: 2-0, J.R. Cheney
1910: 4-1, W.S. Kienholz
1911: 0-1-1, Kienholz
1912: 0-5, Michael C. Long
1913: 2-7, Long
1914: 0-7, J.M. Curnutt
1915: no team
1916: 2-5-1, Bill Haney
1917: 5-2, Karl Haney
1918: no team
1919: 6-4, Karl Haney
1920: 8-2-1, Haney
1921: 9-1-1, Haney
1922: 6-5, Haney
1923: 7-2, Haney
1924: 7-1, Forrest McDaniel
1925: 2-5, McDaniel
1926: 1-7-1, McDaniel
1927: 6-4, McDaniel
1928: 8-3-1, Manuel Laraneta
1929: 6-2-2, Laraneta
1930: 9-1, Laraneta
1931: 2-3-3, Laraneta
1932: 3-5-1, Laraneta
1933: 2-1-5, Laraneta
1934: 2-6, Laraneta
1935: 0-7, Laraneta
1936: 3-3, Laraneta
1937: 4-3-1, Harry Brubaker
1938: 3-2-1, Brubaker

1939: 5-3, Joe Berry
1940: 6-0-1, Berry
1942: 6-2, Bill Vorhees
1943: 3-2-1, Vorhees
1944: 1-4-1, Wilmer Leibrock
1945: 1-4-1, John Santschi
1946: 5-2-1, Santschi
1947: 5-2, Santschi
1948: 4-3, Santschi
1949: 3-4, Santschi
1950: 7-1, Santschi
1951: 4-3, Santschi
1952: 5-3, Bob Tabing
1953: 5-3, Tabing
1954: 6-2, Tabing
1955: 5-3-1, Tabing
1956: 2-6, Tabing
1957: 5-2-1, Bill Seixas
1958: 4-4, Seixas
1959: 6-1-1, Seixas
1960: 4-3-1, Seixas
1961: 8-2, Seixas
1962: 5-3, Seixas
1963: 1-7, Seixas
1964: 3-5, Seixas
1965: 1-7, Seixas
1966: 0-8, Dick Carter
1967: 2-5-1, Carter
1968: 6-2, Mel Mothershead
1969: 2-6, Mothershead
1970: 3-5, Mothershead

1971: 2-6, Mothershead
1972: 4-4, Mickey Teora
1973: 4-2, Teora
1974: 3-6, Teora
1975: 5-4-1, Teora
1976: 2-7, Teora
1977: 4-5, Teora
1978: 4-5, John Misetich
1979: 2-7, Misetich
1980: 3-6, Misetich
1981: 2-6-1, Misetich
1982: 5-4, Henry Pacheco
1983: 6-3-1, Pacheco
1984: 6-5, Pacheco
1985: 8-2, Pacheco
1986: 5-4, Pacheco
1987: 6-4, Pacheco
1988: 3-7, Pacheco
1989: 5-6, Pacheco
1990: 4-6, Pacheco
1991: 8-5, Mike Walsh
1992: 12-1-1, Walsh

1993: 13-1, Walsh
1994: 7-5, Walsh
1995: 10-4, Walsh
1996: 14-0, Walsh
1997: 13-1, Walsh
1998: 6-5, Walsh
1999: 10-3, Walsh
2000: 9-4, Walsh
2001: 4-6, Walsh
2002: 6-5, Walsh
2003: 8-3, Walsh
2004: 6-5, Walsh
2005: 9-3, Walsh
2006: 12-2, Walsh
2007: 7-4, Walsh
2008: 12-1-1, Walsh
2009: 7-4, Walsh
2010: 8-4, Walsh
2011: 12-1, Walsh
2012: 8-4, Walsh
2013: 8-4, Walsh

Coaches' Records

1. Mike Walsh: 209-75-2 (.734)
2. Henry Pacheco: 48-39-1 (.551)
3. Karl Haney: 42-16-2 (.717)
4. Manuel Laraneta: 35-32-12 (.519)
5. Bill Seixas: 33-27-2 (.548)
6. Bob Tabing: 23-17-1 (.573)
7. Mickey Teora: 22-28-1 (.441)
8. Forrest McDaniel: 16-17-1 (.485)
9. John Santschi: 15-15-2 (.500)
10. Mel Mothershead: 13-19 (.406)
11. Joe Berry: 11-3-1 (.766)
12. John Misetich: 11-24-1 (.319)
13. Bill Vorhees: 9-4-1 (.679)
14. Harry Brubaker: 7-5-2 (.571)

15. W.S. Kienholz: 4-2-1 (.643)
16. J.R. Cheney: 2-0 (.1000)
17. Bill Haney: 2-5-1 (.313)
19. Michael Long: 2-12 (.143)
20. Dick Carter: 2-13-1 (.156)
21. Wilmer Leibrock: 1-4-1 (.250)
22. Jim Curnutt: 0-7 (.000)

Totals: 355-197-26 (.637)

COACH MIKE WALSH

Mike Walsh, who played football for San Pedro High himself, became head coach of the Pirates in 1991 and proceeded to obliterate every previous record. He has over 150 more wins than Henry Pacheco, who is second on the list.

In response to a question about how he thinks other coaches survive without frequently winning, Walsh said, "I can't answer for other coaches who haven't had success. The thought of it scares me. I have no idea how they are able to go on [year after year]. The reason for our success is we never tire of doing the same things over and over until we get them completely right. By the way, that never happens. Things could always be better."

Yeah? Well not much. Walsh has had seasons of 12-1-1, 13-1, 14-0, 13-1, 12-2 and 12-1, as well as two city championships, in twenty-three years of coaching at San Pedro.

Born in Torrance, the youngest of six siblings who didn't play sports, Mike started playing Little League baseball when he was about eight and then flag football at Holy Trinity in San Pedro. He played tackle at the now-defunct Fermin Lasuen High School from ninth through eleventh grade before transferring to San Pedro High his senior year when Lasuen closed. After that, he played at Harbor College in 1972 and 1973 and earned a scholarship to Cal Poly Pomona, where he played in 1975 and 1976 and won several awards. After college, he coached baseball and basketball at Sierra Vista High School in Baldwin Park from 1977 to 1981. Then he taught at Jones Junior High in Baldwin Park, the Pomona Psychiatric Hospital and

Sierra Vista High School. After earning a master's degree, he eventually came to San Pedro High School in 1981, coaching JV football and serving as a varsity assistant before being named head coach in 1990.

Walsh married Kathleen Bogdanoff in 1979, and they have two sons, Brian, twenty-nine, and Corey, twenty-three, both of whom played baseball and football at San Pedro. Mike has so many good memories about his coaching days that it is hard to recall them all.

In 1991, Walsh's first year as head coach, he made his mark as his team went 8-5 and made it to the semifinals, where they lost to Crenshaw, 14–11. "They scored with less than two minutes in the game and went on to be city champ," Walsh remembers. "Rino Marconi was our quarterback my first year. He went on to become the University of Redlands' all-time leading passer." Five players made all-city that year, including defensive backs Bryant Thomas and Bryan Castaneda, running back Ambrose Russo, lineman Greg Cukrov and defensive lineman Mike Spelich.

The team was even better in 1993, finishing 13-1 and winning the championship with a 31–7 victory over Fremont. "We were back-to-back 3A city champs in 1992–93," said Walsh. Top players included quarterback Chris Pappas, tailbacks Russo and Jeff Williams and receiver/defensive back Castaneda, who was named City Player of the Year. Walsh continued:

> We went to the city 4A championship game in 1995, 1996 and 1997. We lost in the last minute to Dorsey in 1995 and beat Taft in '96 and '97. 1996 was special. Omar Butler went on to a Division I scholarship at San Diego State and his junior year was defensive MVP on a team that only lost one game…We stayed unbeaten in the sixth game of that year by driving eighty-one yards against Narbonne in the final nineteen seconds of the game. Tony Banks started for the University of Arizona; defensive tackle Travis White signed with St. Mary's and was a preseason All-American his senior year. Steve Smith, who played at Oregon, was drafted by Jacksonville and played one year in the NFL. Offensive lineman Dominic Furio was drafted out of the University of Nevada–Las Vegas in 2003 and played for the Philadelphia Eagles and now is with Team Michigan of the All American Football League.

Walsh said that Holmon Wiggins, 1997 City Player of the Year, later started at the University of New Mexico and is currently coaching at Memphis State. Quarterback Melvin Yarbrough was City Player of the Year in 1996.

More success was just around the corner. Walsh continued:

The 2000–02 team had Mario Danelo, who played fullback/linebacker and went on to be the USC kicker during their championship season. Tams from 2000 starred at Washington State like Bryant Thomas from the 1992 team. In 2006, we won twelve games and lost badly in the championship game to Birmingham. My son Corey was a junior on that team and started at outside linebacker. In 2008, quarterback Barry Heads engineered one of the greatest drives in Pedro history in the final six seconds in the Coliseum, the game ending in a 21–21 tie with Narbonne. Benny Weischedel caught two TD passes in the final six minutes as the clock expired. 2011 was the Kenny Potter show. He had one of the greatest seasons I have ever seen. Kenny was our quarterback, and in 2013 at Long Beach City College, he was named the offensive player of the year in their league. Kenny personally beat the city champs [Narbonne, 49–42] that year in game nine. He was incredible.

And Mike Walsh's career with San Pedro has been just that—incredible.

CHAPTER 25

JUNIPERO SERRA HIGH SCHOOL CAVALIERS

A small Catholic high school of six hundred students in Gardena has become a paragon of academic and athletic excellence in the state of California.

Junipero Serra High School won its second consecutive national championship in the Catholic Math League in 2011, outscoring twenty-nine top high schools from around the country. Athletically, it has few peers. It has won several state championships in track and three in football (1990, 2009 and 2012). In addition, in 2009–10, Serra became the first school in California history to win state football and basketball titles in the same academic year.

But we are talking football here, and Serra, under Coach Scott Altenberg (son of UCLA football great Kurt Altenberg), has few peers today. Since Altenberg became head coach in 2000, the school's record is 141-34-2 for a percentage of .802. Wow! More incredibly, in the last eight years, the Cavaliers have lost just thirteen games and won ninety-four, a percentage of .879. That isn't even possible, yet they have done it!

Cavaliers who have played professional football include Theo Viltz (1961) for Houston, Tim Boyer (1970) for Hawaii in the World Football League, Phil Smith (1977) for Philadelphia, Ollie Williams (1977) for Baltimore, Kevin Biggers (1980) for San Francisco, David Williams (1981) for Chicago, Eugene Profit (1982) for Washington, Joe Cormier (1981) for the Oakland Raiders, Rocen Keton (1986) for the New York Jets, Deon Figures (1988) for the Pittsburgh Steelers, Frank Rice (1996) for Denver, Kris Tichard (1997) for the Seattle Seahawks, Sea Weston (1999) for Kansas City, Duke Ihenacho

(2007) for Denver, DaJohn Harris (2012) for Tennessee and Robert Woods (2010) for Buffalo.

Current (as of this writing) players at major colleges include Nick Usher at the University of Texas–El Paso, Darrel Fuery and Suli Faletuipapal at Fresno St., Kache Palacio at Washington State, Marquise and George Farmer at USC, Jason Gibson at Cal Berkeley, Conner Preston at SMU, Woodson Geer and Paul Richardson at Colorado, Anthony Parker at Washington State, Sione Tuihalamaka at Arizona and Sean Bacon and Bene Benwikere at San Jose State.

That's not all. The great Leo Hand was named State Coach of the Year in 1989 and Scott Altenberg in 2009. Woods, the great USC receiver and now a starter for Buffalo, was named State Athlete of the Year in 2009–10. This is pretty impressive for a small school.

The Cavaliers started playing football under Chuck Shoendienst in 1953, finishing with a 2-6 record their first year. Guard Pat Reagan was first-team All-Catholic, and halfback Roger Metoyer received an honorable mention. Serra improved to 3-6 in 1954, but then Coach George Strohmeyer took over in 1955 and had excellent years in 1956 and '57, going 6-2 both times. The Cavaliers beat San Gabriel 26–0, Cantwell of Montebello 26–0, Pius X of Downey 25–6 and Loyola 18–12. The team accumulated 1,855 yards rushing, and quarterback Mike Thornton, halfback Steve Davis, receiver Frank Marinko and halfback Bob Musella were all outstanding.

The 1957 season was even better, as the Cavaliers rushed for 2,356 yards. Besides Thornton and Musella, Robert Easton, Mike Gurrola and Al Gonzales were all great. Serra wiped out Palos Verdes 31–0, Loyola 37–14, Cathedral 32–19 and Notre Dame of Sherman Oaks 46–6.

After a lull in the early '60s, Pete Lopez took over as coach and guided the Cavaliers to successive seasons of 6-1-2 in 1968 and 7-2 in 1969. In 1968, victims included St. Anthony (12–0), St. Monica (35–13) and St. Bernard's (20–7). Great players included guards Terry Ruzicka and Doug Wheelhouse, quarterback Randy Hammon, tailback Steve Frederick, end Ed King, tackle Dale Maduri and center Steve Morrissey. Even better was 1969, when Serra wiped out Piux X 30–0, Daniel Murphy 27–9 and Bishop Montgomery 28–0.

The next great year was the third season under Coach Dale Washburn, when the team went 11-2-1. Fullback Ron Strong and tailback Robert Currie were first-team All CIF, while tight end Joe Cormier received an honorable mention. The Cavaliers lost in the finals to Schurr High School of Montebello, 21–3.

The Cavaliers were again Camino Real champs in 1984 under Washburn as Serra went 7-2 behind quarterback Darryl Jackson, running back Tim

George Strohmeyer went 6-2 in 1956 for Gardena's Serra Cavaliers. *Courtesy of Serra High School.*

Hazure and back Steven Williams. They had great wins over Cantwell and St. Anthony of Long Beach, both 48–0.

Washburn was even better in 1987, as Serra won nine and lost only two. They lost to Monrovia, 16–14, in the CIF playoffs, but not before beating the likes of Pasadena (26–15), Palos Verdes (19–14) and Verbum Dei (29–20). Outstanding players included Andre Howard, Steven Danzy, Lamont Butler, Mark Davis and Deon Figures, later a star in the NFL.

Then two of the great years in Serra history followed under the unbelievable Leo Hand, who abruptly left after losing only one game in two seasons. "The 1989 Cavaliers were an extremely unselfish group," Hand said in the Serra yearbook. "It was indeed an extraordinary honor to see a group of talented young men, growing up in a narcissistic society, accomplish such great things through altruism and hard work." The Cavaliers were great in the playoffs, beating Arroyo Grande 32–25, Notre Dame of Sherman Oaks 12–3 and Lompoc 34–31 in the championship. Quarterback Fred Safford, running back Tim Trahan, tackle Kenny Thomas and wide receiver Donald Godden were all instrumental in the victories.

The feat was almost duplicated in 1990, as the Cavaliers finished 11-1 but were unfortunately trounced by Arroyo Grande, 31–0, in the finals. Before

Leo Hand is one of the great coaches in South Bay history. His record was 25-1 in 1989 and 1990. *Courtesy of Serra High School.*

that, they had beaten Trabuco Hills 34–21 and La Mirada 34–6. Jerald Henry, Kevin Jordan, Brian Wynne, Donald Huston, Marzette Williams and Leonard Pollard were all outstanding. During the regular season, they had pulverized their opponents, including Miraleste (52–3), St. Anthony (54–3) and Verbum Dei (54–14). Hand summed up his offensive philosophy by saying that he has one favorite play: the one where a player pitches the ball to the ref after crossing the goal line. The result was forty touchdowns in seven games.

Hand left the Cavaliers to pursue graduate studies and write a football book. He ended up coaching high school football in Texas and writing more than fifteen books on football, including *Coaching Football's 3-3-5 Defense*, *Coaching Football's Double Eagle Double-Flex Defense* and *Coaching Football's Modern T Offense*.

Joe Dimalante had success for one season in 1991, going 8-3, while Kevin Crawley was 7-4 in 1992. Charles Nash won twenty-nine games as head coach for five seasons and then went 6-5 in 1993 with co-coach Crawley.

Then it was Scott Altenberg's turn (see accompanying story). The son of great UCLA receiver Kurt Altenberg, Scott is apparently a natural coach. And with records of 13-1, 10-2, 13-1, 15-0, 1-1, 14-2 and 13-1 under his belt, you can rest assured that Cavaliers football is in good hands.

Serra Win-Loss Records

1953: 2-6, Chuck Shoendienst
1954: 3-6, Shoendienst
1955: 3-6, George Strohmeyer
1956: 6-2, Strohmeyer
1957: 6-2, Strohmeyer
1958: 1-7-1, Strohmeyer
1959: 2-4-3, Hub Maikowski
1960: 2-5-2, Maikowski
1961: 4-5, Maikowski
1962: 3-6, Maikowski
1963: 4-5, Maikowski
1964: 3-6, Maikowski
1965: 1-8, Maikowski
1966: 1-7-1, Pete Lopez
1967: 3-6, Lopez
1968: 6-1-2, Lopez
1969: 7-2, Lopez
1970: 4-5, Lopez
1971: 0-8, Ray Kalinich and
 Marty Garrison
1972: 6-4, Kalinich and Garrison
1973: 4-4-1, Ron Smith
1974: 7-4, Smith
1975: 3-5-1, Smith
1976: 3-6, Smith
1977: 6-4-1, Gene Simon, John
 Campa and Gale Hipes
1978: 2-7, Dale Washburn
1979: 6-4-1, Washburn
1980: 11-2-1, Washburn
1981: 5-5-1, Washburn
1982: 1-8-1, Tony Jeter

1983: 2-7, Ira Crenshaw
1984: 7-2, Washburn
1985: 5-6, Washburn
1986: 6-5, Washburn
1987: 9-2, Washburn
1988: 7-4, Joe Griffin
1989: 14-0, Leo Hand
1990: 11-1, Hand
1991: 8-3, Joe Dimalante
1992: 7-4, Kevin Crawley
1993: 6-5, Crawley and
 Charles Nash
1994: 7-5, Nash
1995: 6-5, Nash
1996: 5-5-1, Nash
1997: 6-5, Nash
1998: 5-5, Nash
1999: 1-8-1, Scott Altenberg
2000: 5-5-1, Altenberg
2001: 8-1-1, Altenberg
2002: 13-1, Altenberg
2003: 7-4, Altenberg
2004: 5-5, Altenberg
2005: 7-5, Altenberg
2006: 9-3, Altenberg
2007: 10-2, Altenberg
2008: 13-1, Altenberg
2009: 15-0, Altenberg
2010: 14-1, Altenberg
2011: 8-3, Altenberg
2012: 14-2, Altenberg
2013: 13-1, Altenberg

Coaches' Records

1. Scott Altenberg: 142-42-3 (.767)
2. Dale Washburn: 51-33-3 (.603)
3. Charles Nash: 29-25 (.537)
4. Leo Hand: 25-1 (.961)
5. Pete Lopez: 21-14-1 (.571)
6. Hub Maikowski: 19-35-5 (.364)
7. George Strohmeyer: 13-11-1 (.540)
8. Ron Smith: 10-15-2 (.407)
9. Joe Dimalante: 8-3 (.727)
10. Joe Griffin: 7-4 (.636)
11. Kevin Crawley: 7-4 (.636)
12. Ray Kalinich and Marty Garrison: 6-1-2 (.778)
13. Gene Simon, John Campa and Gale Hipes: 6-4-1 (.591)
14. Crawley and Nash: 6-5 (.545)
15. Chuck Shoendienst: 5-12 (.294)
16. Ira Crenshaw: 2-7 (.222)
17. Tony Jeeter: 1-8-1 (.150)

Totals: 358-224-19 (.611)

COACH SCOTT ALTENBERG

Scott Altenberg, coach of Serra High School in Gardena, has a rich football pedigree. His father, Kurt, who died of cancer in 2005 at sixty-one, was a great receiver at UCLA, particularly renowned for his game-winning touchdown pass against USC (20–16) in 1965.

Meanwhile, Scott, who was an All-Angelus League quarterback and kicker at Bishop Montgomery (1989) in Torrance, has become one of the most successful football coaches in California. Since he started in 1999, Altenberg has gone 142-42-3 for a great .767 winning percentage.

Altenberg has coached some of the leading college players of the last several years, notably Sean Weston (1999) of the Kansas City Chiefs, Carl Ihenacho (2006) of the Oakland Raiders, DaJohn Harris (2006) of the Tennessee Titans, Duke Ihenacho (2007) of the Denver Broncos, Robert

Scott Altenberg is the greatest coach in South Bay's recent years. Since 1999, he has 142 wins, 42 losses and 3 ties. *Courtesy of Serra High School.*

Woods (2010) of the Buffalo Bills and Marquise Lee (2011) of the Jacksonville Jaguars. High school All-Americans under Scott's tutelage include linebacker Austin Jackson (2000), wide receiver Eric McNeal (2001), running back Loren Wade (2001), wide receiver Devin Stearns (2002), linebacker Apaiata

Tuihalamaka (2005), wide receiver Anthony Boyles (2006), defensive end Jason Gibson (2010) and wide receiver George Farmer (2010).

And the awards never stop coming. The Cavaliers were league champs from 2001 through 2003 and 2008 through 2010 and Division III state champions in 2009 and 2012. Whew!

Altenberg, who was born in Santa Monica, was a walk-on quarterback at UCLA, graduating in 1994 and later earning a master's at Loyola Marymount University. He coached three years at Bishop Montgomery and one at Redondo Union before becoming an assistant at Serra in 1997 and head coach in 1999. He also teaches U.S. history and American literature at Serra. He and his wife, Amy, have two sons: Luke, ten, and Nate, six.

Things didn't start out that great in 1999, however, as Altenberg went just 1-8-1 and 5-5-1 the following year. But they kept getting better. Altenberg led his team to an 8-1-1 record in 2001. Victories that year included a 45–0 shutout against Gahr of Cerritos, a 38–17 win over Chaminade of West Hills and a 42–21 win over Harvard-Westlake of Studio City. Leading players included Chase Mattox, Bryan Stanfield, Antoine Kidd, Tony Lee and Chris Hemphill.

But it was in 2002 that the Cavaliers came to the fore, finishing 13-1, with the sole loss coming against Lompoc (16–13) in the Division 10 championship game. They had beaten Bassett of La Puente 34–7, Temple City 35–14 and Cathedral 13–8.

The Cavaliers had another outstanding year in 2006, going 9-3 and losing to Oak Park in the CIF, 23–21. They were 10-2 in 2007, beating Pioneer Valley of Santa Maria before losing to Oaks Christian, 44–7, in the CIF playoffs. Ted Landes threw for 1,809 yards that season, while Carl Winslow rushed for 1,854.

Then an incredible run started in 2008. The Cavaliers went 13-1, losing only to Oaks Christian—again—63–28. Landes had an incredible year, passing for 2,712 yards and thirty-seven touchdowns, while Winslow rushed for 1,630 yards.

But then the mother of all years arrived, as 2009 saw the Cavaliers go 15-0 and win a state championship. This team included three of the all-time greatest Cavaliers—wide receivers Robert Woods, George Farmer and Marquise Lee—all of whom went on to play at USC. Senior Woods had sixty-five receptions, junior Farmer had forty-one and sophomore Lee had three. In the final games of the season, Serra beat Oak Park 54–6, Nipomo 48–18, St. Joseph of Santa Maria 49–27, Oaks Christian 42–41 and Marin Catholic of Kentfield, north of San Francisco, 24–20. Quarterback Conner Preston threw for 3,437 yards and forty-four touchdowns, while Shaquille

Richards rushed for 1,042 yards. Outstanding on defense was Brian True, who was in on 101 tackles, and Jason Gibson, with 84.

In 2010, it was more of the same as Altenberg guided Serra to the finals again, only to lose to Folsom, 48–10. In the playoffs, the Cavaliers had beaten Beverly Hills 48–7, Camarillo 40–7 and Paso Robles 41–23. This time, Conner Preston, now a lofty senior, threw for 3,736 yards and forty-four more touchdowns, while Richards gained 1,854 yards. Man! George Farmer, future USC star, had sixty-five receptions for over 1,500 yards.

Then, 2011 was a "poor" year, as the Cavaliers went 8-3 before coming back in 2012 with a 14-2 record. They were upset in the middle of the season by Narbonne (22–9) and Chaminade of West Hills (28–20). But incredibly, they finished off the playoffs with six straight wins: 49–14 over Oxnard, 58–6 over Santa Monica, 34–21 over Lompoc, 30–28 over Chaminade, 21–10 over Edison of Huntington Beach and 42–15 over Oakdale for the state championship. Jalen Greene threw for 2,443 yards and twenty-five touchdowns, and Malik Roberson rushed for 1,506 yards. Did Altenberg have these players ready or what?

Altenberg told collegelevelathletes.com in the fall of 2012 that it was exciting to see so many guys playing so well. "We have three kids in the NFL this year for the first time…It says that we're putting out good kids."

Then, in 2013 (yawn—this is getting boring), the Cavaliers finished 13-1, beating Pacific of Oxnard 48–16, Buena of Ventura 40–6 and St. Francis of La Canada 22–14 before losing to Chaminade, 38–35, in another awesome game. Jalen Greene was back to throw for 2,544 yards and thirty-three more TDs, and rushing for another 1,209 yards. Darrion Naylor also rushed for 1,037 yards, while new superstar Adoree Jackson had thirty-eight receptions and Jordan Lasley thirty-four receptions. On defense, John Houston was in on an incredible 137 tackles. Jackson rushed for 639 yards and had thirty-eight receptions.

Earlier this year, Jackson chose USC over UCLA, also Scott's alma mater. But Altenberg points out that two of his players, wide receiver Jordan Lasley and linebacker Dwight Williams, signed with UCLA. Altenberg, of course a UCLA fan, thinks the Bruins are catching up to USC in football. "It's going to be changing because UCLA is doing so well," he said.

It's doubtful Altenberg will change—except for the better. "I love teaching," he said. "I think high school kids are very receptive to teaching, and you can see the results of your work on a daily basis. I don't know many jobs where you can do that."

Junipero Serra High School, one of the premier secondary football programs in the United States, will certainly continue to be so as long as Scott Altenberg is in charge.

CHAPTER 26

SOUTH HIGH SCHOOL SPARTANS

South High School, which opened in September 1957, has a fine football tradition. In 1959, its first team, coached by Dave Tollefson, tied with Aviation High School in Redondo Beach for the lead in the Pioneer League. Finishing the season at 5-3, the Spartans were led by wingback Joe Austin (future legendary South coach), tackle Mike Czarske, fullback Bill Hargrove, center Dennis Higgins, tailback Bob Wehrhan and end Roger Smith.

In 1960, Tollefson led the team to a 3-4-1 record behind now-quarterback Joe Austin, Rick DeSpain and Bob Wehrhan. In 1963, halfback Walter Wald, guard Ken Hoffman, tackle Gene Cooper, end Greg Madden and quarterback Bruce Sorensen were important players.

In 1964, wingback Ralph Gambin, quarterback Scott Christensen, guard Tom Piper and end Fred Moyers tried to make the team competitive, as did quarterback Snapper Douglas, wingback Dale Hewett, tailback Jeff Arrieta and end Augie Felando in 1965.

But in 1969, the team came into its own under coach Herb Richey, going 6-3. Behind halfback Robbie Andrews, linebackers Keith Brewer and Mike Costello and Player of the Year tackle Paul Wheeler, the Spartans excelled. Victims included Inglewood (33–7) and Redondo Union (42–0).

However, it was under former star player Austin that the Spartans got their footing. Joe, who coached from 1972 through 1988, had fourteen winning seasons. In 1972 and 1973, the team went 6-3 each year behind players like Sam Vaiana, John Hooks, Dave Kiley, Gary Miller, John Winner, Jess Gregory and Jim Allen.

Johnnie Morton is one of the South Bay's greatest athletes. After starring at South High in 1989, he was an All-American at USC and then played for the Detroit Lions in the NFL. *Courtesy of Torrance Historical Society.*

Their best year came in 1978, when they went just 7-5 but beat Rio Mesa 19–6 in a CIF playoff game before losing to Antelope Valley, 13–8. Quarterback Jack Finley, Chris Pettle, Martin Montago and Kevin McDonald helped the team to key wins over Leuzinger (19–0), Beverly Hills (16–0) and Torrance (14–0).

And things just kept getting better. The Spartans went an excellent 7-3 in 1979, but they were just getting started. Coach Austin led them to nine consecutive winning seasons, coming out on top in sixty-nine games.

The 1981 season was probably the Spartans' biggest, as they went 9-2 behind players like Mike Castillion, Scott Bargar, Oscar Tamago, Chris Scott, Rich Harger and Adrian Diaz. Austin went 8-2 in 1985 and 8-3 in 1986, beating Arcadia 23–21 in the playoffs before losing to Antelope Valley, 41–7. Top players included Steve Kujawa, who passed for 1,283 yards; Brett Austin; Brian Kelly; Alan Barsi; Mark Merrit; Dan Spahr; and Tim Drevno. The Spartans had great wins over Bishop (35–15), Mira Costa (32–23) and Palos Verdes (28–8).

Another great year was 1987, when the team finished 9-3 with quality wins over Mira Costa (36–14), West (34–7) and Redondo (35–21). Quarterback Mike Wyrick worked behind an offensive line of Brett Austin, Tony Fee and Dan Spahr.

1988 was a great year for the first of the football-playing Morton brothers, Johnnie. He went on to a great career at USC, where he will always be remembered for catching a touchdown pass from quarterback Todd Marinkovich to beat UCLA 45–42. (Later, in 1999, his little brother, Chad, ran for 143 yards in USC's 17–7 win over UCLA). As of this writing, Johnnie, who turned out to be one of the South Bay's greatest football players, ranks third on the Detroit Lions' lists for all-time receptions (469) and yards gained (6,499).

It took a couple years, but new coach Don Morrow brought the team to 8-3 in both 1991 and 1992. The second year featured a big 9–0 upset of North behind lineman John Calas, tight end/linebacker Doug Posey and linebacker Josh Waybright, the team's future coach. Chad Morton was a part-time running back in 1992, a wide receiver in 1993 and a running back in 1994 but was hampered by a broken collarbone. But Morton, like his brother, starred at USC and went on to play seven years in the NFL for New Orleans, the New York Jets, Washington and the New York Giants.

The team's next big year came in 1999, when Brett Peabody, a former star player for Miraleste High School, led the Spartans to a 10-2-1 record and the Ocean League championship and was also named Coach of the Year. The team did great in the playoffs, beating Basset High School of La Puente 36–6 and Santa Ynez 21–19 before bowing to Palos Robles, 27–10.

The 2002 season under Coach Don Gereau was not a great one (5-6), but the Spartans went down fighting in the CIF playoffs, losing to a strong Lompoc team, 42–20. The brightest star of the year was Chauncey Washington, who ran for 1,549 yards on 140 carries for an average of 11.1 yards per carry and had twenty-three touchdowns despite missing five games with a knee injury. Washington went on to play for USC before spending four years in the NFL with Jacksonville, St. Louis and Dallas.

Former star linebacker Josh Waybright was named coach in 2003 and made an immediate impact, going 7-3. Outstanding players included Davon Brown, a returning Washington, Brent Dean, Jeff Trott, Mick Sands and Josh Commacho. Key wins were over West (34–7), Centennial (72–0), Torrance (48–12) and Palos Verdes (47–0).

South went 7-3-1 in 2006 and made it to the CIF playoffs, although they lost 7–0 to Pioneer Valley of Santa Maria. Key players were Jonathan Hokama, Mike Mandel, Kyle Kimberlake and Chris Cooper. Quality victories were over Hawthorne (17–0), Serra (28–1) and Torrance (44–14).

The Spartans made the playoffs again in 2008, only to be blown out by powerhouse Oaks Christian, 64–14.

As a new season approaches, the South High Spartans will gird for battle as always and will probably be victorious.

South High Win-Loss Records

1959: 5-3, Dave Tollefson
1960: 3-4-1, Tollefson
1961: 3-5, Tollefson
1962: 4-4, Tollefson (estimated)
1963: 0-9, Tollefson
1964: 0-8, Tollefson
1965: 0-9, Tollefson
1966: 3-4, Tollefson
1967: 3-2-1, Ken Swift
1968: 1-6, Herb Richey
1969: 6-3, Richey
1970: 4-3, Richey
1971: 3-6, Richey
1972: 3-6, Richey
1973: 6-3, Joe Austin
1974: 2-7, Austin
1975: 6-3, Austin
1976: 5-4, Austin
1977: 4-5, Austin
1978: 7-5, Austin
1979: 7-3, Austin
1980: 8-3, Austin
1981: 9-2, Austin
1982: 8-2, Austin
1983: 7-3, Austin
1984: 4-6, Austin
1985: 8-2, Austin
1986: 9-4, Austin

1987: 9-3, Austin
1988: 5-6, Austin
1989: 5-3, Don Morrow
1990: 4-6, Morrow
1991: 8-3, Morrow
1992: 8-3, Morrow
1993: 7-2-1, Austin and Mike Christensen
1994: 6-3-1, Christensen
1995: 5-5, Christensen
1996: 5-7, Christensen
1997: 5-5, Christensen (estimated)
1998: 5-4-1, Brett Peabody
1999: 10-2-1, Peabody
2000: 6-6-1, Peabody
2001: 5-6, Peabody
2002: 5-6, Don Gereau
2003: 7-3, Josh Waybright
2004: 2-8, Waybright
2005: 3-7, Waybright
2006: 7-3-1, Waybright
2007: 5-5, Waybright
2008: 5-6, Waybright
2009: 4-6, Waybright
2010: 12-2, Waybright
2011: 6-6, Waybright
2012: 4-7, Waybright
2013: 2-8, Waybright

Coaches' Records

1. Joe Austin: 112-57 (.663)
2. Josh Waybright: 57-63-1 (.479)
3. Don Morrow: 31-19 (.620)
4. Brett Peabody: 26-18-3 (.585)
5. Dave Tollefson: 18-46-1 (.285)
6. Mike Christensen: 21-20-1 (.511)

7. Herb Richey: 14-18 (.438)
8. Don Gereau: 5-6 (.455)
9. Ken Swift: 3-2-1 (.583)

Totals: 286-248-7 (.535)

COACH JOE AUSTIN

Joe Austin, regarded as one of the finest athletes to ever come out of South Torrance High School, is also an award-winning football coach. From 1973 through 1988, Austin won 111 games and lost 56 for a fine .638 percentage and twelve winning years.

Austin, who was born in Glendale, started playing sports when he was ten. He excelled in football, basketball and baseball all four years at South High School. He made All-League in all sports, although he says basketball was his best sport.

When John McKay offered him a football scholarship, Austin went to USC but switched to baseball his senior year, becoming an All-Conference first baseman for the Trojan team that won the national championship in 1963.

After college, Austin played a couple years of minor-league baseball before he started teaching and coaching at West High School with Fred Petersen. He stayed at West until 1973, when he became head coach at South High.

Austin had many great teams at South, but thinks his 1981 team (8-2) was the best. "Those two losses were to the two teams [Santa Monica and Long Beach Poly] that played for the CIF championship," Austin said. "We just missed being one of them." The Spartans were led by Rich Hargar, the *Daily Breeze* Player of the Year and "the best all-around player ever," Austin said. "He kicked points after, field goals and kickoffs; played wide receiver; and was one of the best man-to-man cornerbacks ever to play at South." Also on that team was All-CIF tight end Chris Scott, who went to the University of Pacific; Wes Jordan, who played at UCLA and was an All-CIF tackle; and Oscar Tomayo, who Austin said was "the best linebacker I have ever coached."

One of Austin's greatest memories was seeing Rich Hargar make a ninety-six-yard catch to beat West High School in 1981. "He caught the ball from quarterback Mike Castillion, another fine player, back-handed it and

Joe Austin was not only one of the greatest athletes to ever play at South, but he also was a great coach with over 110 wins. *Courtesy of Joe Austin.*

outran everyone to the goal line." Other great players on that team were wide receiver Dean Halverson, defensive back Brian Damianakes, guards Dave Baker and Dave Schmaeling and tackle Scott Dickson.

Another great team, Austin said, was the 1986 team (8-3), with *Daily Breeze* Player of the Year Steve Kujawa, who rushed for over 1,500 yards. One of that season's most memorable moments occurred when the Spartans played Arcadia in the quarterfinals. "We were down 21–0 at halftime," recalled Austin. "We came out and scored twenty-three unanswered points without throwing a pass and won 23–21. We went to the CIF semifinals and lost to Palmdale. We had an All-American tackle, Brian Kelly, who went to UCLA, and tackle Tim Drevno, who attended Cal State Fullerton." Other great players from 1986 included fullback/linebacker Paul Hill, tackle Mike Downs and center Mark Merritt.

The 1987 team was another favorite because "my son Brett made All-CIF tight end. I was so proud that he had such a great year and was such a good football player. He was our kicker also." (Brett was a starting tight end at El Camino before a career-ending neck injury.) That same year, Austin had his "best quarterback," Zak Krislock, who passed for 2,216 yards. Austin said the "biggest turnaround of a player" was turned in by Mike Wyrick, "a running back who was kicked off the team when he was a sophomore. He came to me the next year and begged to be let back on the team. We let him come back, and he was one of the best running backs I ever had. He outgained everyone his senior year [1987], with 1,725 yards." Also outstanding in 1987 were linebacker Mark Derossett and guard Dan Spahr.

The 1988 team featured Johnnie Morton, an All-CIF performer who became an All-American at USC and went on to a nice career in the NFL with Detroit and Kansas City.

Austin, who married his wife, Kathie, his freshman year at USC in 1962, has two children, Jennifer, fifty, and Brett, forty-six, and four grandchildren: Nick, twenty-four; Mike, twenty-two; Andrew, fourteen; and Hailey, twelve.

Austin started his career at South in 1973 by going 6-3 with such players as halfback Sam Vaiana, center Jess Gregory, kicker Jim Allen, tackle Russ Burns, guard Eric Riegleman, defensive end Bill Landers, fullback Chris Vasiliu, guard Randy Leopold, wide receiver Jim Holman and quarterback Ron Leetz. He was 6-3 again in 1975, beating Palos Verdes 26–8, North 28–10 and Santa Monica 26–6. The team made the playoffs but lost to powerhouse Loyola, 27–13. Quarterback George Crew, tight end Duane Lamarr, center Dave Freeman, end Tom Byrne, wide receiver Wayne Vanderleest, tackles Lester Mystofsky and Jim Schlatter and running back Pat Stibbie were outstanding.

The Spartans went to the playoffs again in 1978 behind Austin with a 7-5 record. They beat Rio Mesa in the first round of the CIF, 19–6, but lost to Antelope Valley, 13–8. Quarterback Jack Finley and halfback Chris Pettle led such players as center Ken Blanks, tailback Martin Montano, tackle Tom

Mushaney, Kevin McDonald and John Mitchell. Key wins were shutouts over Leuzinger (19–0), Beverly Hills (16–0) and Torrance (14–0).

Good year after good year followed as the Spartans went 7-3 in 1979, 8-3 in 1980, 9-2 in '81, 8-2 in '82, 7-3 in '83 and 8-2 in '85. Outstanding players in 1979 included defensive backs Stacey Gilcrest and Scott Ferguson and tackle Steve Volucci, as well as Sam Ohta, Chris Andrews, Harold Plotkin and Steve Lizardi. The 1980 gang included guard Dave Schmaeling, quarterback Mike Castillion, Richard Contreras and Adrian Diaz. 1982 players included defensive end Ron Knox and center Guy Bunyard. 1983 players included quarterback Greg Hokuf, guard Rex Zumwalt, Scott Barger, Gerald Liether, Rick Shulz and Pat Murphy. The 1984 team had great wins over West (22–18), Simi Valley (17–7), Redondo (20–0) and Mira Costa (20–0). Quarterback Kainoa Ozawa had 1,465 yards passing, and wide receiver Derek Sholl, Ken Dossey and Mike Delew all stood out. 1985 (8-2) was also good year, with such players as fullback Glen Ewing, tackle Alan Banks, defensive end Matt Williams, John Lopez, Kevin Samera, Tim Windorff and Tom Mace.

Austin did not quit after he left South, continuing to coach three years at North High, where he won sixteen games. He went 10-2 in 1992 before one last year at South in 1993, when he was co-coach with veteran Mike Christensen and helped lead South to a 7-2-1 record.

Austin is now retired and proud of what he accomplished as a high school coach. But for those coaches who plod on year after year with little success, he has a few words of advice: "If you're not good at it, get out."

That sums up Joe Austin: a great athlete and a great coach who does not suffer fools gladly.

COACH JOSH WAYBRIGHT

This is the story of a coach who has persevered for the past eleven years with a few winning seasons and a lot of happy ball players.

"These kids showed up every week," said Coach Josh Waybright, who has won fifty-seven games in eleven seasons at South, in a January 5, 2011 *Daily Breeze* article written by Tony Ciniglio. "14 weeks—well, 15 weeks with the scrimmage. They played hard every game at such a high level, and they fought to the end."

Josh Waybright has won fifty-seven games at Torrance's South High School since taking over as coach in 2004. *Courtesy of Torrance Historical Society.*

It took half a century for South to reach the CIF finals in 2010, where the Spartans almost made a dream come true before losing to Lompoc, 20–14. Under Waybright, the team finished 12-2 for the season, the most wins in South's history.

As a result of this great showing, Waybright was named the 2010 *Daily Breeze* Coach of the Year. Waybright, who was a linebacker for South in the early 1990s, dreamed of some day taking South to the finals. "Day to day he has always worked hard," said Mira Costa coach Don Morrow, who coached Waybright at South. "He goes to a million clinics…He's super devoted. Sometimes he has had seasons that have not gone the way he wanted, so for him to hang in and have this kind of season is a testament to him as a person and as a coach."

Waybright, who was born in Bakersfield, started playing baseball and soccer at the age of five. "I was too big to play Pop Warner," he said, "so I had to wait until high school to start playing football. Coach Morrow had just taken over the program, and he is one of the main reasons that I coach today. I was lucky enough to have him all four years he was here."

Waybright, who is single, played two years at Butte Community College in Chico and was going to continue to play at Eastern Oregon but then started coaching at South in 1996. He graduated from Long Beach State with a degree in kinesiology.

Waybright became coach at South in 2003, leading his team to an excellent 7-3 record behind star running back Chauncey Washington, who has played for several teams in the NFL. That year was particularly impressive, as the Spartans had big wins over LaQuinta (63–0), Centennial (72–0) and Palos Verdes (47–0). He had another great year in 2006, when the team went 7-3-1 before losing to Pioneer Valley, 7–0, in the playoffs.

But Waybright's biggest year came in 2010. The Spartans' résumé featured three great wins in the CIF playoffs—41–10 over Santa Paula, 33–12 over Morro Bay and 35–7 over Templeton—before losing to Lompoc in the finals, 30–14. Quality regular-season wins were over El Segundo (38–3), Lawndale (46–0) and Peninsula (43–15). Key players included Anthony Peters, Vinnie Bjazevich and Brandon Chavez.

Waybright's record has not been outstanding the last three years, but the Spartans made it to the CIF playoffs in 2012, losing to Bishop Diego of Santa Barbara. They won a CIF playoff game in 2011, beating St. Bernard 55–41 before bowing to Templeton, 58–13.

But the South Spartans remain competitive each year, and that will continue as long as a gritty former linebacker Josh Waybright remains their coach.

CHAPTER 27

ST. BERNARD HIGH SCHOOL VIKINGS

S t. Bernard, a small Catholic high school of just over two hundred students, has done itself proud in the big world of Southern California football. The Vikings have had some good seasons, including going an incredible 8-1 in 1960, 8-2 in 1975, 8-3 in 1983 and 8-4 in 1998. This culminated in Larry Muno's 10-1 season in 2011, when the Vikings had a fantastic year until they lost the first game of the playoffs to South Torrance, 55–41.

St. Bernard Win-Loss Records

1960: 8-1, Phil Bolger
1961: 6-3-3, Bolger
1962: 3-6, Bolger
1963: 5-4, Bolger
1964: 5-5, Bolger
1965: 4-5, Bolger
1966: 4-5, Bolger
1967: 6-4, Bolger
1968: 4-4-1, Bolger
1969: 2-7, Bolger
1970: 5-4, Bolger
1971: 6-3, Mark Shaughnessy
1972: no record, Shaughnessy

1973: 1-8, John Circuto
1974: 7-5, Circuto
1975: 8-2, Charlie King
1976: 6-3, King
1977: 3-6, Gary Hinman
1978: 4-5, Hinman
1979: 2-7, Greg Pearman
1980: no record, Pearman
1981: no record, Pearman
1982: no record, Pearman
1983: 8-2, Bill Seward
1984: 8-3-1, Seward
1985: 7-4, Duke Dulgarian

1986: 4-6, Dulgarian
1987: 3-7, Dulgarian
1988: 5-5, Dulgarian
1989: 2-7, Jerry Campbell
1990: 4-6, Campbell
1991: 2-8, Tom Strickland
1992: 5-5, Strickland
1993: 6-6, Bob Yarnall
1994: 5-5, Yarnall
1995: 4-6, Yarnall
1996: 5-6, Greg Dixon
1997: 6-5, Dixon
1998: 8-4, Dixon
1999: 4-7, Dixon

2000: 7-3-1, Dixon
2001: 1-9, Dixon
2002: 4-6-1, Dixon
2003: 8-4, Dixon
2004: 0-10, Dixon
2005: 2-8, Dixon
2006: 3-8, Dixon
2007: 8-5, Dixon
2008: 4-6, Dixon
2009: 3-7, Dixon
2010: 3-7, Dixon
2011: 10-1, Larry Muno
2012: season canceled
2013: 5-5, John Bibb

Coaches' Records

1. Greg Dixon: 65-95-1 (.407)
2. Phil Bolger: 52-56-4 (.482)
3. Duke Dulgarian: 19-22 (.463)
4. Bill Seward: 16-5-1 (.750)
5. Bob Yarnall: 15-16 (.484)
6. Charlie King: 14-5 (.737)
7. John Circuto: 8-13 (.381)
8. Larry Muno: 10-1 (.909)
9. Gary Hinman: 7-11 (.389)
10. Tom Strickland: 7-13 (.350)
11. Mark Shaughnessy: 6-3 (.667)*
12. Jerry Campbell: 6-13 (.316)
13. John Bibb: 5-5 (.500)
14. Greg Pearman: 2-7 (.222)*

* incomplete record

Totals: 232-262-6 (.470)
(four years unaccounted for)

CHAPTER 28

TORRANCE HIGH SCHOOL TARTARS

Torrance High School, one of the oldest continuous schools in California, opened its doors on September 11, 1917, but didn't really get into organized football until the 1920s. The first coach was Bob Mitchell in 1924, who lasted for four seasons with a record of 3-25. The Tartars, however, didn't give up, going through several years and coaches until Bernie Donahue carried them to a Marine League championship in 1934 with a record of 7-1. "If this mighty Tartar team had a weakness, no Marine League rival found it," wrote sportswriter Bill Henry. The team was led by All-Marine tackle and captain Roger McGinnis, who had help from All-Marine halfback Jack Javens, right end John McFadden and left end Gar Johnson. Also standouts on that team were guard Chuck Smith and Harry Bond, who excelled on defense and offense. Theodore Adzovich was the bruising fullback, while Harold Watson stood out at halfback. Their victims included Jordan (13–12), Gardena (17–12), South Gate (6–0), El Segundo (33–0), Leuzinger (20–6) and Narbonne (13–0).

After a flurry of coaches that included Roy Cochrane, Bob Barr, Charles Hoffar and John Winfield, World War II hero Louis Zamperini's brother, Pete, came to the rescue. In 1946, the Zamperini-led Tartars (their football field is named after Louis) went 6-1-1. Halfback Ralph George was the MVP of the league, while halfback Darrell Comstock was also All-League. The team's other outstanding players included quarterback Bud Smith, guards Dick Malin and Dom Donatoni and fullback Tom Faren.

After that great season, there were mediocre ones peppered by Eddie Cole going 6-3 in 1948 and Cliff Graybehl ending up 5-3-1 in 1953 and

McGINNIS   C. SMITH   BOND   SELBY

Roger McGinnis was an important contributor to the 1934 Torrance High team that finished 7-1 under Bernie Donahue. *Courtesy of Torrance Historical Society.*

5-3 in 1954. Dick Turner took his troops to two good years in 1958 (5-3) and 1959 (5-2-1).

Then came 1960 and three remarkable years led by Coach Irv Kasten. The Tartars were co-champions of the Pioneer League, led by All-League players Howard Taylor, Cliff Weimer and Tom Holdsworth. Also outstanding were ends Irv Palica and Dennis Albright and tackles Mike Sargent and Howard Achenbach. Some of the team's great wins included a 47–6 pasting of Beverly Hills, a 39–6 blowout of Lawndale, a 19–6 victory over Inglewood and a 21–6 bashing of Aviation.

1961 was equally impressive. Led by quarterback John Gambon (nineteen touchdowns), halfback and captain Jerry McLean, receiver Bob Clark, end Steve Northington and tackles Steve McGuire and John Carlson, this team handed out beatings to Palos Verdes (33–13) and Lawndale (43–21).

Kasten took his team to the Pioneer League title again in 1962 with a 7-3 record. This team was also the first in history to go to the CIF playoffs, losing to South Pasadena, 39–6. Guard Bruce Hendrex, tackles Joe Solis

Irv Kasten led Torrance to six wins in both 1960 and 1961 and seven wins in 1962. *Courtesy of Torrance Historical Society.*

and Bob Sonju, halfback Mike Cicchini and defensive back John Ricci were all outstanding.

The years 1963 through 1967 were pretty dismal, but then Harold Warfle led the Tartars to a 5-5-2 record in 1968. Coach Dick Harris had a good year in 1976 at 5-2-2, but things didn't really look up again until 1984, when Rich Busia and Rick Hood took the Tartars to an 8-2-1 season and the Ocean League championship. The stellar defense held opponents to just 7.6 points and a measly sixty-one yards a game. Wow! Big wins came over North (17–14) and Hawthorne (7–6). The Tartars, behind quarterback Scott McLachlan and receiver Zoltan Harvath, advanced to the CIF playoffs but lost to Santa Maria, 14–6. Other outstanding players included Ty Bradford, Ricky Kirkwood and running back Rob Jones. "I am happy to have worked with this team and am proud of their accomplishments," Coach Rick Hood said. "Torrance High football finally has the respect it deserves."

Things were quiet until 1990, when Bushia went 8-4 with Jason Kendall (who played fourteen years in the big leagues as a catcher for the Pittsburgh Pirates) at quarterback. Kendall was the co-back of the year, while All-League on defense were David Haemaker, Keith Jones,

Jason Kendall, a great quarterback at Torrance High in 1990, went on to play thirteen years as a catcher in the major leagues. *Courtesy of Torrance Historical Society.*

Kurt Stonebary, Antoine Williams and Scott Hagerman. All-League on offense were Ralph Martinez, Wade Owens, Jae Schmutz, Tony Lomelii and Colby Kapua.

Then the popular Rock Hollis took over as head coach in 1994, leading the team to the playoffs, where the Tartars lost to Hart of Newhall, 42–13. The team was led by quarterback Babak Farrokh-Siar, followed by co-captains tailback Andre Hilliard and fullback Kevin Campbell, free safety and wide receiver Dave Lechman (yes, we're related), linebacker Anthony Martinez and tackle Damian Martinez. Other key contributors included tight end John Mondabaugh (who scored the winning touchdown in the final seconds of the Tartars' victory over Hawthorne, securing a playoff spot) and special teams phenomenon Shawn Felis.

Rock and the Tartars made the playoffs in 1997, 1998 and 2004, when they beat Monrovia 43–31 before losing to Lompoc, 49–0. They also made the playoffs the next three years running but lost in the first round to Cabrillo (42–31) in 2005, St. Joseph of Santa Maria (35–8) in 2006 and Harvard Westlake (42–16) in 2007. In 2012, they made the playoffs again but lost to Whittier Christian, 38–28. They returned in 2013, where they beat Azusa 42–20 before bowing to Nordhoff of Ojai, 38–20.

The Torrance Tartars face the 2014 season with a never-say-die attitude and hope to have as many victories off the field as on.

Torrance Win-Loss Records

1924: 0-6, Bob Mitchell
1925: 3-3, Mitchell
1926: 0-8, Mitchell
1927: 0-8, Mitchell
1928: 0-7-1, Sig Nylander
1929: 0-9, Nylander
1930: 2-3-2, Earl Fields
1931: 0-7-1, Fields
1932: 3-4-1, Bernie Donahue
1933: 2-6-1, Donahue
1934: 7-1, Donahue
1935: 5-2-1, Donahue
1936: 4-4, Donahue
1937: 1-3-3, Roy Cochrane
1938: 3-3-1, Bob Barr
1939: 0-6, Barr
1940: 1-4-1, Barr
1941: 2-4, Barr
1942: 1-7, Charles Hoffar
1943: 1-6, John Winfield
1944: 2-5, Winfield
1945: 4-2-1, Winfield
1946: 6-1-1, Pete Zamperini
1947: 5-4-1, Eddie Cole
1948: 6-3, Cole

1949: 3-6, Cole
1950: 4-4, Rex Welch
1951: 4-5, Cliff Graybehl
1952: 4-5, Graybehl
1953: 5-3-1, Graybehl
1954: 5-3, Graybehl
1955: 1-7-1, Don Porer
1956: 1-6-1, Jack Miller
1957: 4-3-1, Dick Turner
1958: 5-3, Turner
1959: 5-2-1, Turner
1960: 6-2, Irwin Kasten
1961: 6-2-1, Kasten
1962: 7-3, Kasten
1963: 1-7-1, Kasten
1964: 2-7, John Trantham
1965: 2-6-1, Trantham
1966: 3-6, Harold Warfle
1967: 0-8-1, Warfle
1968: 5-2-2, Warfle
1969: 4-4-1, Warfle
1970: 2-6-1, Warfle
1971: 2-7, Warfle
1972: 2-7, Warfle
1973: 2-7, Warfle

1974: 0-9, Dick Harris
1975: 0-9, Harris
1976: 5-2-2, Harris
1977: 6-5, Harris
1978: 3-6, Mark Knox
1979: 2-7, Knox
1980: 3-6, Lonnie Roberson
1981: 5-5, Roberson
1982: 1-9, Roberson
1983: 4-6, Rich Busia and
  Rick Hood
1984: 8-2-1, Busia and Hood
1985: 3-7, Busia
1986: 3-7, Busia
1987: 2-8, Busia
1988: 2-8, Busia
1989: 4-6, Busia
1990: 8-4, Busia
1991: 3-7-1, Bill Bynum
1992: 3-7, Bynum
1993: 4-5-1, Bynum

1994: 5-6, Rock Hollis
1995: 5-5, Hollis
1996: 2-8, Hollis
1997: 5-6, Hollis
1998: 6-5-1, Hollis
1999: 2-8, Hollis
2000: 2-8, Hollis
2001: 4-6, Hollis
2002: 4-6, Hollis
2003: 4-6, Hollis
2004: 6-5-1, Hollis
2005: 5-6, Hollis
2006: 5-6, Hollis
2007: 7-4, Hollis
2008: 7-3, Hollis
2009: 2-8, Hollis
2010: 2-7-1, Hollis
2011: 8-5, Hollis
2012: 5-6, Hollis
2013: 5-7, Hollis

Coaches' Records

1. Rock Hollis: 91-121-3 (.430)
2. Rich Busia: 34-48-1 (.416)
3. Bernie Donahue: 21-17-1 (.551)
4. Irwin Kasten: 20-14-2 (.583)
5. Cliff Graybehl: 18-16-1 (.529)
6. Harold Warfle: 17-41-5 (.310)
7. Dick Turner: 14-8-2 (.625)
8. Eddie Cole: 11-7-1 (.605)
9. Dick Harris: 11-25-2 (.316)
10. Bill Bynum: 10-19-2 (.355)
11. Lonnie Roberson: 9-20 (.310)
12. John Winfield: 7-13-1 (.357)
13. Pete Zamperini: 6-1-1 (.929)
14. Bob Barr: 6-14-2 (.318)
15. Mark Knox: 5-13 (.278)

16. Rex Welch: 4-4 (.500)
17. Bob Mitchell: 3-25 (.107)
18. Earl Fields: 2-10-3 (.233)
19. Jack Miller: 1-6-1 (.188)
20. Roy Cochrane: 1-3 (.250)
21. Charles Hoffar: 1-7 (.125)
22. Don Porer: 1-7-1 (.167)
23. Sig Nylander: 0-16-1 (.031)

Totals: 296-461-30 (.395)

COACH ROCK HOLLIS

Rock Hollis is one of the great football names in South Bay history. Going into his twenty-fourth year at Torrance High School, Rock has proven that you can be a great coach and an asset to the school and the community without winning every game. Hollis—who has won ninety-one games, fifty-seven more than the next winningest coach—has developed an outstanding program that builds football players and young men. He's the "rock" who has provided the leadership and stability to develop a program of which players, parents and the administration can be proud.

The Rock might not have a truckload of wins since taking over for Bill Bynum in 1994, but he has had plenty of winning seasons. Just last year, the Tartars soundly beat Azusa in the CIF playoffs, 42–20, and in 2011, they beat Lompoc 56–21 and Santa Ynez 50–14 before losing a heartbreaker to Nordhoff, 34–33.

The Torrance High area has not been a bedrock of talent over the years, but there has to be a reason that Hollis is looking forward to his twenty-fourth year. "I love it," Rock laughed. "They come in as young boys, and in four years they leave as young men. 'You are my heroes,' I tell them." Rock said he has had a great time with great coaches, players, parents and the administration.

Born in Pampa, Texas, Rock came to the South Bay when he was ten. He attended Torrance High School and played football, of course. "I was a 110-pound tackle when I was a freshman," he laughed, which Rock does a lot. He said he played four years and ended up with an appointment to

Rock Hollis (right) is Torrance High School's number-one coach, having won ninety-one games through the 2013 season. *Courtesy of Torrance Historical Society.*

the U.S. Naval Academy, where he stayed for nineteen months before he "figured out the military life wasn't for me."

But he went on to play basketball and attend Cal State Dominguez Hills while at the same time becoming involved in his family's fourth-generation electrical business, Hollis Electric in Torrance.

Everything changed in 1990, said Hollis, who is married to wife, Theresa, and has two children—Desiree and Rocky II. "Bill Bynum, whom I had known since 1967, asked me to help coach the football team," Rock said. After three years as an assistant, he became head coach, and he has been there ever since.

When asked how someone learns to be a head coach, Hollis indicated that it was a lot of work. He went to seminars and coaching clinics and hired the right assistants. One of those assistants is Hansen Champlin, a stockbroker, who has been his offensive coordinator for eleven years and helped Rock introduce the double-wing offense. "I've met so many great coaches and people," Rock said, indicating he wouldn't trade his life for anything.

Rock started out by winning five games in his first year and has never looked back. Some seasons, there were only two victories, but on the whole, he has carried his team and school heroically and successfully. The Tartars won fourteen games in 2007 and 2008 and thirteen in 2011 and 2012. One of his favorite players was Tyrone Taylor, a great athlete who just signed a $750,000 contract with the Milwaukee Brewers. "What a great kid," Rock said. Taylor scored thirty-four touchdowns one year. Carl Holmes, another great running back, went to Fresno State.

"What I want to do is create a family atmosphere," said Rock. "And from the results, the kids love it."

"I just love that guy," said David Lechman, one of his ex-players. "There's nobody like Rock. He's fun, he's tough, he's fair and he knows football. Long live the Rock!"

And that seems to be the general feeling of players, parents, fellow coaches and administrators. It seems that Hollis is going to be the "rock" upon which Torrance football is built for a long time to come.

CHAPTER 29

WESTCHESTER HIGH SCHOOL COMETS

The greatest period in Westchester High School football was the era of Wein and few losses. That's Wein as in Larry Wein, the coach from 1983 to 2002, who had a record of 161-51-3 for a .755 percentage. Wow! Wein had years of 9-2, 9-1-1, 10-1, 9-1, 12-1, 12-1, 9-2, 10-2, 8-3 and 9-1. You can't get much better than that. Too bad the years from 1958 through 1982 are unaccounted for, or Westchester would reign along with the gods of football in this book.

Westchester Win-Loss Records

1958–82: no records
1983: 8-3, Larry Wein
1984: 7-2-1, Wein
1985: 9-2, Wein
1986: 3-6-1, Wein
1987: 7-3, Wein
1988: 6-4, Wein
1989: 6-3, Wein
1990: 8-3, Wein
1991: 6-4, Wein
1992: 9-1-1, Wein
1993: 10-1, Wein
1994: 9-1, Wein

1995: 7-4, Wein
1996: 12-1, Wein
1997: 12-1, Wein
1998: 9-2, Wein
1999: 10-2, Wein
2000: 8-3, Wein
2001: 9-1, Wein
2002: 7-5, Wein
2003: 2-8, David Williams
2004: 3-8, Williams
2005: 6-6, Williams
2006: 4-7, Adrian Ivory
2007: 4-7, Ivory

2008: 3-7, Ivory
2009: 8-4, Ruffin Patterson
2010: 6-5, Patterson

2011: 7-4, Seka Edwards
2012: 2-8, Edwards
2013: 2-8, Tim Lenderman

Coaches' Records

1. Larry Wein: 162-51-3 (.755)
2. David Williams: 11-22 (.333)
3. Adrian Ivory: 11-21 (.344)
4. Ruffin Patterson: 14-9 (.609)
5. Seka Edwards: 9-12 (.429)
6. Tim Lenderman: 2-8 (.200)

Totals: 209-124-3 (.626)
(twenty-four years unaccounted for)

CHAPTER 30

WEST HIGH SCHOOL WARRIORS

The football program at West High School, which became the fourth Torrance public high school in 1962, started slowly. However, it took only three years for opponents to find out that they had chosen their nickname, the Warriors, wisely.

In '62, Bill Parton became the first coach, and had a tough time with the West neophytes ending up with 1-6-1, 2-7 and 2-7 seasons. The school's first victory came over Victor Valley, 6–0, and outstanding players like quarterback Crane Nuzzo, fullback Miles Moore, running back Dave Yeskin, wide receiver Russ Douglas and defenders Ken Burge, George Mount, Marty Kehoe and Richard Grossman served notice of things to come.

The lone victory in 1963 was a 16–6 win over future power Carson High. Running backs Bob Vroman and Jim Thompson, quarterback Lindy Nuzzo and end John Cochrane led the way. Things looked up in 1964, as the Warriors beat Palos Verdes High 14–13 and Bell Gardens 6–0 behind All-League players Gary Lloyd, Lenny Meullich, Jim Barnes and Fred Schwanbeck.

But then Coach Fred Petersen arrived in 1965, establishing a winning program almost immediately with a 7-2 record. The team went only 3-6 in 1966 but set the tone for things to come, as Bill Breitzman, Allen Coward, Steve Sirridge and Steve Renz were All-League performers.

Then two remarkable 9-1 seasons followed. In 1967, the year was marred only by a 14–7 loss to Bellflower in the CIF playoffs. The feat was duplicated in 1968, as the Warriors beat everyone except Lakewood, losing 24–6 in the first round of the playoffs. LaPuente (22–0), Fermin Lasuen (27–12) and South

(31–7) were some of their regular-season victims. Another galaxy of All-League players included Coy Hall, Jim Strofe, Gary Kendrick, Jim Yates, Paul Johnson, Gary Hulsey, Chuck Farrah, Richard Pierce, Jim Parton and Tom Alnes.

In their next good season, 1970, the Warriors went 6-3 and beat Blair of Pasadena 19–12, Santa Monica 21–14 and Redondo Union 14–0. All-South Bay were center Bob Hansen, halfback Craig Kelly, defensive end Doug Helte, tackles Kurt Davis and Mike White and safety Dave Vint.

West went 7-3 in 1972 before losing to Dos Pueblos of Goleta, 21–6, in the CIF playoffs. The Warriors outscored Long Beach Wilson 14–13, Hawthorne 30–26 and Torrance 7–0. Leading the team were quarterback Tracey Harmon, receiver Pat Schmidt and Dave Hill, Jim Sandhofner and Tom Farrell on defense.

Petersen's other remarkable years are delineated in the accompanying profile. When he closed out in 1983 and moved over to El Camino, John Black and Mark Knox took over.

The duo took the Warriors to an outstanding 8-3 season in 1985. The Warriors beat Inglewood, Oxnard and Simi Valley before losing to Hart of Newhall in the finals. Running back Kevin Maher gained over 1,200 yards, and Chris Ramirez was a standout receiver.

All-Leaguers Jeff Creek, Shayne Mihalka and Ted Holloway excelled in 1987, while quarterback Paul Myro, receiver Chad Smith, end Matt Vincent and MVP running back Dean Dougherty defined the 1988 team.

Then, 1989 was a different story, as Black and Knox took their charges to a 10-2 record, including their first playoff win, before losing to Temple City. Running back Josh Moor, quarterback John Walsh, wide receiver James Kim and linebacker Joe Kim excelled.

New coach Kerry Crabb took over in 1991, leading the team to a 9-4 record in 1992. After beating Beaumont and St. Joseph's of Santa Maria in the CIF playoffs, the Warriors lost to Bishop Diego of Santa Barbara, 41–26.

Then Coach Greg Holt arrived. Holt, who starts his twenty-first season in 2014, has won 112 games, second only to Petersen.

"I didn't feel any pressure per se," said Holt in a 2012 *Daily Breeze* article by Phil Collin. "It's called living up to the standard, and that's kind of what I've been trying to do." And he's done it well, boasting seasons of 9-1-1 (1998), 9-1 (2003), 12-1-1 (2006), 7-3-1 (2007), 10-4 (2012) and 10-3 (2013). Holt continued, "There's been some bumps in the road, no question. We've had some high times, and we've had some real low times. But all in all, it's what kind of program do you run? Are you doing the right things? I am motivated by the rich tradition of the guys who have been here—Knox, Black, Petersen. There was a standard that was set, and we always try to live up to it. We don't always do it, but we try

Coach Greg Holt (shown here in 2011) led West Torrance to ten-win seasons in 2012 and 2013. *Photo by Scott Varley; courtesy of the* Daily Breeze.

to do it. We try run a clean program, try to run it to the point where we're class on the field."

After Holt, who was raised in Lompoc and played football at Allan Hancock College in Santa Maria, took over in 1994, his first outstanding year was 1998, when the team went 9-1-1. Quarterback Chad Munson passed for over two thousand yards and twenty touchdowns, and running back Robert Ramirez was outstanding. Great victories were over Morningside (46–0), South (34–6) and Torrance (24–0).

Kicker Sean Silver, quarterback Jim Toti and running backs Tom Cleveland and Dwayne Watts helped out in 2001, while quarterbacks Matt Roquemore and Toti led the team in 2002.

But 2006 was Holt's defining season, as the Warriors finished 12-1-1 and rolled through the playoffs, beating Knight of Palmdale 31–7, Culver City 58–29 and St. Paul 26–4 before losing to Dominguez of Compton, 28–21. To say they were dominating is an understatement, as they annihilated El Segundo 60–0, Hawthorne 50–0 and Redondo 39–3.

In 2009, West was 7-4, losing to Warren of Downey, 51–21, in the playoffs behind quarterback Ronnie Clark, fullback Luke Trunowski and linebacker Dan Henggeler.

In 2012, another outstanding season (10-4) featured great playoff wins over St. Joseph of Santa Maria (45–20), Mira Costa (49–42) and Atascadero (37–6) before losing to Palos Verdes, 35–14. Quarterback Zach Heeger, wide receivers Trevor Lewis and Jonathan Wright, linebackers Jimmie Giardini and Benton Shortridge and offensive linemen Chinedu Ojukwu and Josh Allen were outstanding. The 2013 season was almost a repeat as the Warriors finished 10-3, defeating Canyon of Canyon Country 35–27 and Palmdale 17–14 before bowing to Hart of Newhall, 42–7.

Regardless of the challenges the Warriors face, Greg Holt and his charges seem to be up to the task.

West Torrance Win-Loss Records

1962: 1-6-1, Bill Parton
1963: 1-7, Parton
1964: 2-7, Parton
1965: 7-2, Fred Petersen
1966: 3-6, Petersen
1967: 9-1, Petersen
1968: 9-1, Petersen
1969: 4-3-3, Petersen
1970: 6-3, Petersen
1971: 3-6, Petersen
1972: 7-3, Petersen
1973: 4-5, Petersen
1974: 5-5, Petersen
1975: 11-1, Petersen
1976: 10-2, Petersen
1977: 6-3, Petersen
1978: 5-5, Petersen
1979: 4-5-1, Petersen
1980: 5-5, Petersen
1981: 8-4, Petersen
1982: 14-0, Petersen
1983: 8-2, Petersen
1984: 5-6, John Black and
   Mark Knox
1985: 8-3, Black and Knox
1986: 6-5, Black and Knox
1987: 1-7-1, Black and Knox

1988: 3-6, Black and Knox
1989: 10-2, Black and Knox
1990: 9-3, Black and Knox
1991: 1-8-1, Kerry Crabb
1992: 9-4, Crabb
1993: 5-6, Crabb
1994: 4-6, Greg Holt
1995: 4-6, Holt
1996: 5-5, Holt
1997: 2-8, Holt
1998: 9-1-1, Holt
1999: 5-6, Holt
2000: 1-9, Holt
2001: 3-7, Holt
2002: 4-6-1, Holt
2003: 9-1, Holt
2004: 5-5, Holt
2005: 4-6, Holt
2006: 12-1-1, Holt
2007: 7-3-1, Holt
2008: 2-8, Holt
2009: 7-4, Holt
2010: 3-7, Holt
2011: 6-4, Holt
2012: 10-4, Holt
2013: 10-3, Holt

Coaches' Records

1. Fred Petersen: 131-60-4 (.686)
2. Greg Holt: 112-100-4 (.535)
3. John Black and Mark Knox: 42-32-1 (.567)
4. Kerry Crabb: 15-18-1 (.456)
5. Bill Parton: 4-20-1 (.180)

Totals: 304-230-11 (.568)

COACH FRED PETERSEN

"He was the ultimate warrior," said Kati Petersen Krumpe in a 2011 *Daily Breeze* article by Tony Ciniglio, "and I don't think we realized until today just how many lives he's affected."

Kati was speaking about her father, Fred Petersen, longtime coach of the Torrance West High School Warriors football team, who died at seventy-nine in 2011.

Steve Sarkisian, now head coach of the University of Southern California Trojans and who played and coached under Petersen, had his own idea. "As a fatherly figure, mentor or coach, he was someone you could constantly lean on," Sarkisian said. "He had such a big impact on so many people's lives. He will be celebrated. Obviously it's a loss, but he will be celebrated and missed." Petersen's son, David, is married to Sarkisian's sister, Amy.

Petersen served as football coach at West High from 1965 to 1983, winning 131 games and seven league titles.

"We lost one of the greatest coaches in the history of South Bay football," El Camino coach John Featherstone said in the same article. "I loved Petey. He was a man's man, a throwback to all the great coaches of the past. He was a no-nonsense guy who had great rapport with the players, and it's a sad day for El Camino College. They broke the mold with Petey."

After West, Petersen became offensive coordinator at El Camino, helping the college win one national championship, one state championship and twelve conference titles.

Born in Nebraska, Petersen lettered in football, baseball, track and wrestling in high school before performing at quarterback for Midland Lutheran College near Omaha. In 1965, he became head coach at West at age thirty-three.

Petersen did not take long to acclimate himself at West Torrance, going 7-2 in his very first season. The year was marked by major wins over Rolling Hills High (32–14), Torrance (21–0), Beverly Hills (40–13) and Lennox (41–6). Key players that year included Paul Gadbois, Ron Norman, Dave La Roche and Mark Knox, the future West coach.

By Petersen's third year, West was dominating, going undefeated until losing to Bellflower, 14–7, in its first-ever CIF playoff appearance. His All-League players included lineman Skip Hogue, MVP Dave Boyd and defensive back Gary Marconi. Major victories were over El Segundo (72–14) and Lennox (33–6). This was followed up by another league

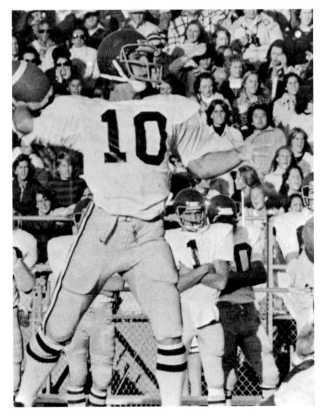

Above: Fred Petersen's record at West Torrance High School was 131-60-4 over nineteen years. *Courtesy of Torrance Historical Society*.

Left: Mark Rhoades was an outstanding quarterback at West Torrance High. *Courtesy of Torrance Historical Society*.

championship in 1968, when Petersen went 9-1, the sole loss coming against Lakewood, 24–6.

Petersen's Warriors were rolling by 1975, when the team went 11-1 behind running back Rick Obema, quarterback Mark Rhoades and a defense led by Mark Norris, Glen Petersen and Corey Hons. "We played awesome football," Petersen was quoted as saying.

The 1976 season was more of the same, as the Warriors finished 10-2, beating Long Beach Wilson 17–14 before losing to Los Altos, 28–14, in the playoffs. Quarterback Dave Weatherman was named Bay League Player of the Year after having passed for 2,221 yards and seventeen touchdowns. Split end Mike Franks had sixty receptions, while running back Bob Hudspeth gained over 1,000 yards. Scott McQueen and Steve Schwartz excelled on defense.

The team had another good year in 1977, finishing 6-3 behind quarterback Todd Hons, who passed for 1,671 yards (and later played one year for Detroit in the NFL). Receiver Kenny Halbert had twenty-eight receptions, while tailback Mark Palmer had twenty-nine carries in just one game.

Good times resumed in 1981, as the Warriors finished 8-4 before bowing to Newbury Park in the CIF playoffs. Quarterback Randy Fayette had 3,699 total yards, while other great players included wide receiver Loren Richey, kicker John Combis, running back Tom LeGardye and defenders Jan Megeff, Tom Yi and David Ahearns. "This is the best team I have ever been associated with," Petersen said at the time. "I'm just proud to be a part of it."

But Petersen's most remarkable year was 1982, when the team went 14-0 and won the CIF championship, throttling Santa Monica 35–21. "The defense just smothered them," Petersen said later. The team had an incredible eight shutouts, and key victories in the CIF came over San Marcos (48–10), John Muir of Pasadena (24–0) and Oxnard (17–8). Running back Jeff Studer accounted for 1,100 yards, while All-South Bay players included flanker Loren Richey, running back John Combs (1,300 yards and twenty-three touchdowns), guard Don Gereau, linebacker Greg Bochesa and defensive end Arnold Fernandez.

Petersen closed out his West career in 1983 with another outstanding year, going 8-2 with quarterback Sean Berry and running back David Petersen leading the way.

One of the most remarkable things about Petersen was his dedication to his sport and his players. "The thing about him is that he remembered all the athletes he ever had," said longtime South Bay Athletic Club president and South High coach Jerry McIlvaine in the *Daily Breeze* in 2011. "His influence at West was enormous. There was a lot of camaraderie among the

Left: Quarterback Todd Hons was a leading contributor to Fred Petersen's 1977 and 1978 teams. *Courtesy of Torrance Historical Society.*

Below: The 1983 West Torrance Warriors finished 8-2 and won two playoff games. *Courtesy of Torrance Historical Society.*

coaches at West, and he was instrumental in keeping that staff functioning and making sure everyone got along."

"He really wanted to help athletes further their education," said Krumpe, a director in the Torrance school system, in that same article. "That was his passion. He wanted athletics to be a pathway to become better students. And he firmly believed that many would not graduate high school without athletics."

Fred Petersen was always there to make sure that did not happen, and he ended up helping thousands of boys' and girls' dreams become realities.

CHAPTER 31

EL CAMINO COLLEGE WARRIORS

E l Camino College and football success are synonymous.
    The Torrance community college has an outstanding record of 446-230-10 from 1947 through 2013, boasting a national championship in 1987 under Coach John Featherstone, twelve seasons with only one loss and one season (1987) with no losses. Outstanding El Camino players who have gone on to grace the gridiron on higher levels include defensive end Fred Dryer (1968) for the Los Angeles Rams and New York Giants; defensive back Keith Ellison (2005) for the Buffalo Bills; guard/center Lynn Hoyem (1958) for the Dallas Cowboys; Jim Obradovich (1974) for New York Giants (and others); quarterback Steve Sarkisian (1994), who went on to become head coach at USC; punt returner Jim Sears (1957) for the Chicago Cardinals; and wide receiver Tom Reynolds (1967) for the Chicago Bears.

Amby Schindler was ECC's first coach, earning a fine 7-2-1 record and going on to win twenty-six games in his five-year career. Schindler was a fine tailback at USC (1937–39) before embarking on a teaching and coaching career.

Norm Verry, another USC star player, had an outstanding career at El Camino, compiling a record of 55-27-2. His first team in 1952 went 8-1, his '53 team went 6-3 and his '54 team had an excellent 9-1 record, its only loss coming to Hinds Junior College of Raymond, Mississippi, in the 1955 Junior Rose Bowl Classic. Great players included Lineman of the Year Fab Abram, back Stan Becker, defensive back Don Greco, offensive lineman Norm Becker and running back Ken Swearingen, who later became an ECC

Above: Gary Kimbrell (pictured here in 1958), who won 180 games coaching at Rolling Hills, Miraleste and Peninsula High Schools, was an outstanding running back at Hawthorne High and El Camino College. *Courtesy of El Camino College.*

Opposite: Coach Norm Verry and his quarterback, Ron Veres, study the action at a game in 1959. Verry led the Warriors to fifty-five wins from 1952 through 1960. *Courtesy of El Camino College.*

coach. Swearingen was at his best in the 27–0 victory over East LA, in which he ran for two touchdowns, passed for another and kicked three conversions. That season included five other shutouts against Ventura (32–0), Modesto (7–0), San Diego (7–0), Valley (13–0) and Santa Monica (14–0).

1955 was another good year, as the Warriors went 7-2-1. Shutout victories came over Modesto (18–0), San Diego (13–0) and Santa Monica (20–0). Linemen Pat Reagan and Roland Rutter; running back Roger Metoyer; quarterbacks Jimmy Lindsey, Phil Shepherd and Jerry Nicholson; and fullbacks Don Kulpaca and Norton Engen all played critical roles on offense, while Joe Zicaro, Bob Bass, Dale Hill and Ted Wall stood out on defense. In 1956, the Warriors were 7-3, shutting out Modesto 13–0, beating Harbor 21–7 and smashing Phoenix 60–6. Future coach Gary Kimbrell was an outstanding running back for the Warriors in 1958.

Verry went 6-4 in 1959, beating Modesto 28–23, Valley 24–6 and Santa Monica 28–12. Outstanding were running backs Ron Goodrich, Jerry Hren

and Glen Kezar; quarterbacks Ron Veres, Dave Long and Bill Crawford; and end Tom Blanch.

Verry coached two more years before a cerebral hemorrhage struck him down at the age of thirty-nine during a game trip. Verry, who was born in Hanford, California, in 1922, was a football star at Visalia High School before attending USC, where he was an All-American guard before entering the U.S. Marine Corps in 1942. He returned to USC in 1944 and played for the Chicago Rockets in 1946 and 1947. He served on the coaching staff at Inglewood High for one year before coming to El Camino in 1950. Verry and his wife, Lois, had two sons, Richard and Steve.

Ken Swearingen, another outstanding El Camino coach, ruled the Warriors from 1962 to 1975. During his playing career, Swearingen was All-Bay League for four years at Redondo Union High School before earning All-Metro honors at El Camino. Swearingen played for the University of the Pacific and came to El Camino in 1962. In his very first year, the Warriors went 7-2 behind running back Jim Reale, end Herb Hinsche (a future high school coach in the South Bay), cornerback Ralph Hughes, quarterback Bob Johnson, wide receiver Ron Bass, defensive back Glen Howell and wide receiver Pat Lininger.

In 1964, the Warriors went 6-3, beating East LA (again) 35–0, Pierce 33–6 and Valley 19–12. 1967 was another great year, as Swearingen led the Warriors to an 8-1 record. One of the players on that team was end John Featherstone, ECC's future Hall of Fame coach. Fullbacks Ed Gillis and Tom Reynolds and quarterbacks Dana Clyde and Jon Robertson were all instrumental. Reynolds scored ninety-six points on 125 carries and thirty-two passes. A series of great years followed: 10-1, 7-2, 6-3, 11-1, 8-1-1, 6-3, 8-1-1 and 6-4. The team's only loss in 1968 was to Fresno City College, 25–0. Quarterback Dan Heck, linebacker Dennis Higgins, defensive back Pat Hamman, defensive end Bryan Cosgove and tackle john Gist all had great years.

But the best was yet to come, as the team finished 11-1 in 1971, losing only to Phoenix, 16–10, in the second game of the season. But the Warriors were unstoppable afterward, annihilating Citrus 14–0, Rio Hondo 51–36 and Santa Rosa 48–14 in the playoffs. Quarterback Coy Hall, running back Doug Jena, guard Jerry Hyatt, lineman Jim Obradovich and defensive back Paul Horn were all great. The 8-1-1 record in 1972 was also impressive as the Warriors polished off Valley 40–0, Laney 34–6 and Fresno 25–13.

In 1974, outstanding players like defensive back Rene Anderson, guard David Applegate, tight end Don Davenport, defensive end Dennis Riggens, tackle Bob Flentye, linebacker Rowen Tupuivao and cornerback Ken McAllister led the team to a 8-1-1 record. The team's only loss was to Pasadena, 28–13.

Bill Vincent, an outstanding lineman for San Diego State, arrived in 1976 after several years as line coach at ECC. Bill went 37-20 in his five years, another outstanding job. He was 7-3 in 1977, when the Warriors beat Harbor 13–6, San Jose 24–18, Reedley 28–7 and East LA 45–15. He finished his stay at ECC in 1981, going 6-3. Vincent, who had also coached six years at Aviation High School in Redondo Beach, will always be remembered for his fine years at El Camino.

Jack Reilly took over in 1983 without much of a letup, going 7-3 in 1982 and 7-2 in '83.

Finally, John Featherstone, the greatest ECC coach of all time, arrived in 1985. It took him only two years to claim the national championship with an 11-0 record. (See accompanying story.)

Some of the great moments in El Camino history follow:

- Linebacker Brian Smith recorded 254 tackles in 2001–02.
- Defensive end Daniel Stewart had twenty-two sacks in 2008–09.
- Steve Sarkisian passed for 7,274 yards and sixty-two touchdowns in 1993–94.
- Kenbrell Thompkins caught 126 passes for 2,052 yards in 2008–09.
- Brian Flowers rushed for 1,557 yards in 2005.
- Running back Zach Swoopshire caught fifty-four balls for 931 yards in 1994–95.

In recent years, a dozen players have accepted scholarships to Arizona, seven to Arizona State, eleven to Cincinnati, three to Florida State, five to Hawaii, three to Missouri, six to Oregon, eleven to Oregon State, five to UCLA, seven to USC, nine to Utah, seven to Utah State, three to Washington and three to Washington State—just to name a few.

Football players in the El Camino Hall of Fame include Fred Dryer (1967); Tom Reynolds (1967); Paul Held (1951); Coaches Swearingen (1962–75), Schindler (1947–51) and Verry (1952–60); Fabian Abram (1954); Jim Clark (1954); Rick Eber (1965); Florencio Torres (1949); Jim Alison (1962); Mike Andrews (1961); Bobby Beathard (1956); Bill Sloey (1970); Bob Weiss (1956); Jerry Witt (1947); Marty Acosta (1948); Gary Kimbrell (1958); and dozens more.

And the Warriors, under Coach John Featherstone, march on.

El Camino Win-Loss Records

1947: 7-2-1, Amby Schindler
1948: 3-7, Schindler
1949: 7-3, Schindler
1950: 8-1-1, Schindler
1951: 1-9, Schindler
1952: 8-1, Norm Verry
1953: 6-3, Verry
1954: 9-1, Verry

1955: 7-1-2, Verry
1956: 7-3, Verry
1957: 4-5, Verry
1958: 3-5, Verry
1959: 6-4, Verry
1960: 5-4, Verry
1961: 5-4, Doug Essick
1962: 7-2, Ken Swearingen

1963: 5-4, Swearingen
1964: 6-3, Swearingen
1965: 5-3-1, Swearingen
1966: 5-2-2, Swearingen
1967: 8-1, Swearingen
1968: 10-1-0, Swearingen
1969: 7-2, Swearingen
1970: 7-2, Swearingen
1971: 11-1, Swearingen
1972: 7-1-1, Swearingen
1973: 6-3, Swearingen
1974: 8-1-1, Swearingen
1975: 6-4, Swearingen
1976: 6-3, Bill Vincent
1977: 7-3, Vincent
1978: 6-3, Vincent
1979: 5-5, Vincent
1980: 7-3, Vincent
1981: 6-3, Vincent
1982: 7-3, Jack Reilly
1983: 7-2, Reilly
1984: 5-5, Reilly
1985: 5-5, John Featherstone
1986: 4-6, Featherstone
1987: 11-0, Featherstone
1988: 9-1-1, Featherstone

1989: 10-1, Featherstone
1990: 9-2, Featherstone
1991: 6-4, Featherstone
1992: 8-3, Featherstone
1993: 0-10, Featherstone
1994: 9-2, Featherstone
1995: 7-4, Featherstone
1996: 8-3, Featherstone
1997: 8-3, Featherstone
1998: 7-4, Featherstone
1999: 8-3, Featherstone
2000: 9-2, Featherstone
2001: 4-6, Featherstone
2002: 3-7, Featherstone
2003: 8-3, Featherstone
2004: 8-3, Featherstone
2005: 11-1, Featherstone
2006: 12-2, Featherstone
2007: 8-2, Featherstone
2008: 10-2, Featherstone
2009: 8-3, Featherstone
2010: 2-8, Featherstone
2011: 8-3, Featherstone
2012: 3-7, Featherstone
2013: 5-5, Featherstone

Coaches' Records

1. John Featherstone: 208-105-1 (.664)
2. Ken Swearingen: 89-29-5 (.743)
3. Norm Verry: 55-27-2 (.666)
4. Bill Vincent: 37-20 (.649)
5. Amby Schindler: 26-22-2 (.530)
6. Jack Reilly: 19-10 (.655)
7. Doug Essick: 5-4 (.555)

Totals: 446-230-10 (.662)

COACH JOHN FEATHERSTONE

The 1987 season was the finest in El Camino College's storied football history, and Coach John Featherstone was the prime instigator of that success.

"You're No 1. You've got it. It's official." Those were the words Featherstone heard after the Warriors dismantled Taft College near Bakersfield 24–6 in the Pony Bowl, giving ECC the undisputed national championship. This turned out to be just the start of Featherstone's storied career at El Camino College. His record going into the 2014 season is 208-105-1 for a percentage of .664. He has the highest winning percentage of any active coach in the Southern Section of thirty-seven community colleges from Bakersfield to San Diego. Featherstone was also named National Coach of the Year in 1987 and 2006 and California Coach of the Year eight times. "I always look at any honor as a coaching staff award because we're all in this together," Featherstone modestly said in an ECC biography.

Featherstone, who has just six losing seasons in twenty-nine years of coaching at El Camino, has also dominated in bowl games, winning by such scores as 49–22 over Saddleback at the Pony Bowl in 1988, 33–6 over LA Southwest College in the 1997 Strawberry Bowl, 49–7 over Southwestern College of Chula Vista in the 1999 South County Bowl, 44–19 over East LA in the 2000 Chips for Kids Bowl and 57–22 over Riverside in the 2005 National Bowl.

Born in Manhattan Beach, Featherstone attended Mira Costa High School, where he participated in track, baseball, volleyball and, of course, football. He played both quarterback and running back but earned All-CIF honors as a wide receiver in 1967. He then played two years at El Camino, earning All-Conference honors, before attending San Diego State, where he played wide receiver for the legendary Don Coryell. In front of fifty-two thousand fans, he led the Aztecs to a win in the Pasadena Bowl, where he made two touchdown catches and was named MVP. The Aztecs finished the season 11-0 and ranked twelfth in the national polls.

After receiving his bachelor's degree in journalism with a minor in physical education from San Diego State in 1970, Featherstone got his MA in physical education in 1973. He started coaching wide receivers at San Diego State in 1971 before coaching quarterbacks and receivers at Grossmont College for four years. In 1975, he became offensive coordinator at Mesa College in San Diego. Then he returned to San Diego State in 1980 to coach wide

Above: El Camino's John Featherstone, one of the greatest community college coaches in the country, has been named National Coach of the Year twice and California Coach of the Year eight times. *Photo by Scott Varley; courtesy of the* Daily Breeze.

Left: Bryan Reeves was an outstanding receiver on the 1988 El Camino team, which went 9-1-1 under Coach John Featherstone. *Courtesy of El Camino College.*

receivers again. In 1982, he joined the Cal Berkeley coaching staff and then returned to offensive coordinator at Santa Ana College before being named head coach at El Camino.

And after twenty-nine years, he gives no sign of retiring. "My job never gets old," a fifty-eight-year-old Featherstone said in an ECC press release after the 2006 season. "Each year is a new challenge. It keeps me going, and every morning I pinch myself because I have he opportunity to go to work and really enjoy what I do. I'm a blessed and lucky man." He is indeed, with a wife, Diane, and four daughters: Terri, Ivy, Keegan and Arianna.

In addition to the hundreds of players who have gone on to play football at four-year colleges, more than three dozen of his players have gone to the NFL, including fullback Marcel Reece (2005) for Oakland, defensive back Mike Harris (2009) for Jacksonville, quarterback Matt Simms (2009) and defensive end Ryan Riddle (2001) for the New York Jets, guard Derrick Deese (1989) for San Francisco, wide receiver Kenbrell Thompkins (2010) for the New England Patriots and linebacker Keith Ellison (2003) for the Buffalo Bills.

Featherstone was elected to the El Camino Hall of Fame in 2005, and he credits his outstanding staff for all his success. "I've had great veteran coaches and some excellent young part-time assistants who have worked hard to build one of the top football programs in the country," he said. "We take pride in winning and representing El Camino in a very professional manner. I also want to thank Don Coryell, my former coach at San Diego State, for having faith in me and giving me my first chance to coach. He is one of the finest men I've had the honor of knowing."

Featherstone has had great year after great year, going 11-0 in 1987; 9-1-1 in 1988; 10-1 in 1989; 9-2 in 1990, 1994 and 2000; 11-1 in 2005; 12-2 in 2006; and 10-2 in 2008.

But 1987 was the greatest year the Warriors ever had. Besides being national champs, quarterback Dan Speltz was a first-team All-American, while linebacker Ken Sale was on the second team and wide receiver Dwight Pickens, defensive back Billy Hugely and linebacker Kaiser Noa all received honorable mentions. On defense, Hughley had 117 tackles, Sale 110 and Noa 105. Defensive back Kevin Harris had six interceptions, and defensive end Tui Suiaunoa had fifteen sacks. Their victims during the year included Mount San Antonio (31–14), Golden West (32–6) and Fullerton (27–26). But their domination was never more evident than in the Pony Bowl, where they beat Taft. Offensive player of the game Speltz was twenty-three for forty-two and passed for 357 yards and three touchdowns to wide receiver

Dwight Pickens. With seven minutes left, defensive player of the game Ken Sale accented the win with a sack and fumble recovery.

El Camino's winning ways under Featherstone continued in 1988, when the Warriors went 9-1-1. First-team All-Conference players included running back Aaron Craver, wide receiver Bryan Burnett, guard Mark Merritt, linebacker Greg Franklin, safety Nui Sale (also a first-team All-American) and punter Dominic Cefalone. Bryan Reeves was an outstanding receiver.

In 1990, the Warriors finished 9-2 behind defensive back Anthony Cole, running back Anthony Daigle, linebacker Willie Crawford and defensive back William Lackey.

And so it goes on for John Featherstone, a continuing saga of winning teams year after year with no end in sight.

CHAPTER 32

LOS ANGELES HARBOR COLLEGE SEAHAWKS

Los Angeles Harbor College became a reality in 1949, and the school established a football program the following year under Coach Joe H. Berry. Berry's best year was 1951, when the Seahawks went 6-4-1. Over the next thirteen years, he would win thirty-five games and establish a football tradition at Harbor.

Berry's 1950 team won four games, beating Taft 27–6, Santa Monica 27–6, Valley 42–12 and San Diego 13–6. There were lots of outstanding players, including quarterback Dave Wallace, fullbacks John Alexander and Jack Allen, tackles James Gannon and Sterling Fordham, guards Carlos Dillenbeck and Kenneth Booth and ends Jack Robertson and Andy Spaar.

The 1952 season didn't turn out very well (1-8), but Manuel Murietta and Don Woolover helped the Seahawks beat Terminal Island 18–0.

Linemen Joe Freeman and Mike King, end Pete Galloni, running back Tim Hewett and kicker Henry Gonzalez helped the Seahawks go 5-6 in 1954.

After Scrappy Rhea's reign (see accompanying story), Bill Young won fifteen games in four years, and then it was time for George Swade to step in. Swade, who won more games (fifty-seven) than any other Harbor coach, coached the Seahawks from 1978 to 1986, from 1995 to 1996 and in 2009. His greatest season was his last, when the Harbor went 9-1, but he also won eight games in 1981 and '82 and went 6-3 in 1986.

There was a lot of action in between Swade's reigns. Chris Ferragamo, the legendary coach at Banning High School, was there in 1987–88 but won just three games. Don Weems coached from 1989 to 1994, winning twenty-four.

1950 Los Angeles Harbor College 1st Football Team

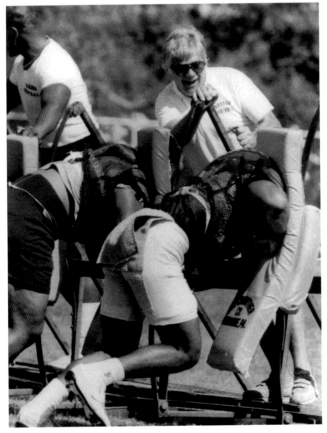

Above: Joe H. Berry coached Harbor College's first-ever football team to a 4-3-1 record in 1950. *Courtesy of Harbor College.*

Left: George Swade coached three different times at Harbor College in Wilmington, accumulating fifty-seven wins, the most in the school's history. *Courtesy of George Swade.*

Tony Bloomfield took over for one year in 1997 (4-6) and Wayne Crawford (2-8) in 1998–99. Steve Schmitz, the coaching icon from South Torrance High, won twenty-one games in four seasons, including an 8-3 year in 2002. Andrew Avilar won twenty-one games from 2004 through 2008, and Brett Peabody, also from South, had fine years in 2010 (8-2), 2011 (7-3) and 2012 (6-5).

The most points ever scored by the Seahawks, seventy-three, came in 1965. The most rushing yards came in the 2010 season, when the Seahawks ran for 538 yards against Antelope Valley and almost 3,000 for the season. The greatest passing game was against Long Beach City College in 2009, when Dominique Blackman threw for 535 yards (and 3,750 for the season). That 2009 game also had the most yards gained ever, 737. Joe Harris has the most yards gained in a season, with 1,562 in 2004, while John White has the most career yards, 2,527 in 2009–10. White also had the longest single run, 97 yards against Long Beach City College in 2009, and school records of 3,943 all-purpose yards and forty-four touchdowns in 2009. Andrew Trudnowski has the highest career passing yardage (5,852), as well as the most touchdown passes (forty-five).

Chris Matthews is the leading pass receiver, with 112 receptions for 2007–08. The record for most touchdowns is held by Deryn Bowser, with nineteen in 2006–07. The record for most career touchdowns belongs to John White, with forty-one in 2009–10. Oscar Cervantes is the leading field goal kicker, with fourteen in 2003–04. Oscar also has the longest field goal, fifty-four yards, which came against Southwest in 2004.

On the defensive side of the ball, the fewest points ever allowed was 231 in 2010 season. The most interceptions (twenty-one) came in 2007 and the most sacks (forty-one) in 2011.

On defense, Steven Juarez leads in career tackles, with 175.5 in 2003–04. The record for most sacks belongs to Alvin Steeb, with twenty-four in 1999–2000. Rakine Toomes leads in career interceptions, with eight in 2002–03.

A new coach, Dean Dowty, takes over the team for the 2014 season. Dowty, who cached at College of the Desert in Palm Desert from 2006 to 2013, led Desert to three bowl games and was named the conference Coach of the Year in 2007.

The Seahawks are hoping that winning days are here again.

Harbor Win-Loss Records

1950: 4-3-1, Joe H. Berry
1951: 6-4-1, Berry
1952: 1-8, Berry
1953: 1-8, Berry
1954: 5-6, Berry
1955: 4-3-2, Berry
1956: 2-7, Berry
1957: 1-7-1, Berry
1958: 2-7, Berry
1959: 3-6, Berry
1960: 0-9, Berry
1961: 4-5, Berry
1962: 2-7, Berry
1963: 6-3, Floyd "Scrappy" Rhea
1964: 9-0, Rhea
1965: 8-2, Rhea
1966: 7-3, Rhea
1967: 4-5, Rhea
1968: 5-4, Rhea
1969: 8-2, Rhea
1970: 1-8, Rhea
1971: 4-5, Rhea
1972: 2-8, Rhea
1973: 3-7, Rhea
1974: 5-4, Bill Young
1975: 5-4, Young
1976: 2-6-1, Young
1977: 3-7, Young
1978: 3-6-1, George Swade
1979: 3-6, Swade
1980: 4-6, Swade
1981: 8-3, Swade
1982: 8-3, Swade

1983: 4-6, Swade
1984: 5-5, Swade
1985: 2-7, Swade
1986: 6-3, Swade
1987: 2-7-1, Chris Ferragamo
1988: 1-10, Ferragamo
1989: 3-7, Don Weems
1990: 5-5, Weems
1991: 3-7, Weems
1992: 8-3, Weems
1993: 5-5, Weems
1994: 0-7, Weems; 2-1, Gene
   Miranda
1995: 5-5, Swade
1996: 0-10, Swade
1997: 4-6, Tony Bloomfield
1998: 2-8, Wayne Crawford
1999: 2-8, Crawford
2000: 3-7, Steve Schmitz
2001: 5-5, Schmitz
2002: 8-3, Schmitz
2003: 5-5, Schmitz
2004: 5-5, Andrew Avilar
2005: 4-6, Avilar
2006: 4-6, Avilar
2007: 5-5, Avilar
2008: 3-7, Avilar
2009: 9-1, Swade
2010: 8-2, Brett Peabody
2011: 7-3, Peabody
2012: 6-5, Peabody
2013: 0-10, Reuben Ale

Coaches' Records

1. George Swade: 57-45-1 (.558)
2. Floyd "Scrappy" Rhea: 53-47 (.530)
3. Joe Berry: 35-80-5 (.313)
4. Don Weems: 24-34 (.414)
5. Brett Peabody: 21-10 (.677)
6. Steve Schmitz: 21-20 (.512)
7. Andrew Avilar: 21-29 (.420)
8. William Young: 15-21-1 (.405)
9. Tony Bloomfield: 4-6 (.400)
10. Wayne Crawford: 4-16 (.200)
11. Chris Ferragamo: 3-17-1 (.167)
12. Reuben Ale: 0-10 (.000)

Totals: 259-335-8 (.437)

COACH FLOYD "SCRAPPY" RHEA

Floyd "Scrappy" Rhea, who died at age ninety in 2010, is one of the great names of South Bay football history. He coached from 1963 through 1973, winning fifty-three and losing forty-seven for a percentage of .530. That doesn't sound great, but Scrappy was also coach of the only undefeated team in Harbor College history—the 1964 Seahawks, who went 9-0. That Harbor team was known as the team that was "unbeaten, untied and unwanted" since it was not invited to any post-season bowl games. The reasons given were that the college didn't have a marching band and could not guarantee the required number of fans. Among the Seahawks' victims that year was Orange Coast College, the 1963 Junior Rose Bowl champ.

The 1964 team was led by quarterback Don Horn and co-captain end Jerry Rodich. Horn, of course, went on to play eight years in the NFL for Green Bay, Denver, Cleveland and San Diego. Also on this great team was Haven Moses, voted the Outstanding Defensive Back, who went on to spend ten years in the NFL with Buffalo and Denver as a wide receiver and was selected to the Pro Bowl twice.

But Scrappy's fame was not relegated to being a junior college football coach. Scrap was an All-American at the University of Oregon in 1942 and 1943, and he went on to play professionally with the Detroit Lions, Chicago Cardinals, Brooklyn Tigers, Boston Yanks and Hawaiian Warriors.

Scrappy was born in 1920 in Rhea's Mill, Arkansas. In the early 1930s, he came to California with his father, who passed away when Floyd was thirteen. The *Daily Breeze* reported that the Fullerton High School principal took Scrappy in and allowed him to work and stay in the restaurant he owned. Rhea attended Fullerton Junior College before going on to Oregon. After professional football and a short stint as a lifeguard in Long Beach, Scrappy taught in elementary schools in Bellflower and Westminster and at Huntington Park High School. He married Carol Weber in 1948 and lived in Long Beach for most of his life. They had a son, Wayne, and two daughters, Helen and Rena, who died in 1997.

Rhea was hired by Harbor in 1958 as a physical education instructor, head baseball coach and assistant football coach. He became head football coach in 1963 and in 1972 added the jobs of athletic director and physical education division chairman.

"The most enjoyable part of my teaching," Scrappy said in a Los Angeles Harbor College press release, "was working with the athletes, seeing them develop and then move on to their own careers. It is rewarding to see those you have guided to the proper channels become productive citizens in our society."

But football was Rhea's primary interest for eleven years. It took only one year with a fine 6-3 record before Rhea's Seahawks went undefeated.

Also outstanding on that undefeated 1964 team were linebacker Sig Frawley, defensive tackle Raul Uranga and defensive end Henry Parks. Named to the All-Conference team were Horn, Moses, Rodich, Steve Cox, Ray Kalinich, Bobby Brooks, Bobby Lowery, John Blakemore and Stuart Horn.

And more outstanding years followed, including 8-2 in 1965, 7-3 in 1966 and 8-2 in 1969.

Rhea understood the travails of coaching in a community college. "Most of the super athletes are picked up by the Oklahomas and the USCs," Rhea said in a *Daily Breeze* article. "We [junior colleges] get the kid who has academic problems or is one year away from being a good athlete. You have to keep on a kid about the academic side. You have to do a good job of teaching. Coaching on the JC level has to be short, simple and sweet. When you get the players molded into a machine, zap, they are gone, scooped up by a four-year-college."

But not before they receive the wisdom and guidance of a very dedicated, successful coach.

RECORDS

South Bay Coaches in Order of Most Wins

Rank	Coach	Starting Year	Record	Winning %
1	Gene Vollnogle of Carson	1963	236-66-1	.781
2	Don Morrow of South and Mira Costa	1993	214-90-2	.703
3	Mike Walsh of San Pedro	1991	209-75-2	.734
4	Gary Kimbrell of Miraleste, Rolling Hills and Peninsula	1964	180-70-3	.717
5	Chris Ferragamo of Banning	1969	178-57-4	.753
6	Larry Wein of Westchester	1983	162-51-3	.755
7	Scott Altenberg of Serra	1999	142-42-3	.767
8	Fred Peterson of West Torrance	1964	131-60-4	.686

Rank	Coach	Starting Year	Record	Winning %
9	Manual Douglas of Narbonne	2002	128-55-1	.698
10	Joe Austin of South and North Torrance	1973	128-72-1	.639
11	Greg Holt of West Torrance	1994	112-100-4	.528
12	Steve Shevlin of El Segundo	1994	101-97-10	.510
13	Gene Simon	1996	100-76-3	.567
14	Dwaine Lyon of Rolling Hills	1964	99-46-5	.677
15	Todd Croce of North Torrance	2001	95-62-2	.604
16	Dino Andrie* of Mary Star	1994	91-80-2	.532
17	Rock Hollis of Torrance	1999	91-121-3	.430
18	Steve Schmitz of North Torrance	1975	88-31-2	.736
19	Edwin Ellis of Chadwick	1941	81-39	.675
20	Dan Robbins of Hawthorne	1991	81-42	.659
21	Ron Tatum of Morningside	1984	79-129-4	.382
22	Gary Willison of Chadwick	2003	73-39-2	.649
23	A.H. Bodenoch of Inglewood	1913	67-71-1	.540
22	Steve Carnes* of Leuzinger	1984	66-30-5	.678
23	Greg Dixon of St. Bernard	1997	65-95-1	.407

Rank	Coach	Starting Year	Record	Winning %
24	Bob Baiz of Fermin Lasuen	1961	59-28-1	.676
25	Ben Camrada of Narbonne	1925	57-14-2	.795
26	Josh Waybright of South	2003	57-63-1	.475
27	Tony Urburu of Peninsula	2000	54-32-4	.622
28	Sid Grant of Chadwick	1986	54-44-3	.535
29	Phil Bolger	1959	52-56-4	.482
30	Dale Washburn* of Serra	1978	51-33-3	.603
31	John Radisich* of Mary Star	1973	50-25-1	.664
32	Russell Striff of Redondo Union	1935	50-36-12	.571
33	Guy Gardner of Palos Verdes	2009	44-15-1	.742
34	Hal Chauncey of Hawthorne	1954	48-14-3	.762
35	Henry Pacheco of San Pedro	1982	48-39-1	.551
36	Steve Newell of El Segundo	1980	48-43-6	.526
37	Richie Braunbeck of Lawndale	1961	46-19-4	.667
38	Harvey Hazeltine of El Segundo	1929	46-27-5	.622
39	Ron Veres of Aviation	1968	45-47-2	.489
40	Les Congelliere of Redondo Union	1975	45-60-4	.431
41	George Swade of Bishop Montgomery	1963	44-23	.657

Rank	Coach	Starting Year	Record	Winning %
42	Ken Russell of Palos Verdes	1974	44-25-1	.636
43	Otto Plum of Hawthorne	1961	44-51-7	.466
44	Karl Haney of San Pedro	1917	42-16-2	.717
45	John Black and Mark Knox of West Torrance	1984	42-32-1	.567
46	Roy Benstead of Lawndale	1969	42-33	.560
47	Ed Levy of North Torrance	1962	39-30-5	.561
48	Bill Judy of Palos Verdes	1983	39-35	.527
49	Joe Dominguez of Banning	1988	38-11-1	.770
50	Leon Wheeler of Morningside	1966	38-13-2	.736
51	Bill Partridge of Gardena	1979	38-33-2	.534
52	Wilbur Lucas of Miraleste	1968	38-36-2	.513
53	Clyde Dougherty	1955	37-35-3	.527
54	Goy Casillas	1987	37-8-2	.809
55	Mike Christiansen of Carson	2006	35-15	.700
56	Manuel Laraneta of San Pedro	1928	35-32-12	.519
57	Bill Norton of Bishop Montgomery	1977	35-37-2	.486
58	Jack Epstein of Narbonne	1978	34-25	.576

Rank	Coach	Starting Year	Record	Winning %
59	Rich Busia of Torrance	1983	34-48-1	.416
60	Bill Seixas of Serra	1957	33-27-2	.548
61	Ed Hyduke of Aviation	1960	33-34-3	.493
62	Don Morrow of South Torrance	1989	31-19	.620
63	Phil Cantwell of Mary Star	1954	31-20-3	.602
64	Chris Hyduke of Redondo Union	1990	31-29	.517
65	Mike Antista of Bishop Montgomery	1969	31-24-1	.563
	Ron Terry of Palos Verdes	1961	31-31-1	.500

* incomplete record

South Bay Teams in Order of Most Wins

1. Carson: 433-179-5 (.706)
2. Banning: 415-282-19 (.593)
3. Redondo Union: 415-404-44 (.506)
4. Gardena: 359-317-21 (.530)
5. Serra: 358-224-19 (.611)
6. San Pedro: 355-197-26 (.637)
7. North Torrance: 347-258-19 (.571)
8. El Segundo: 317-281-29 (.529)
9. Mira Costa: 312-283-24 (.523)
10. Leuzinger: 306-366-17 (.456)
11. West High: 304-230-11 (.568)
12. Inglewood: 297-333-20 (.472)
13. Torrance: 296-461-30 (.395)
14. South Torrance: 286-248-7 (.535)
15. Chadwick: 275-195-6 (.584)

16. Hawthorne: 275-234-18 (.539)
17. Narbonne: 262-307-12 (.461)
18. Morningside: 232-261-21 (.472)
19. St. Bernard: 232-262-6 (.470)
20. Palos Verdes: 224-172-7 (.565)
21. Mary Star of the Sea: 222-206-8 (.518)
22. Bishop Montgomery: 211-324-4 (.390)
23. Westchester: 209-124-3 (.626)
24. Peninsula: 165-92-4 (.642)
25. Rolling Hills: 145-90-9 (.613)
26. Lawndale: 133-131-6 (.504)
27. Miraleste: 122-98-4 (.554)
28. Aviation: 99-85-8 (.536)
29. Lennox: 74-138-2 (.350)
30. Fermin Lasuen: 64-33-5 (.652)

South Bay Teams in Order of Winning Percentage

1. Carson: 433-179-5 (.706)
2. Fermin Lasuen: 64-33-5 (.652)
3. Peninsula: 165-92-4 (.642)
4. San Pedro: 355-197-26 (.637)
5. Westchester: 209-124-3 (.626)*
6. Rolling Hills: 145-90-9 (.613)
7. Serra: 358-224-19 (.611)
8. Banning: 415-282-19 (.593)*
9. Chadwick: 275-195-6 (.584)*
10. North Torrance: 347-258-19 (.571)
11. West High: 304-230-11 (.568)
12. Palos Verdes: 224-172-7 (.565)
13. Miraleste: 122-98-4 (.554)
14. Hawthorne: 275-234-18 (.539)
15. Aviation: 99-85-8 (.536)*
16. South Torrance: 286-248-7 (.535)
17. Gardena: 359-317-21 (.530)*
18. El Segundo: 317-281-29 (.529)
19. Mira Costa: 312-283-24 (.523)
20. Narbonne: 262-307-12 (.461)*
21. Lawndale: 133-131-6 (.504)*

22. Redondo Union: 415-404-44 (.506)
23. Morningside: 232-261-21 (.472)*
24. Inglewood: 297-333-20 (.472)*
25. St. Bernard: 232-262-6 (.470)*
26. Narbonne: 262-307-12 (.461)*
27. Leuzinger: 306-366-17 (.456)*
28. Torrance: 296-461-30 (.395)
29. Bishop Montgomery: 211-324-4 (.390)
30. Lennox: 74-138-2 (.350)*

* incomplete record

BIBLIOGRAPHY

Aviation High School yearbooks
Banning High School yearbooks
Bishop Montgomery High School yearbooks
Carson High School yearbooks
Centinela Valley Historical Society
Chadwick High School yearbooks
Ciniglio, Tony. Various articles for the *Daily Breeze*
Collin, Phil. Various articles for the *Daily Breeze*
Domancich, Sam. *Hit the Line: 100 Years of San Pedro High Football*. N.p.: Out of Mind and into Marketplace, 2006.
El Camino College Library
El Camino College yearbooks
El Camino Public Relations Department
El Segundo High School yearbooks
Fernas, Rob. Various articles for the *Los Angeles Times*
Gardena High School yearbooks
Harbor College Library
Harbor College yearbooks
Hawthorne Historical Society
Lawndale High School yearbooks
Leuzinger High School yearbooks
Manhattan Beach Historical Society

Mary Star of the Sea yearbooks
McLeod, Paul. Various articles for the *Los Angeles Times*
Morningside High School yearbooks
Palos Verdes Peninsula Library Archives
Redondo Union High School Archives
San Pedro Bay Historical Society
Serra High School yearbooks
Sondheimer, Eric. Various articles for the *Los Angeles Times*
Thorpe, David. Various articles for the *Daily Breeze*
Torrance City Library Online Resources
Torrance High School yearbooks
Torrance Historical Society
Trani, Nick. *Thin Ice on the Gridiron.* N.p.: Academy Guild Press, 1927.

REFERENCE WEBSITES

baninghs.org
bmhs-la.org/ (Bishop Montgomery High School)
calpreps.com (California high school sports)
carsonhs-lausd-ca.schoolloop.com
chadwickschool.org
collegelevelathletics.com
elsegundohigh.org
gardenahs-lausd-ca.schoolloop.com
inglewood.iusd.net
la-serrahs.org
lawndalehs.org
lennoxlancershome.com/1958Class/
leuzinger.org
maxpreps.com
miracostahs.org
morningside.iusd.net
narbonnehsgauchos.com
northhighschool.org
pro-football-reference.com

pvphs.com (Palos Verdes Peninsula High Schools)
redondounion.org
sanpedrohs.org
shs.tusd.org (South Torrance High School)
stbernardhs.org
ths.tusd.org (Torrance High School)
westchesterhs-lausd-ca.schoolloop.com
whs.tusd.org (West Torrance High School)
wikipedia.com

INDEX

Y

ABOUT THE AUTHOR

D on Lechman, a native of Colorado, worked as a reporter, critic, columnist and editor for the newspaper industry from 1960 to 2005. A graduate of the University of Colorado in journalism and a dedicated Buff, his columns appear regularly in the *Daily Breeze* newspaper in Torrance, California. You can also read him at donlechman.blogspot.com or http://lechman.org. His first two books for The History Press, *Los Angeles Dodgers Pitchers: Seven Decades of Diamond Dominance* (2012) and *Notre Dame vs. USC: The Rivalry* (2012), are available through www.historypress.net. Besides being a devoted fan of baseball, football and basketball, he enjoys writing, reading, traveling, playing the guitar and piano (poorly), watching movies, listening to music, playing basketball, working out and spending time with his wife and three grandchildren. He teaches writing at Los Angeles Harbor College in Wilmington and has been married to artist Pat for forty years and has two children, Laura Ann and David Michael.